Adoption and Implementation of AI in Customer Relationship Management

Surabhi Singh
IMS Ghaziabad, India

A volume in the Advances in Marketing, Customer Relationship Management, and E-Services (AMCRMES) Book Series

IGI Global
PUBLISHER of TIMELY KNOWLEDGE

Published in the United States of America by
IGI Global
Business Science Reference (an imprint of IGI Global)
701 E. Chocolate Avenue
Hershey PA, USA 17033
Tel: 717-533-8845
Fax: 717-533-8661
E-mail: cust@igi-global.com
Web site: http://www.igi-global.com

Library of Congress Cataloging-in-Publication Data

Names: Singh, Surabhi, editor.
Title: Adoption and implementation of AI in customer relationship management / Surabhi Singh, editor.
Description: Hershey, PA : Business Science Reference (an imprint of IGI Global), 2021. | Includes bibliographical references and index. | Summary: "The book covers major perspectives building on the available literature in the CRM domain while attempting to bring out a focused approach in connecting "Theory to Practice" improvising the customer relationships for the organizations with the use of AI"-- Provided by publisher.
Identifiers: LCCN 2021010753 (print) | LCCN 2021010754 (ebook) | ISBN 9781799879596 (hardcover) | ISBN 9781799879602 (paperback) | ISBN 9781799879619 (ebook)
Subjects: LCSH: Customer relations--Management--Technological innovations. | Artificial intelligence--Marketing applications.
Classification: LCC HF5415.5 .A35 2021 (print) | LCC HF5415.5 (ebook) | DDC 658.8/12028563--dc23
LC record available at https://lccn.loc.gov/2021010753
LC ebook record available at https://lccn.loc.gov/2021010754

This book is published in the IGI Global book series Advances in Marketing, Customer Relationship Management, and E-Services (AMCRMES) (ISSN: 2327-5502; eISSN: 2327-5529)

British Cataloguing in Publication Data
A Cataloguing in Publication record for this book is available from the British Library.

Advances in Marketing, Customer Relationship Management, and E-Services (AMCRMES) Book Series

ISSN:2327-5502
EISSN:2327-5529

Editor-in-Chief: Eldon Y. Li National Chengchi University, Taiwan & California Polytechnic State University, USA

MISSION

Business processes, services, and communications are important factors in the management of good customer relationship, which is the foundation of any well organized business. Technology continues to play a vital role in the organization and automation of business processes for marketing, sales, and customer service. These features aid in the attraction of new clients and maintaining existing relationships.

The Advances in Marketing, Customer Relationship Management, and E-Services (AMCRMES) Book Series

addresses success factors for customer relationship management, marketing, and electronic services and its performance outcomes. This collection of reference source covers aspects of consumer behavior and marketing business strategies aiming towards researchers, scholars, and practitioners in the fields of marketing management.

COVERAGE

- Web Mining and Marketing
- Text Mining and Marketing
- Cases on CRM Implementation
- Relationship Marketing
- Telemarketing
- Data mining and marketing
- CRM and customer trust
- B2B marketing
- Online Community Management and Behavior
- Database marketing

IGI Global is currently accepting manuscripts for publication within this series. To submit a proposal for a volume in this series, please contact our Acquisition Editors at Acquisitions@igi-global.com or visit: http://www.igi-global.com/publish/.

The Advances in Marketing, Customer Relationship Management, and E-Services (AMCRMES) Book Series (ISSN 2327-5502) is published by IGI Global, 701 E. Chocolate Avenue, Hershey, PA 17033-1240, USA, www.igi-global.com. This series is composed of titles available for purchase individually; each title is edited to be contextually exclusive from any other title within the series. For pricing and ordering information please visit http://www.igi-global.com/book-series/advances-marketing-customer-relationship-management/37150. Postmaster: Send all address changes to above address.

Titles in this Series

For a list of additional titles in this series, please visit:
www.igi-global.com/book-series/advances-marketing-customer-relationship-management/37150

Handbook of Research on IoT, Digital Transformation, and the Future of Global Marketing
Hatem El-Gohary (College of Business and Economics, Qatar University, Qatar) David Edwards (Birmingham City University, UK) and Mohamed Slim Ben Mimoun (Qatar University, Qatar)
Business Science Reference • © 2021 • 471pp • H/C (ISBN: 9781799871927) • US $295.00

Management and Marketing for Improved Competitiveness and Performance in the Healthcare Sector
José Duarte Santos (Polytechnic Institute of Gaya, Portugal) and Inês Veiga Pereira (ISCAP, Polytechnic Institute of Porto, Portugal)
Business Science Reference • © 2021 • 355pp • H/C (ISBN: 9781799872634) • US $225.00

Advanced Digital Marketing Strategies in a Data-Driven Era
Jose Ramon Saura (Rey Juan Carlos University, Spain)
Business Science Reference • © 2021 • 342pp • H/C (ISBN: 9781799880035) • US $225.00

Blockchain Technology and Applications for Digital Marketing
Rohit Bansal (Department of Management Studies, Vaish College of Engineering, India) Pacha Malyadri (ICSSR, Center for Economic and Social Studies, India) Amandeep Singh (Chitkara Business School, Chitkara University, Punjab, India) and Asif Pervez (Jamia Millia Islamia University, India)
Business Science Reference • © 2021 • 329pp • H/C (ISBN: 9781799880813) • US $225.00

Big Data Analytics for Improved Accuracy, Efficiency, and Decision Making in Digital Marketing
Amandeep Singh (Chitkara Business School, Chitkara University, Punjab, India)
Business Science Reference • © 2021 • 310pp • H/C (ISBN: 9781799872313) • US $215.00

Handbook of Research on Future Policies and Strategies for Nation Branding
Victoria Pistikou (Democritus University of Thrace, Greece) Andreas Masouras (Neapolis University, Cyprus) and Marcos Komodromos (University of Nicosia, Cyprus)
Business Science Reference • © 2021 • 383pp • H/C (ISBN: 9781799875338) • US $295.00

IGI Global
PUBLISHER of TIMELY KNOWLEDGE

701 East Chocolate Avenue, Hershey, PA 17033, USA
Tel: 717-533-8845 x100 • Fax: 717-533-8661
E-Mail: cust@igi-global.com • www.igi-global.com

Table of Contents

Detailed Table of Contents

The Edtech sector has grown with the emergence of new ventures at all levels of education and training. A number of experiments are carried out in this domain across the globe. Artificial intelligence is instrumental in helping institutions to engage students, provide personalised learning, and stay profitable. The chapter provides information about prevalent models being used for instruction design. It also includes examples of best practices of using technology in learning across the globe. Case studies of Yuanfudao (China), Embibe (India), Ruangguru (Indonesia), Tonies (Germany), Virti (UK), Examity (USA), and Packback (USA) are part of this chapter.

Artificial intelligence has led to the automation of traditional manufacturing and industrial processes and practices. The use of artificial intelligence improves customer experience and it's a proven fact that consumers who enjoy their shopping experience end up making more purchases. Retailing is one of the sectors that has seen drastic changes after the inception of artificial intelligence. This transformation can be seen in the supermarkets like Amazon Go store, Alibaba Hema store, IKEA, and many others. The objective of this chapter is to study the impact of artificial intelligence on Indian retail customers. Primary survey was conducted for the study and it was found that retail organizations emphasizing store design/layout and adoption of technological innovation to ease the consumer buying process were more successful in creating loyal customers for their stores. It can be concluded that India is still lacking in the adoption of IT systems in the retail sector and serious efforts are required in this direction.

Personalization is widely used to attract and retain customers in online business addressing one size fits all issues, but little is addressed to contextualise users' real-time needs. E-commerce website owners use these strategies for customer-centric marketing through enhanced experience but fail in designing effective personalization due to the dynamic nature of users' needs and pace of information exposure. To address this, this chapter explores hyper-personalization strategies to overcome users' implicit need to be served better. The research presents a hyper-personalization process with learning (ML) and artificial intelligence (AI) techniques for marketing functions like segmentation, targeting, and positioning based on real-time analytics throughout the customer journey and key factors driving effective customer-centric marketing. This chapter facilitates marketers to use AI-enabled personalization to address customers' implicit needs and leverage higher returns by delivering the right information at the right time to the right customer through the right channel.

The present times are disrupting times for every kind of business and every aspect of a business. It is not about contactlessness; it is about seamlessness. The auto manufacturers have already started "Amazoning" dealerships. Brands are developing customer-specific platforms like jaguar.rockar.com, where one can explore the range, check the price, select dealer, search inventory, and schedule test drives. The brand Cadillac creates virtual reality experiences in Google Search, wherein a car appears in a living room through a phone call. One can see how it looks, walk around it, open the doors, and get a sense of the interior. This chapter explores the transformation of CRM through artificial intelligence.

The use of technology has always provided competitive advantage to organizations. The current approach of adapting a new technology is the long-term planning. AI has become a new paradigm of enhancing organizational capabilities. AI is not a substitute of human intelligence but a strong support in terms of process automation. Apart from this, the decision-making process also gets streamlined. The success of business is when the customer is happy. To create and retain customer loyalty, effective CRM is required. The current chapter focuses on adoption of AI for efficient CRM and the factors for its successful implementation.

Disruptive technologies such as IoT, big data analytics, blockchain, and AI have changed the ways businesses operate, with AI holding immense marketing transformation potential. AI is influencing marketing strategies, business models, sales processes, customer service options, and customer behaviors. AI-CRM's improving ability to predict customer lifetime value will generate an inevitable rise in implementing adapted treatment of customers, leading to greater customer prioritization and service discrimination in markets. CSPs are working through the challenging process of digital transformation, driven by the need to compete with fast-moving OTT and consumer tech players. CSPs need to move quickly and can advance digital transformation with solutions that leverage AI which can drive value across the business from network optimization and data analytics through to customer care and marketing engagement. The chapter tries to identify how AI is impacting the CRM in the telecom industry and leveraging the benefits of this technology for better customer management and growth.

AI-powered technologies allow online B2B companies to serve their customers with accurate and relevant information, 24/7. For example, they experience an increase in requests for information from customers on such aspects as product availability, features, or other services. The chapter aims to explore artificial intelligence in B2B business. The study employed qualitative research, and the data was collected through a focus group for data collection. An AI-powered chatbot enhanced with natural language processing and understanding conversationally-worded requests could instantaneously provide this information without a human representative. This is vital as the added uncertainty around the pandemic means business customers seek real answers and ways to adapt and fast. The findings suggest the critical success factors of AI-driven CRM in B2B markets. The limitations of the study include the data collection being restricted to one B2B company. The implications are that further study can be extended for exploring AI-based CRM in B2B markets.

This chapter portrays artificial intelligence with the improvement of customer experience on online and offline fashion purchases. The presence of AI in the retail business is turning into a vital part of the customer experience. AI attempts to disclose approaches to interpret with the end goal for organizations to make a genuine use out of them, either online or offline. Thus, with this research, the authors additionally give knowledge on how this experience of AI could be improved in later fashion purchases and how it will undoubtedly be part of the everyday customer experience.

AI-oriented CRM has a bright future in business transformation. We're living in the age of the customer. Due to the proliferation of data, customers are more informed than ever. Armed with empowerment, customers are demanding that customer experience be put on a pedestal. According to research by Walker, customer experience is slated

Foreword

The work on the *Adoption and Implementation of AI in Customer Relationship Management* is highly topical and relevant for all organizations that want to succeed in CRM. AI will revolutionize the capabilities and effectiveness of traditional CRM systems.

This book provides an excellent overview of transformation AI-powered CRM will bring to organizations and how it can automate the work of marketing departments and enhance the customization, convenience, and personalization for customers all at the same time.

I am confident that this pioneer work by of Dr. Surabhi Singh and her team will inspire many marketing teams in their AI transformations!

Jochen Wirtz
National University of Singapore, Singapore

Preface

Artificial Intelligence (AI) refers to the ability of machines to demonstrate intelligence, think, and understand. AI is not only storing and collecting data, but also about analyzing, managing, and interpreting facts in managing Customer Relationship Management (CRM). With the help of AI, patterns can be detected to predict behavior and use the same insight to calculate risks in CRM.

The book comprises thirteen chapters in which the first chapter discusses best practices of AI across the globe. The second chapter talks about the impact of artificial intelligence on customer loyalty in Indian Retail. The third chapter focuses on hyper-personalization for customer-centric marketing. The fourth chapter elaborates on transforming CRM through Artificial Intelligence.

The fifth chapter dictates the fostering of CRM through artificial intelligence. The sixth chapter has taken the perspectives of AI and CRM in Telecom Industry. The seventh chapter investigates the critical success factors of artificial intelligence-driven CRM. Chapter 8 has the customer experience in the Fashion industry is AI driven. The ninth chapter includes the zero-customer defection.

The framework to deploy AI-based Smart CRM is contained in chapter ten. The eleventh chapter has the role of AI in the automation of HR. Chapter 12 has conceptualization of the use of Artificial Intelligence in Customer Relationship Management and Quality of Services: A Digital Disruption in Indian Banking System. The thirteenth chapter has mention of Artificial Intelligence in Retail: Enhancing Customer Experience & Profitability.

Surabhi Singh
IMS Ghaziabad, India

Acknowledgment

I extend my most profound thankfulness to all the researchers and mentors for their constant supervision, support, and guidance. I would thank Prof Jagdish Sheth and Prof Jochen Wirtz whose guidance and insights on Customer Relationship Management encouraged me to take up this project.

I would also thank all the authors whose ideas were useful in finalizing this book. Their extensive studies helped me in the completion of this book. I feel that words are not sufficient to express the immense contribution given by all the researchers of this area in the conclusion of this book.

I am grateful to all family members for their tremendous support during the past few years in the successful completion of the book work. I compliment and congratulate the publisher IGI Global and also thank them for inviting me to contribute to this pioneering work.

Surabhi Singh
IMS Ghaziabad, India

Chapter 1
Artificial Intelligence and E-Learning:
Best Practices Across the Globe

Renu Sharma
Amity University, Noida, India

Mamta Mohan
Amity University, Noida, India

ABSTRACT

The Edtech sector has grown with the emergence of new ventures at all levels of education and training. A number of experiments are carried out in this domain across the globe. Artificial intelligence is instrumental in helping institutions to engage students, provide personalised learning, and stay profitable. The chapter provides information about prevalent models being used for instruction design. It also includes examples of best practices of using technology in learning across the globe. Case studies of Yuanfudao (China), Embibe (India), Ruangguru (Indonesia), Tonies (Germany), Virti (UK), Examity (USA), and Packback (USA) are part of this chapter.

INTRODUCTION

E-learning segment is going through a major transition with multiple offerings and pedagogical innovations. Covid pandemic proved an accelerator for this sector as all the schools, universities, corporate trainings were forced to move online. This unexpected development led to number of experiments and new offerings in education.

DOI: 10.4018/978-1-7998-7959-6.ch001

Venture capital investment in Edtech sector has grown 32 times since 2010 and it reached a record level of 16.1 Billion Dollars in 2020 (*$16.1B of Global EdTech Venture Capital in 2020 – HolonIQ*, n.d.). Technology, which played a supportive role in classroom, became the centre stage for learning. It also shifted the boundaries of schools and universities making it possible for educators to teach beyond their local areas or regions. This shift made globalisation of education sector and redefined the concept of 'campus' and 'classrooms'. Entire world can become the 'campus' now and student from various countries can study together in one classroom. AI interventions provided viable and sustainable solutions to reach rural areas, people with different abilities. 49% of the global population believes that online learning will provide better access to disabled people (Jenner, 2021).

In addition to conventional learning institutions like schools and universities, reskilling emerged as another growing and profitable sector. Rapid changes in business environments, formats and work from home require unlearning old methods and grasping new concepts in a short time. Almost half of the venture capital transactions (48%) in 2020 are for workforce reskilling compared to 33% for K-12, 16% for higher education and just 3% for pre-K level(*$16.1B of Global EdTech Venture Capital in 2020 – HolonIQ*, n.d.). Key success factors for the reskilling market include autonomy in terms of time, privacy and applications of learning which can be translated into course designs with the help of AI. Virti trained health professionals with the aid of virtual patients and XR 9extended reality).

Although online learning was present prior to pandemic but it gained major traction due to the lockdowns and shutting of physical learning spaces during Covid crisis. In fact the online learning market is likely to increase at a CAGR of more than 13% during 2020-2026 (*Global E-Learning Market - Outlook and Forecast 2021-2026*, n.d.). This quick shift from traditional classroom teaching to online learning is made possible thanks to artificial intelligence. Moreover, AI leads to better retention of key concepts amongst students and improved academic outcomes(*Can Artificial Intelligence Actually Make Classroom Discussion Better? | League for Innovation*, n.d.). It also made education more inclusive by empowering institutions, educators and learners of all abilities(*Unleashing the Power of AI for Education | MIT Technology Review*, n.d.). Edtech companies like Ruangguru is taking education to rural areas of Indonesia. Teachers started to befriend technology to learn the ropes of online delivery, use of video conferencing platforms, and use of multiple tools to enhance student engagement. Micro learning and blended learning have become norms rather than exception in present education scenario (Khan, 2021). Virtual teaching assistants, chatbots, augmented reality, smart text messaging, proctoring services etc. are now widely used in content delivery.

In addition AI can benefit institutions, systems and people working in education domain Data science combined with instruction design principles resulted in numerous successful experiments in online education across various levels around the globe. Be it kindergarten, K-12 schools, higher education, corporate training, tools like natural language processing, machine learning, cloud technology are helping institutions to scale up their operations and improve profitability. According to a study conducted by Microsoft, 99.4% of educators believe that AI will play an important role for their institutions' competitiveness in the coming three years (*Unleashing the Power of AI for Education | MIT Technology Review*, n.d.).

This chapter will take a look at some of the case studies across globe where entrepreneurs made innovative use of AI for education.

This chapter aims to provide the following

1. A brief discussion about some popular instruction design models used in e-learning: These models include REMOTE and RAMP model.
2. Case studies of Edtech companies who are making innovative usage of AI in education: These include Yuanfudao (China), Embibe (India), Ruangguru (Indonesia), Tonies (Germany), Virti (UK), Examity (USA) and Packback (USA).

HOW TO USE THIS CHAPTER?

Instruction design models and case studies provided in this chapter can open up new possibilities for creating and delivering knowledge. More importantly these examples highlight the importance of unlearning some deep rooted practices of formal education. It is not possible to revamp the traditional top-down model of education within a few months. But success of edtech start-ups like Tonies, Yuanfudao, and Embibe etc. can make educational institution to rethink their business models and include AI interventions. Students can learn to take control of the content they wish to learn. Educators can combine the AI tools in their sessions and can also invest in their own reskilling. The cases cited in this chapter can trigger curiosity and can light up the path to mastering a desired skill.

To sum up educators, trainers, students, lifelong learners and institutions can use this chapter to:

- Understand theoretical models and how they can be integrated into practices as exemplified by case studies
- Unlearning deep rooted educational methods which have become redundant in present scenario
- Open up to possibilities created by AI like small group tutoring, personalised learning and mix of autonomy and relatedness

- Blend some of the AI tools/practices in existing ways to improve student engagement
- Become aware about various ways and educational products to reskill oneself

POPULAR E-LEARNING MODELS

Remote

This framework is proposed by Virtual Teaching Task Force of Harvard Business School to guide teachers for making their digital learning more engaged (*REMOTE—A Framework for Teaching Online | Harvard Business Publishing Education*, n.d.). The acronym REMOTE stands for reactions, eye contact, manageable, organised, thoughtful, engagement & evaluation.

Reactions, which may be verbal or non-verbal, are an important dynamic feedback mechanism for teachers. In online classes educators encourage students to respond through emojis, facial expressions, hand gestures and through asking question. Eye contact helps in better engagement also making students and educators the presence of each other. As the time available during online classes shrinks due to internet issues, keeping a simple set up rather than multiple gadgets can make it manageable. As most of the teachers will join their classes from home, it will help if they keep their environment neat and organized. Another important part to emphasize is the compassion and thoughtfulness in student-teacher interaction. To engage students, tools like chats, polls, video, power point slides can be mixed and matched in multiple creative ways. Students should have a clear idea about evaluation criteria. Chats, shared documents, Google Slides etc. can be used for group project works

Remote Technology Task Force of HBS made it possible to access the popular Aldrich classrooms of Harvard Business School to both in-person and remote students through a judicious use of technology (*Creating the HBS Hybrid Classrooms: Collaboration, Experimentation, Equity, and Innovation - News - Harvard Business School*, n.d.). The layout of classrooms was altered to facilitate blended learning. Professors are able to address in-person students along with online students. This solution ensured animated discussions and interaction amongst students and faculty in almost the same way as it used to happen in campus albeit in a safe way.

RAMP Model

As e-learning cannot be strictly monitored and regulated like classroom teaching, the effectiveness of any e-learning programme depends on self-motivation of the participants. Rather than extrinsic motivation like rewards and punishments, learning should provide intrinsic motivation where the process itself becomes joyful. RAMP model (Marczewski, 2013) builds on two key research based models of intrinsic motivation highlighting important components of effective learning. Self Determination Theory (SDT) proposed by Ryan and Deci (Ryan & Deci, 2000) and 'Drive' which is a work of Dan Pink(Pink, 2011). For effective learning SDT focusses on autonomy, competence and relatedness whereas 'Drive' emphasizes autonomy, mastery and purpose. Gamification expert, Marczewski (Marczewski, 2013)combined the key elements of both these models and postulated RAMP model which denotes relatedness, autonomy, mastery, and purpose.

- **Relatedness:** Connection, Social Status, Sense of Belonging
- **Autonomy:** Sense of control, Choice, Responsibility, Freedom
- **Mastery:** Personal Development, Learning, Levels of challenge
- **Purpose:** Meaning, helping others, a reason why

One or more of these intrinsic motivators should be present in the instruction design to sustain engagement of learners. Virti, a UK based edtech company exemplifies the model as it allows students to interact with each other, ask questions, respond to others' queries, at their own pace, and develop their critical thinking skills in the process. Popular learning sites like EDX, Coursera etc. offer self-paced courses, have an inbuilt community building feature through comments and discussions amongst course participants, provide grades for challenge levels and explain the relevance of course content for all modules. Germany's Tonies won numerous awards for their product design as their speakers are designed in a way that a child can use them without adult intervention, making him feel independent.

CASE STUDIES – BEST PRACTICES ACROSS GLOBE

In the higher education segment, both blended learning, which is a mix of online learning and face to face teaching and fully online learning are being used (Lee & McLoughlin, 2010).Initially most of the e-learning started with delivering the traditional class room content online. However, this form of learning resulted in lack of attention and engagement of students. Blended learning includes a mix of various elements like online content with offline interaction, structured content with unstructured content, simulations along with live contents etc. (Singh, 2021). The case studies described in the chapter supports effectiveness of blended learning. Examity makes use of online proctoring for offline exams for educational institutions as well as corporates. Virti combines augmented reality, virtual reality, extended reality and self-paced practice to deliver training to medical professionals.

The selected case studies for this chapter depict the usage of AI in various parts of e-learning like interaction with students, knowledge delivery, collaboration between educators, peer reviews etc. In the self-paced learning segment, Europe, Russia and UK are the dominant consumers (*Global E-Learning Market - Outlook and Forecast 2021-2026*, n.d.). China and India are now the hotspot for Edtech venture garnering more than 70% of global venture capital and having 30% of world's learner population(*China and India Now 70%+ of Global EdTech VC – HolonIQ*, n.d.). As education environment is diverse in different social groups, these case studies span across different countries including China, Germany, India, Indonesia, UK, and USA. These cover diverse areas like K-12, higher education, test preparation, corporate training etc. For this chapter we have compiled following case studies from different countries across the globe:

Yuanfudao, China

Yuanfudao is a leading educational company in China, which caters to pre-school, K-12 school and higher education through its various apps and products. It is the most valuable edtech start up in the world with a valuation of 15.5 billion dollars. . The company has built up a team of educators from diverse areas like pedagogy, psychology, linguistics, literature, English, thinking, and fine arts. Their teaching and research team comprise of professionals from Harvard University, Cambridge University, Peking University and Beijing Normal University. Yuanfudao has 11 curriculum development and teaching centres across China and it caters to 400 million students (*Tencent-Backed Online Education Firm Yuanfudao Raises US$1b in New Round, Garage - THE BUSINESS TIMES*, n.d.). A deep integration of AI and education helped the company in overcoming shortage of high quality educators. During Covid pandemic provided free lessons to more than 5 million students of primary and middle school creating an industry record of maximum number of online lessons in a day.

Services Offered

It provides a variety of education solutions including online lessons, intelligent exercises and problem analysis under it various brands like

- **Yuanfudao App**: multi subject online app catering to K-12 level online tutoring app providing live classes and real time response to questions. It includes Yuankouscian which is an arithmetic questions checking app and Zebra app which classes for children ranging 2 – 8 years

- **Xiaoyuan Souti:** problem solving app which provides video explanations of solutions and includes a search engine for questions
- **Yuantiku App:** personalized target and exercises with specific learning goals .The app includes real previous exam questions, error notebooks and diagnostic reports.
- **Xiaoyuan Kousuan App**: an app where students can get online assignments, submit handwritten responses, get their work corrected and review their incorrect work.

Use of Artificial Intelligence

For creating a behaviour database, billions of data points are collected with interviews of students who topped college entrance exams. Big data, AI and machine learning helps to generate predictive analytics, to collect feedback and improve value propositions.

Multi-sensory, situation interactions are created with the help of artificial intelligence to engage learners.AI helped the company to increase customer retention and secure commendable renewal rates of primary students. Students can scan problems and receive their solution within seconds. The company has invested in developing its own AI research institute with representatives from leading global universities and corporate entities including Peking University and Microsoft(*Yuanfudao Raises US$2.2 Billion in New Financing, Valuing the Company at US$15.5 Billion, Becoming the Most Valued Ed-Tech Company Worldwide*, n.d.)..

A variety of AI tools are deployed by the company and these include handwriting recognition, ancient poetry assistant, voice recognition, photo search, intelligent correction of handwriting responses. It makes use of full link monitoring, online disaster recovery, capacity assessment and fault drills to ensure smooth delivery of live sessions and security, stability and reliability of the system.

Awards/ Achievements

Yuanfudao AI Research Institute shared more than five independent research and development technologies with the industry. The company topped Microsoft's MSMARCO (Microsoft Machine Reading Comprehension) leader board through its MARS system generated by Neuro- linguistic programming team. Using AI, the company topped SQuAD (Stanford Question Answering Dataset) and was named as "Queen of the Internet" It got listed amongst 50 most innovative companies in China in 2019 by Forbes(*Yuanfudao - Global SERS*, n.d.).

Embibe, India

Embibe is an edtech platform that helps students in cracking competitive exams especially engineering and medical entrance exams. Established in 2012 by Aditi Avasthi, the company makes judicious use of AI to provide personalized feedback and specific tips to students (*Embibe: A Teacher's Pet Tool | Forbes India*, n.d.). Analytics point out that 39% of overall performance comes from behavioural attributes and 61% comes from knowledge attributes (*Embibe - AI - Using AI In Education To Maximize Learning Outcomes*, n.d.). Therefore, mere focus on knowledge will not give better results unless behavioural component is also improved. The tech system tracks more than 20 different parameters which comprise of behavioural elements as well as academic elements. Rather than simply giving standard tips for improving test scores, the system studies behaviour and recommends personal behavioural nudges and sets progressive goals for each student.

Embibe has created a personalized content discovery engine after mining attempt data for more than 6 years. The engine tracks parameters like non attempt minutes, where student spent more time on question, provides them an improvement story along with learning strategy to improve their test scores. Content provided to each students vary depending upon its content usage trends, its importance for learning a specific concept, search patterns, remaining time for exam, level of student preparedness etc. Focus on building student intelligence, mentor intelligence and content intelligence sets this venture apart from other players in the same market.

Strength in AI enabled Embibe to offer digitalisation services to other institutions/education providers also. Reliance invested 180 Billion dollars in this venture with a target of making technology accessible to 1.9 million schools and 58000 universities (*RIL Edtech Biz Could Hit $7-8 Bn If It Gets 10% Market Share by CY25: Report*, n.d.).

Services Offered

The company offers Embibe app for students through which students can access the following:

E-books & Exam Preparation: Mock tests for NCERT (National Council for Educational Research and Training) 6th standard to 12th standard.

Entrance Tests Preparation including NEET (National Eligibility cum Entrance Test), JEE Main & Advanced (Joint Entrance Exam), MHT CET (The Maharashtra Common Entrance Test), AP EAMCET (Andhra Pradesh Engineering Agriculture and Medical Common Entrance Test), TS EAMCET (Telangana State Engineering Agriculture and Medical Common Entrance

Test), KCET (Karnataka Common Entrance Test), KVPY(Kishore Vaigyanik Protsahan Yojana Exam) and BITSAT (Birla Institute of Technology and Science Admission Test).

Embibe also offers an app for parents to track progress of their wards and learn strength and weaknesses of their child backed by data insights. Parents can also plan practice test and design lesson plans for their wards.

Use of Artificial Intelligence

Automation helps the company in getting contents from multiple sources across numerous template styles. Based on this content, ingestion models are created using OCR (optical Character Recognition), NLP (Neuro Linguistic Programming) and machine learning that can incorporate historical examples and extract information from unseen documents. Embibe smart tagging system and Embibe concept tagging derives meaning from textual content and images.ML algorithms ranks concept with maximum relevance to a question.

The company uses ESQ (Embibe Score Quotient) which is an algorithm projected on three orthogonal axes, AQ(Academic Quotient comprising of subject knowledge), BQ (Behavioural Quotient to measure student motivation, attention and commitment) and TQ (Test taking Quotient to measure time management and prioritization of questions)(*Embibe - AI - Using AI In Education To Maximize Learning Outcomes*, n.d.). Besides machine learning combines in-house data set with publicly available data sources to tag questions with metadata like difficulty level and time required to solve.

The company invests heavily in instrumentation of rich event types, specific data by property, and learn behaviour data. User interaction is gauged through scrolls, clicks, hovers, tap pressure, location, device position, cursor position. Server side events and client side events including session refreshes, page load, api refreshes, push notifications, page views are captured. Practice attempt level data like answer choice, time spent, visit/re-visit, hint used, and solution viewed etc. and result interaction data including result widget, context, timestamp, widget position etc. is instrumental in surfacing customized recommendations for students. Session level data like question and answer details, voting behaviour, payment details is also automated.

For collection and instrumentation of data, the company has its in-house facilities and also makes use of third party plugins like Heap and segment.io (*Embibe - AI - Using AI In Education To Maximize Learning Outcomes*, n.d.). Amazon Elastic MapReduce helps the company in generating and updating user data. Academic ability profiles and session level data for each user is stored in Elasticsearch clusters.

For generating data related to traffic patterns, search failures, test improvements, log mining is used. The company makes use of Grafana and Kibana dashboards to provide data visualization.

Awards/ Achievements

The company won Amazon Award for Best AI for Education sector (*Amazon AI Awards 2017: Recognising the Future of AI*, n.d.) and is amongst Top AI start-ups in India(*10 Standout Start-Ups Taking an AI Leap in India*, n.d.). Aditi Avasthi, who is the founder of the company, won numerous awards including Accenture Vaahini Innovator of The Year(*Aditi Avasthi: ETPWLA 2019: Embibe Founder Aditi Avasthi Gets "Accenture Vaahini Innovator of the Year" - The Economic Times Video | ET Now*, n.d.), and CEO of the year (EdTech Review). She was listed amongst 100 most influential women by BBC and in '40 under 40' list of Fortune India.

Ruangguru, Indonesia

Established in 2014, Ruangguru is the largest educational technology enterprise in Southeast Asia having operations in Indonesia, Vietnam and Thailand (*Adamas Belva Syah Devara & Iman Usman, 25 & 26*, n.d.).The founders, Adamas Belva Syah Devara and Iman Usman studied from premier educational institutions. Adamas is a Stanford MBA and Harvard Masters of Public administration whereas Iman is Master of International Education from Columbia University. They identified that students are already comfortable with use of technology but teachers, trainers still have resistance for edtech as they were comfortable with the familiar manual ways of teaching. They ideated that use of technology was imperative to create a profitable business venture to reach 52 million students and for connecting 4 million teachers(*MIT Solve | Ruangguru - Solver Spotlight | Youth, Skills & Future Workforce Solver | Ruangguru*, n.d.). It became the largest technology company in Indonesia which provided live streaming of 18 channels of online school for free within one week of lockdown(*The 10 Most Innovative Education Companies of 2021*, n.d.). The company has around 250 videos for teachers' training and gives free access of this mobile library to educators. The platform helps student interaction by giving opportunity for chatting with other students and groups. It caters to 22 million users, has 300,000 educators dealing in more than 100 subject areas and employs 4000 people across the region.

Services Offered

It started as a tutoring marketplace where student can view certifications and qualifications of teachers and then make a decision about what to learn and from whom to learn. Tutors can join this marketplace and upload their credentials to enable students to make a choice. It ensured that a tutor can reach beyond his/her limited geographical areas and students get the power to choose amongst multiple tutors. Ruangguru gradually moved to K-12 education, exam preparation, private tuitions, stepped into corporate executive training and skill building. It also entered non-profit segment to cater to rural children who drop out of formal education and need diplomas to join workforce.

Their diverse range of educational services and products include:

- **Ruangbelajar** provides videos and practice questions for competitive exams.
- **Ruanguji** is a platform to carry online assessments for competitive exams.
- **Ruangles** is for getting private lessons with tutors at home.
- **Ruanglesonline** is where students can ask or resolve questions and problems with online tutors. They will get a response in less than 30 minutes.
- **Ruangkerja** is a training app providing LMS (Learning Management System) for corporates.
- **Ruangkelas** provide distance learning for free.
- **Brain Academy** includes interactive tutoring.
- **Ruanbaca** makes available resources and materials for reading.
- **Roboguru** is where customers can click pictures of their questions and submit them online for getting answers.
- **Skill academy** is meant for technical and soft skilling.
- **English Academy** caters to people who wish to become proficient in English.

Use of Artificial Intelligence

Smart use of Artificial intelligence is an important ingredient of Ruangguru's success. It tracks the learning behaviour and quiz results of its students using AI and guides them to best possible path to gain mastery. It makes use of population level data and probabilistic estimates of each student(*Adamas Belva Syah Devara MPA 2016 Has Spurred Educational Technology in Southeast Asia | Harvard Kennedy School*, n.d.). Another significant factor is their creative use of currents trends in instructional designs for online learning. The platform deploys group chats for peer to peer mentoring and encourages discussions pertaining to test preparation materials. These group chats can be accessed anytime, anywhere.

The company makes use of consumer facing software including cloud services and mobile applications. Cloud services helps them minimize outages and slowdowns (*Ruangguru Case Study | Google Cloud*, n.d.).Technology also helps them in optimizing manufacturing and processes. Machine learning, big data and control systems are part of their digital systems. As a result they could scale up their operations and provide quality education services without hampering their standards. AI is used for providing reports to partners and stakeholders and also to send messages between applications. Technology enabled the company to serve more users, save cost and reduce employee requirements. It also helped them collaborate with other service providers like LINE, which is a popular messaging platform. This collaboration enhanced the reach of their services and helped them in accommodating more traffic.

Awards/ Achievements

For its innovative use of technology in education Ruangguru won numerous awards and prizes including Ernst & Young - Emerging Entrepreneur Award, MIT Solve - Youth, Skills, and the Workforce of the Future Challenge 2017, Google Launchpad Accelerator, Atlassian Foundation "10 in 10" Partnership Prize, Australian Department of Foreign Affairs and Trade (DFAT) Indo-Pacific Development Prize

Tonies, Germany

The company provides small, shockproof, well designed speakers to ignite curiosity and provide education to children away from screen(*Introducing Tonies, The Revolutionary Children's Audio Player And European Toy Sensation Making Its U.S. Debut September 2020*, n.d.). Patric Fabbender and Marcus Stahl are founders of Boxine Gmbh which markets Tonies and Toniebox for children aged 3 and above. The company was started in Germany in 2013 and later on expanded to Austria, Switzerland, UK, Ireland and USA. It has created an extensive library of songs and stories, tailor made to suit the requirements of different countries.

Children learn and engage better when they have a sense of control and autonomy. Smart speakers require parental supervision as many times these devices get the commands wrong especially when kids speak. But with Tonies, the content is pre-loaded and there is hardly any possibility of malfunction. Besides devices like smartphones have flashing screens and result in sensual overload making children lose distracted. With audio content, children can play with their imagination, acquire information and knowledge which can improve their reading and expressive skills. The magnetic figurines make this experience haptic and sensual resulting in focus and play. 'Content tonies' offered by the company have pre-loaded contents whereas creative tonies provide a choice of personalised recording. Educators have started using Tonies for classroom and curriculum. More than 850 teachers are listed on their website as they use Tonies in multiple ways to impart lessons to young children(*Boxine GmbH Company Profile | Düsseldorf, Nordrhein-Westfalen, Germany | Competitors, Financials & Contacts - Dun & Bradstreet*, n.d.)The company has collaborations with publishers of children's books, celebrities, and production houses including Disney, Universal Music Group, DreamWorks, Magiclight, Sony Music. It has 250 employees and it clocked sales of 140 million euros in 2020 (Schweiz, 2020).

Product/ Services Offered

The products include a 5 inch indestructible cube weighing 600 grams made up of water repellent, sustainable fabric. Unlike other devices this cube does not have control screens, rather it has two "ears" for volume control and right, left movement to forward or repeat the content. Therefore, a child can handle this device without adult interventions and feels a sense of autonomy. Little magnetic figurines called"Tonies" have audio content including songs and stories. Besides the recorded content, children and their parents can also create, record and store their own content up to 90 min on "creative tonies".These boxes are offered in multiple colours to attract kids. Tonies are sturdy hand painted figurines measuring 5 to 8 cms tall and inspired from classic stories and movies like Frozen, Cinderella, Pinocchio, Rapunzel, and Nemo etc. Each figure has NFC (Near Field Communication) chip programmed with the book/content, which can be downloaded based on NFC authorisation.

Use of Artificial Intelligence

The company makes extensive use of cloud storage and apps to provide an engaging solution for kids and their parents. The company has partnered with Grand Centrix for IOT services and TonieCloud platform(*Tonies – Grandcentrix GmbH*, n.d.). To create more innovative products, the company established ToniesLab in 2021.

Once the content is uploaded on Tonie cloud and transferred to figurine, it becomes a closed ecosystem(*Toniebox Gives Kids Hours of Screen-Free Entertainment*, n.d.). The child can access it without Wi-Fi and internet.

Awards/ Achievements

Tonies won numerous design awards including Red Dot- Best of the Best, German Design award, Golden Rockin Horse, IF Design award, Creativity Award of the City of Dusseldorf and German Founder award. The company also won the Game Changer

Award given by Bain & Co. and Manager Magazine and got "Best Interactive Toy" award by Made for Mums.

Virti, UK

Started in 2018 by Dr Alexander Young, Virti provides immersive training to doctors and medical students using XR (Extended Reality), AI and gamification. The company is based in UK with offices in Bristol and Los Angeles. Experiential training environment and use of technology makes it possible to train in a cost effective way. Besides training modules are designed to include opportunity for repetitive practice and space for reflection. Each trainee gets objective feedback and insights about his performance based on data. The design of training modules overcomes the shortcomings of both offline and online training programmes. In person /offline sessions are quiet expensive, require coordination in terms of time and availability and are almost impossible during pandemic. Online programmes are cost effective but they are not engaging enough for participants.

During pandemic training of health professionals became a matter of life and death as offline workshops became inaccessible but the need for understanding new concept and procedures became critical. It gave a push to training modules of Virti as it stepped in for NHS (National Health Service), which is a publicly funded facility of UK government (*"Virtual Patient" Helps Train Medics Remotely during Pandemic - BBC News*, n.d.). Doctors and staff of NHS received training for wearing protective gear (PPE), using ventilators, navigating unfamiliar Intensive Care Units (ICUs), handling patients and their relatives. Use of AI makes this training solution scalable, more engaging and affordable.

Training modules of Virti includes soft skills training besides academic knowledge. The company makes use of "Virtual patients" to train medics in communication skills, empathy and mindfulness. Animated human characters act as patients and interact with clinicians. Assessment is based on multiple factors including the questions asked by the doctor, tone and quality of voice, the manner in which instructions are given to patient, accuracy of diagnosis made etc. Based on their scores, the system highlights area of improvement. The doctors can practice back and forth with virtual patients to improve their skills.

Services Offered

Soft skills like communication play a critical role in healthcare sectors. Medics need to understand patient concerns, share diagnosis with them, give instructions, share good/bad news and educate them for healthy behaviour. Besides patients, doctors may be required to interact with family and relatives of patients and also look after their administrative duties. They are under tremendous pressure as their decisions are high stake and need to be taken fast. The trauma of medical conditions, intense listening to woes and problems can adversely impact the well-being of medical practitioners leading to quicker burn outs. Simulated virtual learning alleviates psychological burden of intensive medical training reducing stress and anxiety of medical students(*Medicine & Mindfulness: How VR Training Is Helping Healthcare Through The Pandemic*, n.d.).The company provides following services(*Virti: Home*, n.d.):

- **The Virti Platform:** a cloud based LMS (Learning Management System) which includes a creation suite and analytics engine. Creation suites process behavioural insights through science based methods and create fast, efficient and realistic content in the form of 2 D videos, Virtual Reality and Decision trees.
- **Predictive Analytics:** Using AI, it becomes possible to measure training performance based on objective data. Following parameters can be measured:
    - Performance: measured by completion of task and response under stress
    - Engagement: frequency of activity, peer comparison, extent of simulation usage
    - Sentiment: analysis of soft skills through quantitative techniques
    - Interaction: analysis of user attention through speed of actions, spatial movements, eye tracking
- **Services:** Virti provides experience design services to organisations. It facilitates roll out of digital training modules, curriculum integration and adoption in institutions. Pedagogy for training programmes combines data science with behavioural insights based on scientific evidence and translates it into real world performance. An important content of training programme is retrieval practice based on score data and recall probability. If the user data shows forgotten information, personalised prompts can steer towards retrieval practice and helping the user to retain the learning in long term memory.

Gamification in terms of rewards, peer comparisons, micro interactions can release dopamine and the outcome is high engagement. As modules can be accessed through smartphones, desktop or laptop, trainees feel safe and they can use their failures and mistakes to further their own learning. Moreover reflective practices are in built in all simulations to improve understanding and absorption of training content.

Use of Artificial Intelligence

Virti makes use of machine learning algorithms which can create predictive models using training data to translate it into real world scenarios, and personalised training programmes. This eventually results in better application and retention of learning. These training programmes can be delivered remotely. to tailor content, recommend specific actions and identify outliers.real time analytics and automated assessment generated reports are used

The use of 'virtual patients' simulates the real life scenarios and VR headsets help in making the learning immersive. Valuable insights can be collected through tracking the eye movements, tone of voice, and decisions taken in simulated stress situations(*Artificial Intelligence Trains Doctors to Be More Empathetic to People - The Washington Post*, n.d.).

Hospitals can customise their "virtual patients" in terms of skin colour, age, gender, height, clothes etc. At present more than 60 avatars are available for training.

Deep learning technology helps the company to improve training outcome by more than 230% as claimed by the company(*Training Platform Virti Raises $10M Series A Led by IQ Capital to Teach Soft Skills in VR | TechCrunch*, n.d.)

Awards/ Achievements

Virti is listed amongst the Fast Company's most innovative companies in the world and is also named as Time's Best Inventions of 2020.It won the Best Start Up award given by Tech Spark, National Health Tech Start Up Reward, Mayor of London MedTech Business Awards, VR Healthcare Award, SimGHOSTS Innovation Award, Association of Medical Education Technology Enhanced Learning (TEL) and Technology Innovation Excellence (TIE) awards(*Virti: Home*, n.d.).

Examity, USA

Student assessments are a critical area of formal education system. Examity is a US based company which does learning validation and provides proctoring services to educational institutions including colleges and universities. Started in 2013 by Michael London, it proctors more than three million exams each year. During Covid, educational institutions were forced to conduct online exams. This transition to online delivery proved a challenge for teachers as well as institutions. A smart use of artificial intelligence coupled with human empathy led Examity to help educators in making a cultural shift to online delivery and examinations. It has partnered with more than 500 organisations/ institutions including Amazon, JLL, Elsevier, Coursera, Adobe, Tableau Software, Penn State University, University of Sydney etc. Besides it offers auto and live invigilation services to organisation for recruitment exams and employee validation. It deploys artificial intelligence and proprietary machine learning technology to provide auto proctoring and live proctoring solutions to help teachers conduct online assessments (*Auto Proctoring - Examity*, n.d.).

Trust, transparency, convenience for test taker as well as examiner organisation, variety of proctoring services, test integrity, credential protection, content security and support services are some of the ingredients of Examity's success. As the global online remote proctoring market is expected to grow at a CAGR of 7.7% during 2021-2026(*Online Remote Proctoring (Remote Invigilation) Market 2021 Size, Business Growth, Recent Trends and Future Scenario Till 2026| Examity, ProctorU – The Courier*, n.d.), Examity is poised for robust growth in future.

Services Offered

Examity offers two types of auto proctoring – standard and premium. The difference between these two variants is addition of human audit in case of premium offering. Auto proctoring starts with auto authentication of candidate using photo identity and challenge questions. Entire exam right from the start to end is monitored and recorded. This full video is made available on the dashboard along with time stamp and is reviewed by test administrator. In case of premium auto proctoring, human audit of recorded content is carried out to point out any technology related mistakes.

Live proctoring is available for pre- employment screening, high stakes exams, critical certifications etc., In this case identity authentication is done through a real time webcam and posing a challenge question. Live exam proctor will monitor the test taking environment using a 360 degree camera sweep of the workstation or room. Entire exam session is recorded and artificial intelligence is used to check any unusual activity. The recording is reviewed by Examity proctor and auditor; thereafter it is released to dashboard.

Besides services like Live premium gives on screen, real time support to resolve any technical question, pause/resume the exam in the event of any irregular conduct or do any immediate intervention, if required during the exam.

Use of Artificial Intelligence

With the help of artificial intelligence and machine learning, the company offers flexible proctoring solution with consistent support and integration with systems of client organisation. It makes us of biometric security features including fingerprint authentication through mobiles, facial recognition, test takers' keystrokes recognition(*Creative Ways Students Try to Cheat on Online Exams*, n.d.).It can detect when test takers move out or leave the area or turn their head for a longer period of time, or any irregular voices in the surroundings. Through keystroke analysis, any irregular behaviour can be spotted to know whether the examinee is typing own answer or getting it from the screen. Biometric imaging along with webcam usage can reveal if the test taker is trying to read out from his hands, arms, water bottle etc. The company also deploys high quality audio detectors which can alert proctors if there is anyone whispering answers or for any other suspicious sounds.

Awards/ Achievements

Owing to its innovative use of technology, Examity was listed amongst World's most innovative Companies by Fast Company. It also featured amongst Deloitte's Technology Fast 500 Winners in 2019(us-tmt-fast- & -winners-list, 2019). Michael London, founder of Examity became a finalist for Ernst & Young Entrepreneur of the year award in 2019.Great Hill Partners invested 90 million dollars and acquired majority stake in Examity in May 2019.

Packback, USA

Traditional education system and pedagogy stifles curiosity and does not offer much room for peer to peer interaction. In 2014, Jessica Tenuta, Kasey Gandham, Mike Shannon and Nick Currier established Packback, a question based social learning platform for enhancing critical thinking skills through discussion, interactions and collaboration amongst students and instructors. This pedagogy uses method of enquiry, gives autonomy, and help is mastering learning. More than 3500 instructors 600,000 students have used this platform with more than 17.8 million discussion posts (*Home - Packback*, n.d.).

It encourages students to ask open-ended and effective questions which are responded to by other students. The platform provides a Curiosity score to students which is based on four quality dimensions: curiosity, credibility, communication, and connection (*The Topic of Discussion: How Specific Online Discussion Methodologies Affect Outcomes - Packback*, n.d.).These scores push students to ask tougher questions and substantiate their answers with more credible sources(*Can Artificial Intelligence Actually Make Classroom Discussion Better? | League for Innovation*, n.d.). Students have options to edit a post, upload and embed image/videos, insert formulas and code blocks. Based on the feedback they can edit and re-publish their posts and get a review mail for such moderated posts. When students asks or respond to questions or give/receive responses from others, it builds a sense of community improving connection and communication.

Moreover the platform reduces the work load of instructors by acting as their "Digital Teaching Assistant", who manages discussion amongst student communities.

The platform generates automated scores for participation, insights report and recommended actions. This information pertains to skill level of students and based on the analytics it recommends the suitable posts or discussion to be initiated. Students can practice constructive debates by using counterpoint and supporting points and instructors can give their feedback as private 'coaching' or public 'praise'.

There are distinct styles to fashion an online discussion(*The Topic of Discussion: How Specific Online Discussion Methodologies Affect Outcomes - Packback*, n.d.). Instructor led discussions are highly structured; more controlled and are based on 'call and response' model. Freeform chats are less scripted and are generally used by students to seek help or clarification. These chats fulfil social needs but lack any strong pedagogical design. Inquiry driven discussions leads students to think divergently, provide deeper interaction with peers and better engagement with content as they are directed but still highly autonomous. With the help of AI, the company has enabled an equitable, scalable platform to encourage inquiry driven discussions and gaining mastery through instant feedback. Instructors can invest their time in more strategic matters like research and creation of knowledge.

Services Offered

- **Discussion Pedagogy:** The platform is founded on three pillars inquiry, autonomy and mastery learning. Packback trains students to formulate better questions based on course material. Students have the autonomy to ask or respond to question based on their preference.
- **Packback Platform:** the platform acts as AI enabled 'Digital TA' (teaching Assistant) for instructors and provides engagement tools. Educators can use these tools to guide, engage, redirect, and provide feedback and to celebrate success of their students. Automated participation scoring, insight reports, recommended actions are some other tools to ease burden of teachers and to inculcate critical thinking skills amongst students.

To make the interaction delightful and engaging, the platform offers avatar builder, critical debaters and Sparks.

Use of Artificial Intelligence

Roots of the AI used by Packback comprise of popular pedagogical models including Bloom's Taxonomy of Cognition, Garrison's practical enquiry model, Self Determination Theory, Bloom's 2 Sigma Problem, Garrison's community of Enquiry model.

The company makes use of proprietary algorithm to calculate Curiosity Score. Natural language processing provides instant feedback on multiple points about content moderation like use of paragraphs, tips for citing a particular reference to improve credibility of post and warning in case of passive voice usage.

Besides AI is used for providing instant feedback and to overcome Bloom's 2 sigma problem. As pointed out by Benjamin Bloom, students who learn in small groups have much better learning compared to conventional classrooms(Bloom, 1984). But such kind of tutoring is not viable and it is expensive too. To conceptualise an affordable group instruction method where students can learn in a group, with limited number of participants is termed as Bloom's 2 sigma problem. With the help of AI tools now Packback provides all benefits of tutoring in a small group without burdening the teachers and making it affordable for students.

Awards/ Achievements

The company won Chicago Innovation Award in the 'Up & Comer' category. Mike Shannon, one of the co-founders appeared in 'Shark Tank' series and got investment from Mark Cuban. The founders were listed amongst '20 in their 20's' of Crain's Chicago Business and '50 on Fire' of Chicago Inno. It is ranked 49 amongst America's Fastest growing companies 2021 by Financial Times (*FT Ranking: The Americas' Fastest-Growing Companies 2021 | Financial Times*, n.d.).

REFERENCES

$16.1B of Global EdTech Venture Capital in 2020 – HolonIQ. (n.d.). Retrieved July 26, 2021, from https://www.holoniq.com/notes/16.1b-of-global-edtech-venture-capital-in-2020/

Amazon AI Awards 2017: Recognising the future of AI. (n.d.). Retrieved July 8, 2021, from https://yourstory.com/2017/12/amazon-ai-awards-2017/amp

Artificial intelligence trains doctors to be more empathetic to people - The Washington Post. (n.d.). Retrieved July 12, 2021, from https://www.washingtonpost.com/technology/2021/02/16/virtual-ai-hospital-patients/

Auto Proctoring - Examity. (n.d.). Retrieved June 19, 2021, from https://www.examity.com/solutions/auto-proctoring/

Avasthi. (n.d.). *ETPWLA 2019: Embibe founder Aditi Avasthi gets "Accenture Vaahini Innovator of the Year" - The Economic Times Video | ET Now*. Retrieved July 12, 2021, from https://economictimes.indiatimes.com/news/company/corporate-trends/etpwla-2019-embibe-founder-aditi-avasthi-gets-accenture-vaahini-innovator-of-the-year/videoshow/68636240.cms?from=mdr

Bloom, B. S. (1984). The 2 sigma problem: The search for methods of group instruction as effective as one-to-one tutoring. *Educational Researcher*, *13*(6), 4–16.

Boxine GmbH Company Profile | Düsseldorf, Nordrhein-Westfalen, Germany | Competitors, Financials & Contacts - Dun & Bradstreet. (n.d.). Retrieved July 6, 2021, from https://www.dnb.com/business-directory/company-profiles.boxine_gmbh.3a47fbdf271e382eea4c303c27900ccb.html

Can Artificial Intelligence Actually Make Classroom Discussion Better? | League for Innovation. (n.d.). Retrieved July 16, 2021, from https://leagueforinnovation.wordpress.com/2020/09/17/can-artificial-intelligence-actually-make-classroom-discussion-better/

China and India now 70%+ of Global EdTech VC – HolonIQ. (n.d.). Retrieved July 26, 2021, from https://www.holoniq.com/notes/china-india-now-70-global-edtech-vc/

Creating the HBS Hybrid Classrooms: Collaboration, Experimentation, Equity, and Innovation - News - Harvard Business School. (n.d.). Retrieved June 19, 2021, from https://www.hbs.edu/news/articles/Pages/creating-hybrid-classrooms.aspx

Creative ways students try to cheat on online exams. (n.d.). Retrieved June 24, 2021, from https://www.insidehighered.com/digital-learning/views/2017/09/20/creative-ways-students-try-cheat-online-exams

Devara. (n.d.). *2016 has spurred educational technology in Southeast Asia | Harvard Kennedy School*. Retrieved June 22, 2021, from https://www.hks.harvard.edu/alumni/connect/community-stories/adamas-belva-syah-devara-mpa-has-spurred-educational-technology

Devara & Usman. (n.d.). Retrieved June 22, 2021, from https://www.forbes.com/pictures/fmhd45gdgi/adamas-belva-syah-devara/?sh=727b61393cc9

Embibe: A Teacher's Pet Tool | Forbes India. (n.d.). Retrieved July 8, 2021, from https://www.forbesindia.com/article/checkin/embibe-a-teachers-pet-tool/41195/1

Embibe - AI - Using AI In Education To Maximize Learning Outcomes. (n.d.). Retrieved July 8, 2021, from https://www.embibe.com/ai

FT ranking: The Americas' fastest-growing companies 2021 | Financial Times. (n.d.). Retrieved July 20, 2021, from https://www.ft.com/americas-fastest-growing-companies-2021

Global E-learning Market - Outlook and Forecast 2021-2026. (n.d.). Retrieved June 17, 2021, from https://www.researchandmarkets.com/reports/5327504/global-e-learning-market-outlook-and-forecast?utm_source=BW&utm_medium=PressRelease&utm_code=n8vslb&utm_campaign=1550491+-+Global+E-learning+Market+Outlook+and+Forecast+2021-2026%3A+Market+is+Likely+to+Witness+an+Absolute+Growth+of+About+110%25&utm_exec=chdo54prd

Home - Packback. (n.d.). Retrieved July 20, 2021, from https://www.packback.co/

Introducing tonies, The Revolutionary Children's Audio Player And European Toy Sensation Making Its U.S. Debut September 2020. (n.d.). Retrieved June 19, 2021, from https://www.prnewswire.com/news-releases/introducing-tonies-the-revolutionary-childrens-audio-player-and-european-toy-sensation-making-its-us-debut-september-2020-301136398.html

Jenner, M. (2021). *The future of learning report.* https://www.futurelearn.com/info/insights/self-education-online-learning-the-future-of-education

Khan, B. H. (2021). A Global Framework for E-Learning. In *Challenges and Opportunities for the Global Implementation of E-Learning Frameworks* (pp. 1–14). IGI Global.

Lee, M. J. W., & McLoughlin, C. (2010). Web 2.0-based e-learning: Applying social informatics for tertiary teaching. In *Web 2.0-Based E-Learning: Applying Social Informatics for Tertiary Teaching*. doi:10.4018/978-1-60566-294-7

Marczewski, A. (2013). *The Intrinsic Motivation RAMP*. Academic Press.

Medicine & Mindfulness. (n.d.). *How VR Training Is Helping Healthcare Through The Pandemic*. Retrieved July 13, 2021, from https://www.forbes.com/sites/charlestowersclark/2021/02/19/medicine--mindfulness-how-vr-training-is-helping-healthcare-through-the-pandemic/?sh=30fb425a58b9

MIT Solve | Ruangguru - Solver Spotlight | Youth, Skills & Future Workforce Solver | Ruangguru. (n.d.). Retrieved June 23, 2021, from https://solve.mit.edu/challenges/youth-skills-the-workforce-of-the-future/solutions/2359#solution-subnav-offset

Online Remote Proctoring (Remote Invigilation) Market 2021 Size, Business Growth, Recent Trends and Future Scenario Till 2026| Examity, ProctorU – The Courier. (n.d.). Retrieved June 24, 2021, from https://www.mccourier.com/online-remote-proctoring-remote-invigilation-market-2021-size-business-growth-recent-trends-and-future-scenario-till-2026-examity-proctoru/

Pink, D. H. (2011). *Drive: The surprising truth about what motivates us*. Penguin.

REMOTE—A Framework for Teaching Online | Harvard Business Publishing Education. (n.d.). Retrieved January 20, 2021, from https://hbsp.harvard.edu/inspiring-minds/remote-a-framework-for-teaching-online

RIL edtech biz could hit $7-8 bn if it gets 10% market share by CY25: Report. (n.d.). Retrieved July 8, 2021, from https://www.livemint.com/industry/ril-edtech-biz-could-hit-7-8-bn-if-it-gets-10-market-share-by-cy25-report-11624508424422.html

Ruangguru Case Study | Google Cloud. (n.d.). Retrieved June 22, 2021, from https://cloud.google.com/customers/ruangguru

Ryan, R. M., & Deci, E. L. (2000). Self-determination theory and the facilitation of intrinsic motivation, social development, and well-being. *The American Psychologist*, *55*(1), 68.

Schweiz, D. (2020). *Pressemappe tonies®. 2016–2017*. Academic Press.

Singh, H. (2021). Building effective blended learning programs. In *Challenges and Opportunities for the Global Implementation of E-Learning Frameworks* (pp. 15–23). IGI Global.

standout start-ups taking an AI leap in India. (n.d.). Retrieved July 12, 2021, from https://www.livemint.com/Leisure/u7M3e5ymwmGf6QRLaXBoAJ/10-standout-startups-taking-an-AI-leap-in-India.html

Tencent-backed online education firm Yuanfudao raises US$1b in new round, Garage - THE BUSINESS TIMES. (n.d.). Retrieved July 1, 2021, from https://www.businesstimes.com.sg/garage/tencent-backed-online-education-firm-yuanfudao-raises-us1b-in-new-round

The 10 most innovative education companies of 2021. (n.d.). Retrieved June 15, 2021, from https://www.fastcompany.com/90600179/education-most-innovative-companies-2021

The Topic of Discussion. (n.d.). *How specific online discussion methodologies affect outcomes - Packback*. Retrieved July 16, 2021, from https://www.packback.co/pedagogy/the-topic-of-discussion-outcomes-driven-by-online-discussion-depend-on-implementation-method/

Toniebox gives kids hours of screen-free entertainment. (n.d.). Retrieved July 6, 2021, from https://www.fastcompany.com/90556948/european-kids-love-this-screen-free-storytelling-device-now-u-s-kids-can-get-it-too

Tonies – grandcentrix GmbH. (n.d.). Retrieved July 6, 2021, from https://grandcentrix.net/en/references/tonies/

Training platform Virti raises $10M Series A led by IQ Capital to teach soft skills in VR | TechCrunch. (n.d.). Retrieved July 12, 2021, from https://techcrunch.com/2021/06/29/training-platform-virti-raises-10m-series-a-led-by-iq-capital-to-teach-soft-skills-in-vr/

Unleashing the power of AI for education | MIT Technology Review. (n.d.). Retrieved June 17, 2021, from https://www.technologyreview.com/2020/03/04/905535/unleashing-the-power-of-ai-for-education/

us-tmt-fast-, & -winners-list. (2019). *2019 Technology Fast 500 ™ Ranking Recognizing growth*.

Virti: Home. (n.d.). Retrieved July 12, 2021, from https://virti.com/

"Virtual patient" helps train medics remotely during pandemic - BBC News. (n.d.). Retrieved July 12, 2021, from https://www.bbc.com/news/uk-england-bristol-55202237

Werbach, K., & Hunter, D. (2012). *For the win: How game thinking can revolutionize your business*. Wharton Digital Press.

Yuanfudao - Global SERS. (n.d.). Retrieved July 1, 2021, from https://globalsers.org/company-profiles/yuanfudao/

Yuanfudao Raises U. S. $2.2 Billion in New Financing, Valuing the Company at US$15.5 Billion, Becoming the Most Valued Ed-Tech Company Worldwide. (n.d.). Retrieved June 19, 2021, from https://www.prnewswire.com/news-releases/yuanfudao-raises-us2-2-billion-in-new-financing-valuing-the-company-at-us15-5-billion-becoming-the-most-valued-ed-tech-company-worldwide-301157837.html

KEY TERMS AND DEFINITIONS

Blended Learning: A style of learning where online and electronic media is combined with face-to-face interaction.

CAGR: Compound annual growth rate.

Gamification: Use of game design elements in other areas of activity.

IOT: Internet of things.

LMS: Learning management system.

Micro Learning: It refers to small learning unit or small pieces of knowledge.

NFC: Near field communication.

RAMP: Relatedness, autonomy, mastery, purpose.

REMOTE: Reactions, eye contact, manageable, organised, thoughtful, engagement evaluation.

XR: Extended reality.

Chapter 2
Impact of Artificial Intelligence on Customer Loyalty in the Indian Retail Industry

Kirandeep Bedi
https://orcid.org/0000-0003-3468-5135
Amity University, Noida, India

Monica Bedi
Punjab University, Chandigarh, India

Ramanjeet Singh
Amity University, Noida, India

ABSTRACT

Artificial intelligence has led to the automation of traditional manufacturing and industrial processes and practices. The use of artificial intelligence improves customer experience and it's a proven fact that consumers who enjoy their shopping experience end up making more purchases. Retailing is one of the sectors that has seen drastic changes after the inception of artificial intelligence. This transformation can be seen in the supermarkets like Amazon Go store, Alibaba Hema store, IKEA, and many others. The objective of this chapter is to study the impact of artificial intelligence on Indian retail customers. Primary survey was conducted for the study and it was found that retail organizations emphasizing store design/layout and adoption of technological innovation to ease the consumer buying process were more successful in creating loyal customers for their stores. It can be concluded that India is still lacking in the adoption of IT systems in the retail sector and serious efforts are required in this direction.

DOI: 10.4018/978-1-7998-7959-6.ch002

INTRODUCTION

In the current market scenario, only retailers leveraging innovation and differentiation can survive, and such innovation can come only from the use of creativity and the best available technologies. Technology is the solution to the problem in this digital era. Industry 4.0 brings four major innovations- Internet of things (IoT), robotic and automation, 3D printing, and augmented reality. All these innovations come with further series of technologies like Beacons, body scanner, PoS, EDI tech, etc. These technologies are impacting retail outlook (Berman and Evans, 2010; Rowley and Slack, 2003). All these innovative technologies in the retail sector not only increased the effectiveness of the retail business in terms of better inventory management, better prediction of consumer buying behavior but also improved customer experience due to customization and automation. Technology reduced long checkout lines with benefits of high speed in providing services in the store, loyalty card programs, etc. Artificial Intelligence being adopted these days is the combination of several technologies, which allow software and machines to sense, understand, act and learn on their own or augment human activities and forms the bases of Industry 4.0.

Industry 4.0 in Retailing

India is the world's fifth-largest global destination in the retail space. Indian retail industry has emerged as one of the most dynamic and fast-paced industries and has been on a growth trajectory over the past few years. It accounts for over 10% of the country's Gross Domestic Product (Indian Brand Equity Foundation, 2021). India is considered a booming market and the fourth most attractive nation for retail investment (Gandhi & Chinnadorai, 2017). Indian Retail comprises of organized and unorganized sector in which organized comprises of malls, departmental stores, company outlets, marketing channels, and most important E-commerce. And on the other side, the unorganized sector includes local pan shops, kirana stores, and roundabout stores, etc. in the local market (Aggarwal, 2015). Retail sector growth in India has been greatly facilitated by the e-commerce industry. Online retail is expected to reach 10.7% by 2024 (Equitymaster,2021). During Covid-19, Retail technology investments were made for digitization, decreasing expenditure on store openings and remodels. Due to rising demand during the lockdown, most players recorded a 20-80% surge in order volumes despite challenges such as order delays and cancellations. In a way, the lockdown gradually changed the mindsets of consumers and encouraged them to switch to online retail platforms (IBEF,2021). Artificial Intelligence is being used by retail stores to facilitate customers as to survive in such a competitive environment retailer must retain the existing customer and an existing customer is cheaper to acquire than a new customer in fierce competition. Various researchers found that consumer retention and customer loyalty is essential to the profitability of the retail business (Singh & Imran, 2012; Reinatz et al.,2004; Hennig & Klee, 1997). It has been found that online retailers lose 25% of their customers yearly but a small increase in customer retention can increase profits by more than 25% (Singh & Imran, 2012). Customer loyalty increases intent to return which improves financial results. Loyal customers give positive recommendations to their friends and relatives.

Artificial Intelligence is considered one of the fundamental bases of Industry 4.0 and a great facilitator for the customer and the organization. Artificial intelligence (AI) exhibiting aspects of human intelligence (HI) has become a key source of innovation (Rust and Huang, 2014) and is diffusing boundaries between the physical, digital, and biological spheres. It has enabled industries to consider adopting new technologies as under: **Internet of Things (IoT)** is the foundation of Industry 4.0. IoT is a network of objects and devices connected through the internet. In retailing, it helps in attaining new capabilities like monitoring, control, customization & autonomy (Balaji & Roy, 2017). The network between IoT devices is expected to offer higher efficiency, privacy, convenience, security & high-quality decision-making (Weinberg et al., 2015). According to Porter & Heppelmann (2014) the data generated with the help of IoT devices helps the retailer to gain newer insights into value creation, building effective communication strategies & better positioning. **Augmented Reality** integrates the real world with virtual information, thereby, enhancing specific reality (Lamantia, 2009). Augmented Reality increases the interactions of the consumer with the product which enables them to personalize information in a 3D virtual model (Fiore, Kim & Lee, 2005). **Beacons** are small wireless battery-run sensors that connect with nearby mobile devices through Bluetooth Low Energy (BLE). These interactions provide consumers with detailed information based on their location. This technology enables targeted ads or relevant content directly to the digital devices of the customer. **Multimedia kiosks** bring significant advancement in-store promotions which earlier relied on paper-based catalogs, promotional leaflets which were a very old way of promotion (Rowley & Slack, 2003). Multi-Media kiosks help organizations in gaining control over the point of purchase stage decisions in the marketing cycle. Thus, technology is being used in different forms to benefit both retailers and customers.

Review of Literature

The smart environment is fastening changes in consumer behavior. The e-commerce recommendation system provides information about products that meet customers' preferences. Artificial Intelligence has made interaction between manufacturers and consumers more personal increasing the accuracy of segmentation and targeting the desired customers. It can be taken as a new type of direct marketing, which is a prerequisite for more sophisticated personalized marketing. The technology has substantially influenced the business models, processes, strategies and operations of retail companies (Sorescu et al., 2011). Weijters et al. (2007) found that the average customer purchase is greater for people using innovative technological solutions than that of the customers not using them. Past researches show that digital value proposition is a suitable construct to mediate the explanation of the transformative effects of digital technologies on customer experience (Mollen & Wilson, 2010; Parise et al., 2016; Kalaignanam et al., 2018; Cowan & Ketron, 2019). The advanced technologies benefit both consumers and marketers by providing customized information to customers and information on consumers' behaviour, preferences and market trends to managers. Studies found that online retail provides an adaptive and interactive scenario which is more appealing for consumers, with benefits for the decision-making process (Pantano & Pietro, 2012). Also, studies concluded that artificial Intelligence provides higher enjoyment which strongly influences consumers' attitude towards retailers (Lee et al., 2005). Indeed, enjoyment is found to be positively related to user's satisfaction with specific technology products (Pantano & Pietro, 2012; Woszczynski et al., 2002). Researchers are of the view that rising interest in designing advanced tools also for retailing follows the increasing awareness in the consumers' increasing power and the possibility to choose among alternatives, as well as on the opportunities for co-creating innovative products and services (Berry et al. 2010; Alexander et al. 2009; Eastlick et al., 2012). Also, location-based services allow users to receive integrated information based on time, location and context, enhancing their shopping experience (Sima et al.,2020). Customer experience, which is at the heart of digital transformation, is widely recognized as a source of sustainable competitive advantage (Ziaie et al.,2021).

To conclude, the success of this technology in the retail sector not only depends on retailers but also on the acceptance, attitude, and use of the technology by the consumer. With this background, the present study is conducted to understand the impact of Artificial Intelligence on the customer loyalty of the Indian consumer in the retail industry. Perceived Security, perceived value, product assortment and shopping experience are the dimensions taken into consideration for customer loyalty based on the review of literature.

Perceived security is the extent to which consumers believe that the internet is safe for exchanging information for the business. It greatly affects the customers' adoption of e-tail service (Kim & Shim, 2002). The influence of awareness of personal security was found more on males than females (Chiu, Lin, and Tang, 2005). Perceived Value is the customer's subjective probability that e-tail will efficiently facilitate his or her purchasing (Koufaris, 2002; Taylor & Todd, 1995; Teo, 2001).

Davis et.al. (1989) states that the theoretical foundations for perceived value are derived from several research streams, including self-efficacy theory, a cost-benefit paradigm, and adoption of innovations research. Product Assortment is backed by customer's preference for innovativeness and desire to seek new stimuli and is even more relevant for artificial intelligence (Dabholkar & Bagozzi, 2002). A variety of studies have seen the influence of product assortment on customer loyalty in e-tail (Goldsmith, 2002; Chiu, Lin, and Tang, 2005). Shopping experience is the most effective way to differentiate the organization from the competition. It drives loyalty when customers are engaged on an emotional, intellectual, or even spiritual level, and enjoy the product before, during and after its use. Shopping experience is an important variable of customer satisfaction and loyalty (Weijters et.al. 2007). Perception of adoption of Artificial Intelligence varies across demographic variables (Gender, Age, Education, Marital Status and Income). Demographic variables are commonly used for segmentation as usage of technology varies across different demographic groups. By considering gender differences, e-tailers can better target the right consumers (Chiu, Lin, and Tang, 2005). Additionally, literature on technology adoption has established important role played by demographics in this setting. Acceptance of Artificial Intelligence is more strongly driven by attitude among younger people and men's attitude for its value (Morris & Venkatesh, 2000; Venkatesh et al., 2003). Newness in the form of artificial intelligence is impacted by gender, education and age differences (Robertson and Gatignon, 1991; Im, Bayus, & Mason, 2003; Weijters et.al., 2007). Highly educated people normally adopt artificial intelligence for time preference (Weijters.et.al., 2007; Morris & Venkatesh, 2000). The above literature thus formed the basis of further study.

Objective of the Study

The objectives of the study are:

1. Understanding the impact of Artificial Intelligence on customer loyalty in the Indian Retail Sector.
2. Investigating the Efficacy of Demographics (Gender, Age, Marital Status, Educational Qualification, and Income) as Predictors of Adoption of Artificial Intelligence in Retail Sector.

HYPOTHESES

Based on the review of literature, the following hypotheses have been framed:

H1: There is a significant impact of adoption of Artificial Intelligence on customer loyalty in the retail sector.

H1a: There is significant impact of adoption of Artificial Intelligence on Perceived security in the retail sector.

H1b: There is significant impact of adoption of Artificial Intelligence on Perceived Value in the retail sector.

H1c: There is significant impact of adoption of Artificial Intelligence on Product Assortment in the retail sector.

H1d: There is significant impact of adoption of Artificial Intelligence on Shopping Experience in the retail sector.

H2: There exists a significant relationship between perception of adoption of Artificial Intelligence and Demographic Variables (Gender, Age, Marital Status, Educational Qualification and Income).

H2a: There exists a significant relationship between perception of adoption of Artificial Intelligence and Gender.

H2b: There exists a significant relationship between perception of adoption of Artificial Intelligence and Age.

H2c: There exists a significant relationship between perception of adoption of Artificial Intelligence and Marital Status.

H2d: There exists a significant relationship between perception of adoption of Artificial Intelligence and Educational Qualification.

H2e: There exists a significant relationship between perception of adoption of Artificial Intelligence and Income.

DATA ANALYSIS AND RESEARCH RESULTS

Respondent Profile

The questionnaire included a section on respondent socio-demographic information such as gender, age, marital status, annual income, education level and profession. A total of 125 questionnaires were distributed and a total of 100 questionnaires were found usable for analysis. The sample consists of more males (59.0.%) than females (41.0%). Majority of the population consists of age group of 26-33 years (35%). The second majority consists of age group of 18-25 years (28%). This younger population are more tech savvy; therefore, majority of the population is single (60.4%). There are 39.6% married respondents in the sample. About 40.4% of the respondents are from science background which is highest. 32.5% are from non-science background and others constitute 27.2%. The graduate population forms 37.7% of total sample. 46.8% of people have done their masters. Most of the people earn less than Rs. 20,000 to 60,000 per month (54.0%). Roughly 46.0% of the population earns between Rs. 60,001 to Rs. 1,00,000 per month.

Correlation Analysis

Table 1 illustrates the results of correlation coefficients for the factors mentioned in the hypotheses. The Pearson product-moment correlation coefficient (or Pearson correlation coefficient, for short) is referred to as a measure of the strength of a linear association between two variables and is denoted by r. It can be noted that four constructs of customer loyalty i.e. Perceived Security; Shopping Experience; Product Assortment; Perceived Value is influenced by adoption of Artificial Intelligence in the retail sector. All associations were found to be significant at 95 per cent level, with the strongest association being adoption of Artificial Intelligence and Shopping Experience ($r=0.606$, $p\leq.05$) followed by Product Assortment ($r=0.554$, $p\leq.05$) and Perceived Value ($r=0.541$, $p\leq.05$). However, there was found to be a weak association between adoption of Artificial Intelligence and Perceived Security ($r=0.446$, $p\leq.05$). Hence hypothesis H1a, H1b, H1c, H1d are accepted.

Table 1. Pearson correlation analysis results

Hypotheses	Factors	The Intention of an Individual to Adopt Artificial Intelligence	
		Correlation Coefficient (r)	Significance (Two-tailed)
H1	Perceived Security	0.446	0.005
H2	Perceived Value	0.541	0.025
H3	Product Assortment	0.554	0.002
H4	Shopping Experience	0.606	0.001

Note: Correlation is significant at the 0.05 level (two-tailed)

Regression Analysis

In the next step, to recognize the influence of AI on the customer loyalty, four dimensions i.e. Perceived Security (PS); Shopping Experience (SE); Product Assortment (PA); Perceived Value (PV), multiple regression was applied. The results were found to be significant at $p\leq.05$ level and value of adjusted $R^2=0.349$. Table 2 shows that a significant value of 9.945 for the F-distribution with 3 and 97 df. F-test used as an indicator to assess the significance of the regression, with a $P < 0.05$; so, the results show that a significant relationship exists between AI and customer loyalty. AI predicts 38.88% of the variance in Customer loyalty, as R^2=0.388. Whereas the correlation coefficient indicates a moderate positive linear relationship between the variables (Table 2). According to these expected results, it indicates that AI weakly explained the variance in customer loyalty. Table 2 highlights the beta values that indicate each variables' explanatory power. The constructs, numbered on the basis of importance as shown by beta coefficient(β) which is the standardised regression coefficient, are Shopping Experience (SE) (β=0.558), Product Assortment(PA) (β=.406), Perceived Value (PV) (β=.398), and Perceived Security (PS)(β=.311). The results support the framed hypotheses i.e. H1, H1a, H1b, H1c, H1d. The explanatory variables were thoroughly scrutinized for issues pertaining to multicollinearity. Tolerance Value (TV) and Variance Inflation Factor (VIF) for each explanatory variable was utilized to assess the issue of multicollinearity. It can be seen from Table 2 that TV and VIF are within the permissible limit.

Table 2. Artificial intelligence and customer loyalty

Independent Variable		Standardized Regression Coefficients	T-value	Significance Probability	TV	VIF
Constant		1.612(.247)	6.571	.000		
Shopping Experience		0.558	4.378	.000	0.802	1.248
Product Assortment		.406	3.549	.001	.994	1.006
Perceived Value		.398	3.311	.002	.995	1.006
Perceived security		0.311	2.445	.018	.806	1.241
Multiple *R*	.623					
R^2	.388					
Adjusted R^2	.349					
Durbin- Watson Test	1.70					
F	9.945			.005		
Sample Size	100					

* Beta co-efficient is the standardised regression co-efficient which allows comparison of the relatives on the dependent variable of each independent variable.

** t-statistics help to determine the relative importance of each variable in the model.

Investigating the Efficacy of Demographics as Predictors of Adoption of Artificial Intelligence in Retail Sector

One-way ANOVA was used to measure the perception of adoption of Artificial Intelligence in the retail sector across various demographic variables (Gender, Age,

Education, Marital Status, Educational Qualification and Income). Table 3 shows results of one-way ANOVA for demographic variables as independent and adoption of Artificial Intelligence as the dependent variable. From the results, it can be inferred that there is a significant difference for adoption of Artificial Intelligence across gender at 95% level of significance [F (1, 98) = 4.411, p = 0.038]. Hence hypothesis H2a is rejected.

Table 3. One-way ANOVA

	Gender		Age		Marital Status		Qualification		Income	
	F-value	Sig.	F-value	Sig.	F-value	Sig.	F-value	Sig.	F-value	Sig.
Adoption of Artificial Intelligence	4.411	.038*	3.049	.052	7.094	.009*	3.483	.035*	2.836	.042*

Table 3 also shows that there is no significant difference on adoption of artificial intelligence across age. Hence hypothesis H2b is rejected. From the table, one can conclude that there is a significant effect of marital status on adoption of artificial intelligence at 95% level of significance [F (1, 98) = 7.094, p = 0.0094]. Hence hypothesis H2c is rejected. Moreover, there is found to be a significant difference in adoption of Artificial Intelligence at the p<.05 level across Educational Qualification [F (2, 97) = 3.483, p = 0.035]. Hence hypothesis H2e is rejected. Also, there is found to be a significant difference for adoption of artificial intelligence across income at 95% level of significance [F (3, 96) = 2.836, p = 0.042].

CONCLUSION, RECOMMENDATIONS AND LIMITATIONS

This study helps to expand understanding of how AI enhances the customer loyalty. In the present study, the customer loyalty was operationalized by four constructs of customer loyalty being Perceived Security; Shopping Experience; Product Assortment; Perceived Value. Correlation analysis was used to measure the relationship among the variables. The results found that there is a positive relationship between AI and all four constructs of customer loyalty and that there is a direct and strong relationship between providing Shopping Experience and AI. Perceived Security is an important factor for retailers to consider when introducing technologies and deploying AI. Artificial intelligence (AI) is revolutionizing the way customers interact with retail stores. In time of slow economic growth and disrupting developments, retail firms are competing with each to survive and expand customer base. Retailers attempt to enhance the base of customers by providing convenience and personalization of retail services (Kaur et.al., 2020). There is a need to do a detailed analysis of their consumer preferences and buying behaviour. Introduction of Artificial intelligence will enable retailers to make higher revenues. It is recommended that companies in the retail industry can utilize artificial intelligence to enhance the customer experience across the customers' buying process especially the awareness stage. Retailers should try to offer more personalized services to customers which will result in influencing their overall experience with a better understanding of the services and products. Digital transformation and automation is an ongoing process that is continuously improving and AI is one of the most important components of this revolution. Indian industry has not yet taken full advantage of artificial intelligence technologies for increasing business performance. The strengthening belief of customers on technology will bring a major change in the Indian retail industry and consumers who enjoy their shopping experience will make more purchases.

To augment the customer loyalty requires the adoption and deployment of appropriate information technology infrastructure which leads to enriching the customer experience through the usage of innovated tools and solutions of artificial intelligence. Undoubtedly, AI will improve the consumer experiences & their interaction with products and services, hence, impacting customer loyalty. The research suffers from few limitations which should be taken into consideration in future work. A larger sample size is required to get better model fit and more generalised results. Secondly, this is because the implementation of many of artificial technologies are recent and the benefits are not feasible to be obtained in the short term. Further, studies should be conducted to investigate the ethics and security of AI technology from a consumer perspective.

REFERENCES

Aggarwal, A., & Yadav, V. K. (2015). Impact of Technology in E- Retailing Operations: A Consumer Perspective. *Procedia: Social and Behavioral Sciences*, *189*, 252–258. doi:10.1016/j.sbspro.2015.03.220

Alexander, A., Nell, D., Bailey, A. R., & Shaw, G. (2009). Theco-creation of a retail innovation: Shoppers and the earlysupermarket in Britain. *Enterprise and Society*, *10*(3), 529–558. doi:10.1093/es/khp016

Balaji, M. S., & Roy, S. (2017). Value co-creation with Internet of things technology in the retail industry. *Journal of Marketing Management*, *33*(1-2), 7–31. doi:10.10 80/0267257X.2016.1217914

Berman, B., & Evans, J. R. (2010). *Retail Management: A Strategic Approach* (11th ed.). Pearson Education, Inc.

Berry, L. L., Bolton, R. N., Bridges, C. H., Meyer, J., Parasuraman, A., & Seiders, K. (2010). Opportunities for innovation inthe delivery of interactive retail services. *Journal of Interactive Marketing*, *24*(2), 155–167. doi:10.1016/j.intmar.2010.02.001

Chiu, Y. B., Lin, C. P., & Tang, L. L. (2005). Gender differs: Assessing a model of online purchase intentions in e-tail service. *International Journal of Service Industry Management*, *16*(5), 416–435. doi:10.1108/09564230510625741

Cowan, K., & Ketron, S. (2019). A dual model of product involvement for effective virtual reality: The roles of imagination, co-creation, telepresence, and interactivity. *Journal of Business Research*, *100*, 483–492. doi:10.1016/j.jbusres.2018.10.063

Dabholkar, P. A., & Bagozzi, R. (2002). An attitudinal model of technology-based self-service: Moderating effects of consumer traits and situational factors. *Journal of the Academy of Marketing Science*, *30*(3), 184–201. doi:10.1177/0092070302303001

Davis, F. D., Bagozzi, R. P., & Warshaw, P. R. (1989). User acceptance of computer technology: A comparison of two theoretical models. *Management Science*, *35*(8), 982–1003. doi:10.1287/mnsc.35.8.982

Eastlick, M. A., Ratto, C., Lotz, S. L., & Mishra, A. (2012). Exploring antecedents of attitude toward co-producing a retailcheckout service utilizing a self-service technology. *International Review of Retail, Distribution and Consumer Research*, *22*(4), 337–364. doi:10.1080/09593969.2012.690775

Fiore, A., Kim, J., & Lee, H. (2005). Effect of image interactivity technology on consumer responses toward the online retailer. *Journal of Interactive Marketing*, *19*(3), 38–53. doi:10.1002/dir.20042

Gandhi, B. M., & Chinnadorai, K. M. (2017). Retail in India. *International Journal of Engineering Development and Research*, *5*(1), 433–435.

Goldsmith, R. E. (2002). Explaining and predicting consumer intention to purchase over the internet: An exploratory study. *Journal of Marketing Theory and Practice*, *10*(1), 22–28. doi:10.1080/10696679.2002.11501913

Henning, T. T., & Klee, A. (1997). The Impact of customer satisfaction and relationship quality on customer retention: A critical reassessment and model development. *Psychology and Marketing*, *14*(8), 737–764. doi:10.1002/(SICI)1520-6793(199712)14:8<737::AID-MAR2>3.0.CO;2-F

Im, S., Bayus, B. L., & Mason, C. H. (2003). An empirical study of innate consumer innovativeness, personal characteristics, and new-product adoption behavior. *Journal of the Academy of Marketing Science, 31*(1), 61–72. doi:10.1177/0092070302238602

Kalaignanam, K., Kushwaha, T., & Rajavi, K. (2018). How Does Web Personalization Create Value for Online Retailers? Lower Cash Flow Volatility or Enhanced Cash Flows. *Journal of Retailing, 94*(3), 265–279. doi:10.1016/j.jretai.2018.05.001

Kaur, J., Arora, V., & Bali, S. (2020). Influence of technological advances and change in marketing strategies using analytics in retail industry. *International Journal of System Assurance Engineering and Management, 11*(5), 953–961. doi:10.100713198-020-01023-5

Kim, Y. M., & Shim, K. Y. (2002). The influence of internet shopping mall characteristics and user traits on purchase intent. *Irish Marketing Review, 15*(2), 25–34.

Koufaris, M. (2002). Applying the technology acceptance model and flow theory to online consumer behavior. *Information Systems Research, 13*(2), 205–223. doi:10.1287/isre.13.2.205.83

Lamantia, J. (2009, August 17). Inside out: interaction design for Augmented Reality. *UXMatters*. https://www.uxmatters.com/mt/archives/2009/08/inside-out-interaction-design-for-augmented-reality.php

Lee, M., Cheung, C., & Chen, Z. (2005). Acceptance of Internet-based learning medium: The role of extrinsic and intrinsic motivation. *Information & Management, 42*(8), 1095–1104. doi:10.1016/j.im.2003.10.007

Mollen, A., & Wilson, H. (2010). Engagement, telepresence and interactivity in online consumer experience: Reconciling scholastic and managerial perspectives. *Journal of Business Research, 63*(9-10), 919–925. doi:10.1016/j.jbusres.2009.05.014

Morris, M. G., & Venkatesh, V. (2000). Age differences in technology adoption decisions: Implications for a changing work force. *Personnel Psychology, 53*(2), 375–403. doi:10.1111/j.1744-6570.2000.tb00206.x

Pantano, E., & Pietro, L. (2012). Understanding Consumer's Acceptance of Technology-BasedInnovations in Retailing. *Journal of Technology Management & Innovation, 7*(4), 483–492. doi:10.4067/S0718-27242012000400001

Parise, S., Guinan, P., & Kafka, R. (2016). Solving the crisis of immediacy: How digital technology can transform the customer experience. *Business Horizons, 59*(4), 411–420. doi:10.1016/j.bushor.2016.03.004

Porter, M. E., & Heppelmann, J. E. (2014). How Smart, Connected Products Are Transforming Competition. *Harvard Business Review*, *92*, 64–88.

Reinatz, W., Manfred, K., & Wayne, H. D. (2004). The Customer Relationship Management Process: Its Measurements and Impact on Performance. *JMR, Journal of Marketing Research*, *41*(3), 293–305. doi:10.1509/jmkr.41.3.293.35991

Robertson, T. S., & Gatignon, H. (1991). How innovators thwart new entrants into their market. *Planning Review*, *19*(5), 4–13. doi:10.1108/eb054333

Rowley, J., & Slack, F. (2003). Kiosks in retailing: The quiet revolution. *International Journal of Retail & Distribution Management*, *31*(6), 329–333. doi:10.1108/09590550310476060

Rust, R. T., & Huang, M. H. (2014). The Service Revolution and the Transformation of Marketing Science. *Marketing Science*, *33*(2), 206–221. doi:10.1287/mksc.2013.0836

Sima, V., Gheorghe, I. G., Subić, J., & Nancu, D. (2020). Influences of the Industry 4.0 Revolution on the Human Capital Development and Consumer Behavior: A Systematic Review. *Sustainability*, *12*(10), 4035–4063. doi:10.3390u12104035

Singh, R., & Khan, I. (2012). An Approach to Increase Customer Retention and Loyalty in B2C World. *International Journal of Scientific and Research Publications*, *2*(6), 1–5.

Sorescu, A., Frambach, R. T., Singh, J., Rangaswamy, A., & Bridges, C. (2011). Innovations in Retail Business Models. *Journal of Retailing*, *87*, 3–16. doi:10.1016/j.jretai.2011.04.005

Taylor, S., & Todd, P. A. (1995). Understanding information technology usage: A test of competing models. *Information Systems Research*, *6*(2), 144–177. doi:10.1287/isre.6.2.144

Teo, T. S. H. (2001). Demographic and motivation variables associated with internet usage activities. *Internet Research*, *11*(2), 125–137. doi:10.1108/10662240110695089

Venkatesh, V., Morris, M. G., Davis, G. B., & Davis, F. D. (2003). User acceptance of information technology: Toward a unified view. *Management Information Systems Quarterly*, *27*(3), 425–478. doi:10.2307/30036540

Weijters, B., Rangarajan, D., Falk, T., & Schillewaert, N. (2007). Determinants and outcomes of customers' use of self-service technology in a retail setting. *Journal of Service Research*, *10*(1), 3–21. doi:10.1177/1094670507302990

Weinberg, B. D., Milne, G. R., Andonova, Y. G., & Hajjat, F. M. (2015). Internet of things: Convenience vs. privacy and secrecy. *Business Horizons*, *58*(6), 615–624. doi:10.1016/j.bushor.2015.06.005

Woszczynski, A. B., Roth, P. L., & Segars, A. H. (2002). Exploring the theoretical foundations of playfulness in computerinteractions. *Computers in Human Behavior*, *18*(4), 369–388. doi:10.1016/S0747-5632(01)00058-9

Ziaie, A., Shami Zanjani, M., & Manian, A. (2021). Systematic review of digital value propositions in the retail sector: New approach for digital experience study. *Electronic Commerce Research and Applications*, *47*, 101053. doi:10.1016/j.elerap.2021.101053

Chapter 3
Hyper-Personalization:
An AI-Enabled Personalization for Customer-Centric Marketing

Darshana Desai
https://orcid.org/0000-0001-5458-4994
Indira College of Engineering and Management, India

ABSTRACT

Personalization is widely used to attract and retain customers in online business addressing one size fits all issues, but little is addressed to contextualise users' real-time needs. E-commerce website owners use these strategies for customer-centric marketing through enhanced experience but fail in designing effective personalization due to the dynamic nature of users' needs and pace of information exposure. To address this, this chapter explores hyper-personalization strategies to overcome users' implicit need to be served better. The research presents a hyper-personalization process with learning (ML) and artificial intelligence (AI) techniques for marketing functions like segmentation, targeting, and positioning based on real-time analytics throughout the customer journey and key factors driving effective customer-centric marketing. This chapter facilitates marketers to use AI-enabled personalization to address customers' implicit needs and leverage higher returns by delivering the right information at the right time to the right customer through the right channel.

PERSONALIZATION AND ARTIFICIAL INTELLIGENCE

Recent growth in online business has resulted in increased use of different personalized services to develop one to one customer relationships, effective marketing, and to attract

DOI: 10.4018/978-1-7998-7959-6.ch003

users and retain customers. Ecommerce websites use personalization as an effective strategy by providing one to one services like product recommendation, information and ratings of the product by satisfying individual users' needs. Personalization is used in different dimension like information, interface and structural navigation of the website on one to one basis, information and navigation personalization increase satisfaction level with highly relevant content which reduces cognitive efforts on ecommerce website over information overload (Desai 2019). Ecommerce Websites like Amazon.in provide product recommendations based on collaborative filtering techniques and also suggest some frequently buy items with people having similar interest in products. User's' navigational behavior and search is analyzed and extracted knowledge is used to target users by showcasing advertisements catering their implicit need e.g. Facebook.com, and gmail.com. Personalization of Social Networking websites have also shown significant impact of control to develop trust towards website (Desai 2021) which can be significantly used as an effective marketing tool for advertisement. Vendors are also using personalization to match advertising and promotions with customers' individual needs and preferences in what is known as targeted or behavioral advertising. Personalization is widely used and has always been one of the key drivers of creating enhanced customer experience in the digital business to remain in the marketplace across industries. A Gartner survey in 2019 found that 38% of customers stop interacting with the e-commerce website and unsubscribe if they find personalization efforts by the business are irrelevant and creepy. Marketing leaders strive to achieve a highly tailored message to customers to cater to the dynamic needs of the customer. However, with evolving customer awareness, digital marketing, and brand promotion in business need to elevate and redesign marketing strategies to push personalization to different levels by enabling adaptive content, functionality, and interaction in real-time in the digital landscape.

Personalization is extensively used in marketing but struggles in design of marketing strategies for customer centricity due to its dynamic needs. Hyper-personalization has emerged as an advanced way of marketing with real-time analytics of data, Artificial intelligence, and automation to bridge the gap. Artificial Intelligence is not only used in the ecommerce sector it is emerging to facilitate customers from various other domains like financial, healthcare, ecommerce services etc. Recent studies focus on handling strategic marketing issues to achieve personalization and its impact like unstructured data handling to integrate with existing areas of marketing, recent studies trying to tackle strategic marketing issues. Balducci and Marinova 2018 identified use of unstructured data for several areas of marketing, Agarwal et al. 2020 explored use of analytics for consumer value in healthcare, Tong et al. 2020 used machine learning technique for prediction with personalized mobile marketing, and Kumar et al. 2019 used AI for engaging customer using personalization, also Desai 2019 found positive impact of personalization on customer satisfaction.

AI enabled personalization caters highly contextualized experience to individual consumers to meet distinct implicit and explicit needs across each touch point consumer journey using real-time data analytics, 360-degree customer view, and providing communication of the right product or service, at the right place, right time, and right channel. Hyper-personalization gives more insight to understand customers better, dives deep to analyze their behavior, preferences, likes, and understand needs and wants of customers. Hyper-personalization leverages real-time data analytics and AI to generate a highly contextualized customer experience.

IBM Watson uses AI to provide personalized services for delivering real-time, automated personalized information having data-driven customer insights which makes customer centric marketing endeavors more feasible. Although AI based services are in the market, it is having only 13% of usage and technology adoption for customer centric personalized marketing. Hyper personalization continues to provide a unique experience throughout the customer journey with the business creating customer gnomes having details like customer demographics, interaction with the website, purchase history, location, and preferences. This chapter introduces hyper-personalization in section one subsequently describing hyper-personalization stages for effective marketing, application of AI enabled personalization across different verticals and the future areas.

HYPER-PERSONALIZATION FOR CUSTOMER CENTRIC MARKETING

Hyper-personalization is used as a customer-centric marketing strategy in e-commerce and social networking websites to influence through improved personalized customer experience. This empowers businesses for effective marketing by delivering timely information dissemination, recommendation, tailored content, and communication to the customers that lead to higher satisfaction.

Hyper personalization is the continuous process to deliver information or services to the customer based on their implicit analyzing users' web space behavior and purchase habits. As hyper-personalization requires real-time data to meet ever-changing customer demand and interaction it is implemented throughout the interaction with the business from marketing, to purchase, after-sales service, and recommendation for future business. Customer centric marketing through hyper personalized experience is about customizing all activities and, as a result, building fierce consumer loyalty. Companies do this in a number of ways; customizing products is the most obvious, but it is just as important to personalize the shopping experience. This can be done by tailoring recommendations and by mapping the customer journey—personalizing the customer experience across all interactions and all channels. This provides the ability to constantly analyze consumer feedback in order to build the best possible shopping experience from first contact to becoming a repeat buyer.

Users' unique 360-degree profile is created with continuous intelligent learning and inferring need hyper-personalization uses customer information to tailor content, products, and services to a customer's wants and preferences. **User modeling** of data includes customers' demographic information, profile, geographic locations data captured through mobile location, usage trail on website, purchase history, and social media presence and likings. These details are highly contextualized to deliver real-time offerings and recommendations to the users. Hyper-personalization pulls highly relevant information, product recommendations, or services understanding user real-time sentiments, through Internet of Things (IoT) data predictive analytics and prescriptive analytics which deepens personalization and takes it to a higher level of contextualization

Hyper-personalization helps businesses to engage more effectively with existing customers and attract new prospective customers with prescriptive analytics. Highly contextualized interaction, information sharing, and communication to the right customers help to build a stronger relationship. This eventually helps businesses to cater to customers' individual needs, boost customers' trust and satisfaction to build brand loyalty and effective marketing(Desai 2021). Though hyper-personalization has inherent benefits, it requires more real-time attention, higher collaborative work to build relevant personalization strategies for individual customers, this not only demands efforts but the huge investment to implement real-time analytics involving data capturing, addressing privacy concerns, and highly proactive, built-in analytics systems.

PREREQUISITE FOR HYPER PERSONALIZATION

To provide a hyper-personalized experience to the customer, marketers need to construct user modeling covering all the aspects of customers through AI-enabled technologies, customers' dynamic profile, social interactions, likings, preferences, purchase behavior, and lifestyle tracing. Hyper-personalization is a prevailing tool for online marketing in the technology space integrating data from various system sources to build a collaborative model presented to address different customer segments. The Genomes of the customer is created with 360-degree details of the customer to build strength to the system with technologies like big data analytics, artificial intelligence (AI), machine learning, and advanced data analytics to hold personalization.

Hyper-personalized marketing strategies can be enabled for customer-centric unique experience using:

- **Real-time customer data**. The marketer needs to take control and be tech-savvy to produce the result of dynamic customer data to provide a real-time personalized experience and design a marketing strategy. Real-time data regarding customers' social interactions, geo locations, online behavior, and search history need to be mapped to the existing genome details of the customer for effective marketing.
- **Customer modelling with unifying data sets to achieve a 360-degree customer view (Creating customer Genome).**

The data stored inside different sources individually do not create value but can provide insightful information to design marketing strategy by connecting all scattered information through real-time analytics using big data technologies. The genome of Customer or 360-degree view of customer helps marketers to design marketing strategies which are highly customer-centric to provide a unified view. This amalgamation of data from various sources empower marketers to create a highly personalized experience for their customers which leads to higher customer satisfaction and build trust (Desai 2019, Desai 2020)

- **Proactive customer engagement. A unified view of each customer and centralized data of customer** facilitate marketers to not only generate micro-segment of customers by collaborative filtering presentation to address like-minded customers to disseminate relevant information through different communication channel for advertisement at various geo-location and engage the customer with proactive action to provide the right information at right time through the right channel for effective personalization and create a hyper-personalized experience for the customer.

HYPER-PERSONALIZATION PROCESS FOR STP (SEGMENTATION, TARGETING AND POSITIONING)

Hyper personalization is the constant process to cater users' individual needs on a real-time basis based on the level of interaction of the users. This involves following processes in order to achieve hyper personalized, customer centric services and product recommendations produced to retain existing customers and attract new users to convert into customers and leverage the business.

AI and Data Collection

Recent studies focus on data collection based on AI for personalization like customer profiling and intelligence include consumer data, their activity trails on website interaction, environments through their used connected devices (Cooke and Zubcsek 2017), retail analytics like use of heat maps, video surveillance (Kirkpatrick 2020), Internet of Things based services enables tracking of consumer their product consumption, location (Ng and Wakenshaw 2017), location based services and advanced analytics can capture customer unstructured data through online presence and interaction (Balducci and Marinova 2018), consumers driving behavior analysis and tracking used to determine personalized insurance premiums(Soleymanian et al. 2019).

Getting the information about the customers' needs and preferences is an important step towards personalized recommendation offerings in the form of services or products. Data Collection automation facilitates through various instruments such as connecting technologies like IoT, social networking sites, mobile apps, and sensor based technologies like remote sensing and detectors and wearable devices like smart watches, fit bits. Customer Data Platforms (CDP) is maintained with integration of the users' information from their website interactions with web analytics, CRM data maintained in the form of transaction history, customer support interaction and demographic data. Geo-location of the customer, average spending and satisfaction level of customers and sentiments fetched through reviews and social media comments also plays a major role in the process of hyper personalization.

AI and ML Techniques for Marketing Strategy (STP) in Hyper-Personalization

Recent studies demonstrated numerous use of AI & ML techniques like predictive and prescriptive analytics for market analysis. Consumer research uses automated text analytics for marketing insights like prediction and customer understanding, consumer research and heuristics based analytics (Humphreys and Wang 2018, Berger et al. 2019, Dzyabura and Hauser 2011). Data generated from diverse big data sources and various forms like structured data like customer transactions and unstructured in the form of reviews and comments are now used for big data analytics for marketing insights and strategy formation (Wedel and Kannan 2016; Berger et al. 2019; Liu et al. 2016).

Customer Segmentation

In marketing practice, predictive analytics are commonly used to predict volatile market trends and customers' heterogeneous preferences. After data collection the customer information base with segments is prepared by analyzing information using machine learning techniques clustering and classification. Customer Segmentation is used to produce hyper personalized messaging, and offerings to the likeminded customers' requirement after identifying customers purchase habits. Hyper personalization uses automated segmentation of customers considering the dynamic nature of customer choices and needs making interactions producing more trust and satisfaction (Desai 2019, Desai 2021). Supervised Learning methods like classification algorithms are used to model for categorizing loan approval, customer segmentation based on sparse learning for preferences by customer (Netzer et al. 2019; Chen, Iyengar, and Iyengar 2017), micro segment for retail big data (Dekimpe 2020). Unsupervised Learning method like clustering used for customer unlabeled data like behavior for segment generation to decide marketing strategies and actions based on price, product, promotion and place or channel.

Customer Targeting

After segmentation of customers recommendation is generated based on derived personalization rules from ML for targeting customer with marketing strategies. Hyper personalized recommendation is generated with collaborative filtering techniques by analyzing purchase history, purchase pattern, items in the cart, related and liked items, products liked and bought by other customers. Prior studies used ML for target optimization for promotions to new customers and digital profiling (Simester et al. 2020; Neumann et al. 2019), targeting customers based on ML for brand promotion in retailing through right channel (Danaher et al. 2020), adaptive personalized systems design for targeting customer with 360 degree view based on real-time analytics (Chung et al. 2016; Liebman et al. 2019; Dzyabura and Hauser 2019), Deep Learning techniques for personalized recommendations (Guo et al. 2018) and collaborative filtering based automated recommendations of videos, music or products through recommender systems(Lu, Xiao, and Ding 2016).

Positioning

Analytics results in the previous phase generates possible paths for hyper personalized interaction with the customers which help to select appropriate channels, timing of messages or offerings produced at the right time to the right customer satisfying customer implicit real-time needs. Personalization benefits, due to its ability to recognize patterns from data (e.g., text mining, speech recognition, facial recognition). Any marketing functions and activities that can benefit from personalized outcomes should consider thinking AI. The most common applications in marketing are various personalized recommendation systems (Chung et al. 2009; Chung et al. 2016), such as Netflix movie recommendations and Amazon cross-selling recommendations. Data Mining techniques used for positioning a perceptual map for various customer base (Daabes and Kharbat 2017), trained conversational AI chatbots for brand promotion and customer relationship management at various stages for brand personality (Wilson and Daugherty 2018, Luo et al. 2019), AI based personalized marketing engagement and customer service throughout journey, brand reputation tracking through sentiment analysis on social media platforms reviews, ratings and comments (Kumar et al. 2019, Huang and Rust 2020)

Continuous feedback must be taken on every hyper personalized interaction in order to improve recommendation and generating highly contextualized and relevant offerings to the customers in future, this also helps in evaluating existing process and accuracy of the algorithms through various metrics on a real-time basis.

HYPER-PERSONALIZED CUSTOMER-CENTRIC MARKETING PROCESS

E-commerce websites use personalization tools as an effective marketing strategy but AI-enabled real-time analytics on big data have captured the market through hyper-personalization. Digital Marketing is recently revolutionized with innovative, highly contextualized, direct-to-consumer brands or products to lead the consumer through hyper-personalized experiences to cater to individual needs and make them feel special. Hyper-personalization creates unique, relevant, and highly cognitive experiences for the customer at every interaction with the brand. Companies like Netflix, Amazon, Starbucks and many other giants have raised the bar of personalization and changed the game of digital personalized marketing for competitors. Cutting through this glut of communications requires four R's for effective marketing: (1) reaching the right consumer, (2) with the right product, (3) at the right time, and (4) through the right channel.

CUSTOMER JOURNEY AND HYPER-PERSONALIZED OFFERINGS

Hyper-personalization can be effectively used to reach out to a large customer base through analyzing existing customers' connections to attract new and retain existing

Figure 1. Hyper-personalization process for customer centric marketing

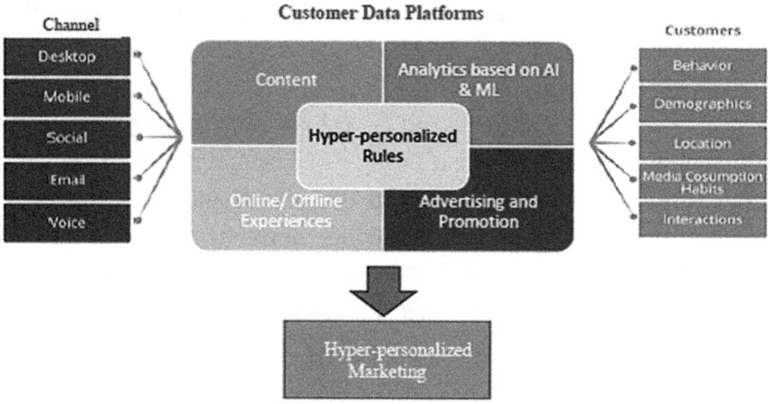

customers for all the interaction with the personalized landing page, personalized services, dynamic pricing, etc. Hyper personalized advertising uses customer basic profile, geo-location, and purchase history, interaction with the website, likes, and preferences to generate personalized content, targeted advertisement.

CONCLUSION

Hyper-personalization is an emerging technology with AI-enabled personalization. This chapter presents an overview of hyper-personalization and its current use in e-commerce marketing by business giants. Artificial Intelligence and Machine Learning algorithms can be effectively used for designing marketing strategy segmentation, targeting and positioning with recommendations, personalized offerings of the product and services also personalized interaction for effective customer relationship management. Business owners need to integrate with existing customer demographic profile data, location, transaction details, preferences of the customers to store in customer Data Platform for efficient analysis and derivation of hyper-personalized rules to serve customer better and customer centric marketing to leverage the business. Further technical implementation with real time case study can be developed based on the suggested way of Machine Learning Techniques to produce hyper-personalized experience to the users.

Figure 2. Customer journey and hyper-personalized offerings

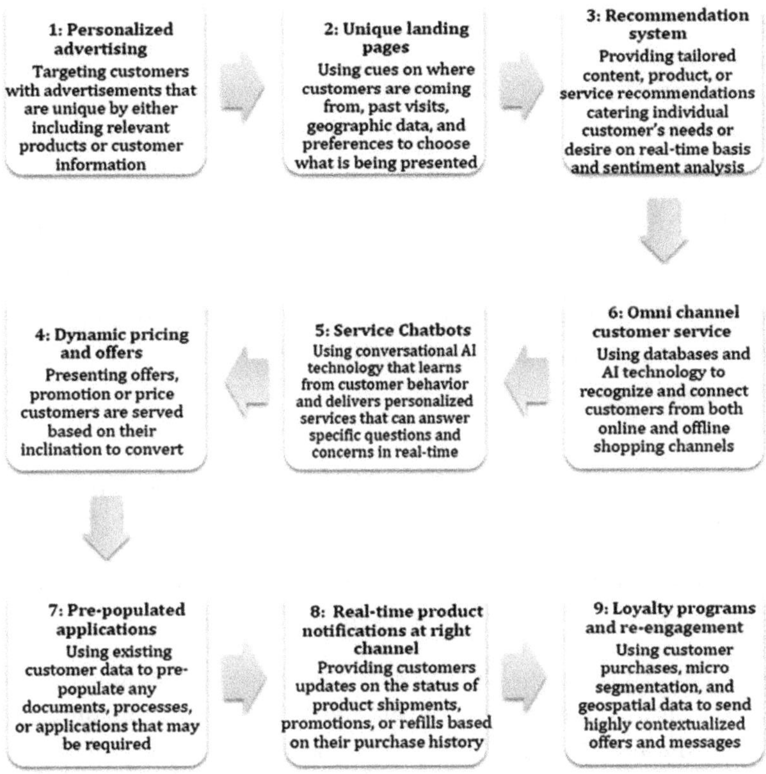

REFERENCES

Abbott, J., & Minasian, P. (2020). The Modern Retailer Imperative: Creating Hyper-personalized. *Connected Customer Experiences*, 1–12.

Abdollahpouri, H., Adomavičius, G., Burke, R., Guy, I., Jannach, D., Kamishima, T., Krasnodebski, J., & Pizzato, L. (2019). *Beyond Personalization: Research Directions in Multi Stakeholder Recommendation*. doi:10.1007/s11257-019-09256

Agarwal, R., Dugas, M., Gao, G., & Kannan, P. K. (2020). Emerging technologies and analytics for a new era of value-centered marketing in healthcare. *Journal of the Academy of Marketing Science, 48*(2), 9–23.

Balducci, B., & Marinova, D. (2018). Unstructured data in marketing. *Journal of the Academy of Marketing Science, 46*(4), 557–590.

Berger, J., Humphreys, A., Ludwig, S., Moe, W. W., Netzer, O., & Schweidel, D. A. (2019). Uniting the tribes: Using text for marketing insight. *Journal of Marketing, 84*(1), 1–25.

Chen, Y., Lee, J. Y., Sridhar, S., Mittal, V., McCallister, K., & Singal, A. G. (2020). Improving cancer outreach effectiveness through targeting and economic assessments: Insights from a randomized field experiment. *Journal of Marketing, 84*(3), 1–27.

Ciuffo, J. (2019). Artificial Intelligence in Marketing. *Artificial Intelligence and Machine Learning for Business for Non-Engineers,* 71–76. doi:10.1201/9780367821654-6

Cooke, A. D. J., & Zubcsek, P. P. (2017). The connected consumer: Connected devices and the evolution of customer intelligence. *Journal of the Association for Consumer Research, 2*(2), 164–178.

Daabes, A. S. A., & Kharbat, F. F. (2017). Customer-based perceptual map as a marketing intelligence source. *International Journal of Economics and Business Research, 13*(4), 360–379. doi:10.1504/IJEBR.2017.084381

Dekimpe, M. (2020). Retailing and retailing research in the age of big data analytics. *International Journal of Research in Marketing, 37*, 3–14.

Desai, D. (2019). An Empirical Study of Website Personalization Effect on Users Intention to Revisit E-commerce Website through Cognitive and Hedonic Experience. In V. Balas, N. Sharma, & A. Chakrabarti (Eds.), *Data Management, Analytics, and Innovation. Advances in Intelligent Systems and Computing* (Vol. 839). Springer. doi:10.1007/978-981-13-1274-8_1

Desai, D. (2021). Role of Privacy Concern and Control to Build Trust in Personalized Social Networking Sites. In A. Sheth, A. Sinhal, A. Shrivastava, & A. K. Pandey (Eds.), *Intelligent Systems. Algorithms for Intelligent Systems.* Springer. doi:10.1007/978-981-16-2248-9_10

Dzyabura, D., & Hauser, J. R. (2019). Recommending products when consumers learn their preferences weights. *Marketing Science, 38*(3), 365–541. doi:10.1287/mksc.2018.1144

Gartner. (2019). *Gartner Survey Shows Brands Risk Losing 38 Percent of Customers Because of Poor Marketing Personalization Efforts.* https://www.gartner.com/en/newsroom/press-releases/2019-03-11-gartner-survey-shows-brands-risk-losing-38-percent-of

Grewal, D., Hulland, J., Kopalle, P. K., & Karahanna, E. (2020). The future of technology and marketing: A multidisciplinary perspective. *Journal of the Academy of Marketing Science*, *48*(1), 1–8. doi:10.100711747-019-00711-4

Guo, J., Zhang, W., Fan, W., & Li, W. (2018). Combining geographical and social influences with deep learning for personalized point-of- interest recommendation. *Journal of Management Information Systems*, *35*(4), 1121–1153.

Hanson, J., Wei, M., Veys, S., Kugler, M., Strahilevitz, L., & Ur, B. (2020). *Taking Data Out of Context to Hyper-Personalize Ads*. doi:10.1145/3313831.3376415

Huang, M.-H., & Rust, R. T. (2021). *A strategic framework for artificial intelligence in marketing*. doi:10.1007/s11747-020-00749-9

Humphreys, A., & Wang, R. (2018). Automated text analysis for consumer research. *The Journal of Consumer Research*, *44*(6), 1274–1306. doi:10.1093/jcr/ucx104

Hyper-Personalization: A new way of customer-centric marketing. (2019). *Academe*, *97*(5).

Instapage. (2019). *Hyper-Personalized Marketing: How to Do It Right with 3 Examples to Prove It.* https://instapage.com/blog/hyper-personalization

Jain, G., Rakesh, S., Kamalun Nabi, M., & Chaturvedi, K. R. (2018). Hyper-personalization – fashion sustainability through digital clienteling. *Research Journal of Textile and Apparel*, *22*(4), 320–334. doi:10.1108/RJTA-02-2018-0017

Kirkpatrick, K. (2020). Tracking shoppers. *Communications of the ACM*, *63*(2), 19–21.

Kumar, V., Rajan, B., Venkatesan, R., & Lecinski, J. (2019). Understanding the role of artificial intelligence in personalized en- gagement marketing. *California Management Review*, *61*(4), 135–155. doi:10.1177/0008125619859317

Liebman, E., Saar-Tsechansky, M., & Stone, P. (2019). The right music at the right time: Adaptive personalized playlists based on sequence modeling. *Management Information Systems Quarterly*, *43*(3), 765–786. doi:10.25300/MISQ/2019/14750

Liu, X., Singh, P. V., & Srinivasan, K. (2016). A structured analysis of unstructured big data by leveraging cloud computing. *Marketing Science*, *35*(3), 363–388. doi:10.1287/mksc.2015.0972

Luo, X., Tong, S., Fang, Z., & Qu, Z. (2019). Frontiers: Machines versus humans: The impact of AI chatbot disclosure on customer pur- chases. *Marketing Science*, *38*(6), 937–947.

Maddodi, S., & Nandha Kumar, K. G. (2020). *Artificial intelligence and hyper-personalization for improving customer experience*. Retrieved from www.drsrjournal.com

Netzer, O., Lemaire, A., & Herzenstein, M. (2019). When words sweat: Identifying signals for loan default in the text of loan applications. *Journal of Marketing Research, 56*(6), 960–980.

Neumann, N., Tucker, C. E., & Whitfield, T. (2019). Frontiers: How effective is third-party consumer profiling? Evidence from field studies. *Marketing Science, 38*(6), 918–926.

Ng, I. C. L., & Wakenshaw, S. Y. L. (2017). The internet-of-things: Review and research directions. *International Journal of Research in Marketing, 34*(1), 3–21.

Okazaki, S., Eisend, M., Plangger, K., de Ruyter, K., & Grewal, D. (2020). Understanding the Strategic Consequences of Customer Privacy Concerns: A Meta-Analytic Review. *Journal of Retailing*, *96*(4), 458–473. doi:10.1016/j.jretai.2020.05.007

Position Paper-Hyper-Personalization. (2016). www.nem-initiative.org

Richrelevance, A. W. F. (2019). *Hyper-Personalization: The Pinnacle of Personalization for Marketers*. Academic Press.

Simester, D., Timoshenko, A., & Zoumpoulis, S. I. (2020). Targeting prospective customers: Robustness of machine-learning methods to typical data challenges. *Management Science*, *66*(6), 2495–2522. doi:10.1287/mnsc.2019.3308

Sodhi, A. (2018). *Hyper-Personalization: A Marketing Primer for Enhanced Customer Experience*. Academic Press.

Soleymanian, M., Weinberg, C. B., & Zhu, T. (2019). Sensor data and behavioral tracking: Does usage-based auto insurance benefit drivers? *Marketing Science, 38*(1), 21–43. doi:10.1287/mksc.2018.1126

Tong, S., Luo, X., & Xu, B. (2020). Personalized mobile marketing strategies. *Journal of the Academy of Marketing Science*, *48*(2), 64–78. doi:10.100711747-019-00693-3

Wedel, M., & Kannan, P. K. (2016). Marketing analytics for data-rich environments. *JournalofMarketing*, *80*(6), 97–121.

Wilson, H. J., & Daugherty, P. R. (2018, July). Collaborative intelligence: Humans and AI are joining forces. *Harvard Business Review*, 114–123.

Zanker, M., Rook, L., & Jannach, D. (2019). Measuring the impact of online personalization: Past, present, and future. *International Journal of Human-Computer Studies*, *131*, 160–168. Advance online publication. doi:10.1016/j.ijhcs.2019.06.006

Chapter 4
Transforming CRM Through Artificial Intelligence

Abhinav Chaturvedi
Bennett University, India

Mukesh Chaturvedi
Management Development Institute, Gurgaon, India

ABSTRACT

The present times are disrupting times for every kind of business and every aspect of a business. It is not about contactlessness; it is about seamlessness. The auto manufacturers have already started "Amazoning" dealerships. Brands are developing customer-specific platforms like jaguar.rockar.com, where one can explore the range, check the price, select dealer, search inventory, and schedule test drives. The brand Cadillac creates virtual reality experiences in Google Search, wherein a car appears in a living room through a phone call. One can see how it looks, walk around it, open the doors, and get a sense of the interior. This chapter explores the transformation of CRM through artificial intelligence.

INTRODUCTION

The present times are disrupting times for every kind of business and every aspect of a business. It is not about contactless; it is about seamlessness. The auto manufacturers have already started "Amazoning" dealerships. Brands are developing customer-specific platforms like jaguar.rockar.com, where one can explore the range, check the price, select dealer, search inventory, and schedule test drives. The brand Cadillac creates Virtual Reality experiences in Google Search, wherein a car appears in a

DOI: 10.4018/978-1-7998-7959-6.ch004

living room through a phone call. One can see how it looks, walks around it, opens the doors, and get a sense of the interiors.

The store salespersons are no more required to stand around in empty stores; they can connect live with the shoppers. The shoppers can speak with the salespersons via video chats, preview new products, and see features and demonstrations. That is why brands like Citroen are experimenting with small formats. Croma is also trying Gadgets-of-Desire format, about 2,000 square feet, Half Sore-Half App, that will stock key SKUs with the remaining range augmented by digital tools.

The quick-service restaurants use analytics, based on big data and artificial intelligence, to work out the joints' location. They use multiple data points like demographics and cell phones, and social media activity. Besides the right location, this model can give the kind of revenue that will be generated.

The packaging was meant for the safe carrying and safekeeping of the product. Over time, it became a medium of promotion of the product as it displayed the brand name and, sometimes, the picture of the product. Now, with the help of AI, packaging can create immersive experiences for the customers. A QR code or an image, either internal or external, on the package could engage customers through gamification and create a direct reward or loyalty program.

Mass marketing is an age-old concept. Today, with AI, each customer is a customer by itself. This way, marketers can create customized promotions or curated store views based on past purchases.

Customers are in an old habit of checking the expiry date and nutrition value on the product package. With AI, shoppers can open their cameras, point them at the product, and get all the relevant information about the contents on their cameras.

With the real estate and the inventory costs rising, the retail store's size has been shrinking. There are not many aisles loaded with all the SKUs. AI can help stores with sizing down without losing revenue. Interactive catalogs can store thousands of products, and, with one click, the selected item could land in the shopping basket and get delivered home. The checkout counters are also less as the payments are contactless. AI can make even small profits.

The marked emergence of CRM as a business strategy has radically transformed the operations of an organization. A change in business focus from transactional to relationship marketing has taken place in which at the center of all activity lies the customer, and organizations are now desperately trying to restructure their processes around their strategically significant customers' needs. Such a shift is the realization of a customer to be a business asset by organizations. The crucial catalyst of such a seismic change to customer focus recognizes that customers are an asset for the business. Managing relationships can derive a continuous and sustainable economic benefit for an enterprise when handled effectively.

THE CRM ERA

The late 1990s and early 2000s are unforgettable as it was an era where CRM was the weapon of choice for organizations to attain competitive advantage where managers plowed millions of dollars in building solid relationships with the customers. It was a trip of a life for enterprises that invested millions of dollars in developing CRM Systems. CRM systems were developed as part of the overall strategy to efficiently and instantly respond to changing customers' desires. Strategic initiatives like these were in line to bolster both revenues and customer retention to lower marketing costs (Rigby & Ledingham, 2004). After the initial hype, there was a disappointment as the expected results were nowhere, and sales plummeted for CRM systems, causing a decline in IT expenses in the years 2000-2002. The fate of CRM was now being linked with that of the overhyped ERP systems. However, in 2003, the Annual Management Tools Survey done by Bain & Company reported growth in adopting the CRM systems (Rigby, 2003). In the 2003 annual survey, out of the total respondents, "78 percent said they use CRM systems, compared with 35 percent in 2000" (Rigby, 2003, p. 6). According to the survey, the defection rates of about 18% in 2000 had plummeted to 3% (Rigby, 2003, p. 7). The question is, what changed, and where are we now? Plus, are we again at the cusp of another massive change?

With the great pandemic behind us, we have once again made technology act as a savior, whether it was working from home via systems like Zoom, MS TEAMS, or shopping online. If something benefited most from the pandemic, it was growth in the CRM software market, now expected to be around $80 billion in revenues by 2025 from close to $40 billion currently (Taylor, 2021). There is growth expected but fueled by an increase in IT investment by many organizations in the past year. It is proving that change is close. The reason for growth today and in 2003 are almost similar. The reason that turned disappointment to satisfaction back then in 2003 and ready to fuel the expected growth is the strategy to harness CRM Systems successfully. The current digital age and the pandemic have furthered the need to better connect with the customers to recognize their needs and desires for organizations better. The attention is being paid to clearly define problems in the customer relationship cycle to solve them rather than using CRM to transform the entire business (Rigby & Ledingham, 2004).

However, solving customer problems is essential but full of challenges for organizations despite customer centricity being the topmost priority. While customer-centricity remains a priority at the same time, it is a challenge for CRM teams. Many organizations have established specialized CRM teams to engage in all possible activities and have a dialogue with key stakeholders about putting the customer first. Nevertheless, somehow, organizations still struggle to achieve the same despite all possible efforts and investing heavily in CRM systems. So, what are some of the critical challenges faced by CRM teams today?

Before we attempt to answer the above question, it is essential to understand a growing complexity in the business environment. The complexity aids in rapidly growing data, making it difficult for organizations to execute their strategy correctly. Despite a lack of a truly customer-centric organization, CRM professionals continue to commit themselves because being customer-centric happens to be a state-of-mind and various mindsets block genuine customer-centric innovations in organizations (Selden & Macmillan, 2009). In a recent survey titled *2021 the State of CRM,* [1] it has been found that more than data and tools, the most significant missing piece from the CRM industry is the availability of clear strategic advice. In other words, there is a paucity of clarity of the path and the starting point in executing the CRM strategy. Thus, making CRM teams battle various challenges. Hence, the challenges troubling the CRM teams today are:

1. Retention of customers – Despite heavy investment and several touchpoints available with the organizations, various CRM teams are growing concern to retain customers better. The CRM teams are day in day out trying to work in the direction of increasing customer lifetime value by increasing customer loyalty. There are various attempts to improve retention by creating a better overall experience for customers. CRM teams are finding better ways of targeting and segmentation as well. Due to technology advancement, there is a constant change in consumer behavior which creates challenging situations for CRM teams to better retain customers due to low switching costs and substitutes.
2. Growing Marketing pressure – The recent pandemic (COVID-19) has been a game-changing year for many industries for good and evil. Technology has enabled many firms to adopt new channels for connecting with the customers; the need of the hour for all marketers is now to develop a strategy that facilitates MultiChannel Planning. Thus, putting pressure on marketing functions to think of ways to involve customers to build better future relationships.
3. Integration of Data with relevant tools – The fourth industrial revolution has made the customers equally powerful as it has benefited organizations investing in CRM systems. The reason is that now, through numerous channels such as mobile phones and social media, there is an enormous amount of data generated, and this data is flowing at a rapid pace. The growing rate of data has added to the complexity of storage, normalization, and cleaning. The complexity is not only a painstaking hurdle but is becoming a costly affair for organizations to overcome. New tools are required to support CRM teams to manage data and push strategy to the next level. However, the challenge can also be the pace

of integration as there are bound to be internal challenges about processes, strategy, and adoption.

4. Frugal approach to Automation – Automation per se is not a challenge for organizations since many have already established automated campaigns and automated customer journeys. However, automation needs not be forgotten as it is like a backbone for CRM teams that continue to provide quick wins both in revenue and efficiency. The challenge is to automate manual tasks by streamlining processes for long-term efficiency and cost-saving.

CRM practices are promising for any organization, but the challenges may become perilous in reality. CRM benefits are numerous, like developing mutually beneficial relationships to improve the customers' overall experience and convert them into loyalists (Nguyen & Mutum, 2012; Payne & Frow, 2005). However, researchers provide evidence that various businesses employ advanced level CRM systems and tools to reap benefits for themselves (Jayachandran, Sharma, Kaufman, & Raman, 2005) at the customers' cost (Haenlein, 2017).

One of the main concerns growing across is that CRM implantation may exploit customers' vulnerabilities going forward as technology becomes sophisticated (Nguyen, Jaber, & Simkin, 2020). Such a growing concern results in certain new forms of challenges such as privacy concerns, asymmetric information, and vulnerabilities that may become causes of distrust (Nguyen et al., 2020). However, organizations at the strategic level should pay attention to trust and fairness while implementing any CRM initiatives to avoid possible concerns (Phan & Vogel, 2010). An example is when an organization invests in specific CRM tools to achieve superior customized advertising while giving minor importance to customer privacy and fairness. Besides, across various industries such as banking, telecom services, car rentals, and even credit card services by banks attempt to deliberately bind customers in contracts, as well as exploit customers with fees and at times bewilder them with fine prints leading to customer annoyance (Frow, Payne, Wilkinson, & Young, 2011; McGovern & Moon, 2007; Nguyen et al., 2020). In contexts as mentioned, there seems to be clear proof of how companies strategic focus is short-term oriented towards increasing its profits and not about long-term customer relationship building (Daunt & Harris, 2012). As we move forward, some of these challenges shall dynamically evolve in response to the developing novel technologies for instance the Internet of Things, Big Data, 5G, Blockchain, and artificial intelligence.

However, what is interesting is how can this dark side be tackled, and can the growing reliance on machine learning and artificial intelligence be a much-needed antidote to the growing challenges.

THE DAWN OF ARTIFICIAL INTELLIGENCE

Artificial Intelligence (AI) is referred to as "a system's ability to correctly interpret external data, to learn from such data, and to use those learnings to achieve specific goals and tasks through flexible adaptation" (Kaplan & Haenlein, 2019, p. 15). Although Artificial Intelligence (AI) has to be considered valuable and meaningful for an organization, it is essential to view it from a business capability lens rather than just technology (Davenport & Ronanki, 2018). AI is a culmination of various fields like engineering - robotics, mathematics, psychology, economics, and political science. However, right from the 1980s, when the fascination rose amongst the business community, increasing use of different AI categories has been employed. Such a variety provided frameworks for the development of cognitive capabilities that would help solve business problems.

Speaking about solving business problems, AI is capable of meeting three broad needs of any business. First, it is about enabling the automation of various business processes. Second, it is about analyzing data to generate valuable insights. Finally, one of the areas where AI recently is making a significant impact is engagement with customers and employees (internal customers of any organization), better known as "cognitive engagement" (Davenport & Ronanki, 2018). Natural language processing Chatbots, intelligent agents providing 24/7 service, and recommendation systems assisting in health treatment, automobile purchase, and systems that assist retailers in personalizing various customer services are examples of such cognitive engagements slowly gaining popularity. Such cognitive engagement projects' popularity has profoundly impacted the marketing paradigm, especially marketing communication and Customer Relationship Management (CRM) (see Foltean, Trif, & Tuleu, 2019; Mangold & Faulds, 2009). Under this context, new media technologies that deliver new ways for businesses to reach out, interacting with, and customizing customer messages are fundamental to the CRM process (Hennig-Thurau et al., 2010).

Now, the strategic challenge for organizations is to make the best use of AI for addressing the challenges of CRM. AI capabilities can transform CRM into AI-CRM and help in better engagement with customers by improving an organization's ability to predict customer lifetime value (Libai et al., 2020). In CRM, AI enables firms to analyze data faster or interact with customers at a large scale and provides better prediction models. Such AI-enabled CRM services also lower cost as more personalized services can be created, impacting the nature of services designed for "implementing adapted treatment of customers, leading to greater customer prioritization and service discrimination in markets" (Libai et al., 2020, p. 44).

However, there is a growing fear that AI shall ultimately replace humans as it is getting better in many "Human Jobs" such as disease diagnostic, language translation, and recently providing an exceptional customer service level (through bots). Such fear is just a misnomer as with the rise of machine intelligence, and such technologies will have a more profound impact in complementing and augmenting humans' capabilities, not replacing them in any manner. It would be a new era of better known as "collaborative intelligence" (Paschen, Wilson, & Ferreira, 2020; Wilson & Daugherty, 2018).

The Human and AI Collaboration

The human and machine relationship is long and has only advanced over time. It all started when Alan Turing raised a question - 'Can machines think?' (Turing, 1950). Since then, both humans and machines have co-exited and built on each other's complementarity rather than replacing each other. Organizations that have deployed AI for short-term gains have experienced low productivity and attempt to replace employees by deploying more technology to increase their loss. Organizations need to optimize the collaboration to benefit from this relationship. For such a collaboration to work, both humans and machines need to assist one another. Let us see how it can be achieved.

Human Assistance Towards Machine

According to research (see Paschen et al., 2020; Wilson & Daugherty, 2018), there are few roles that humans must perform in order to make this relationship worthwhile.

Training

There must be adequate training of the machine-learning algorithms in an organization to understand how a particular task needs to be performed. Big data sets must be used to teach various applications how to perform under multiple use cases. Also, AI systems must be taught about handling effective interactions with humans. Some examples, Microsoft's AI-based assistant Cortona, or Amazon's Alexa, as well as the famous Siri by Apple. Such bots are extensively trained to develop just the appropriate type of personality. To instill qualities in such bots, countless hours are spent by individuals from various fields – such as poet, artist, musician, etc. Also, various start-ups such as Koko, an offshoot for MIT labs, are investing in mimicking human emotions such as sympathy. This only indicates that this complementarity is going to grow shortly.

Guiding

It is not only about training but in specific fields such as medical, law and so on, an expert's opinion matters. AI works through processes that happen to be largely opaque, handling wicked problems. Thus, AI systems have a dependency on human experts in the growing field to elaborate on such systems' evolving behavior to users who are non-experts. Such experts are becoming not only necessary but integral too in industries where there is a possibility of a machine's output being challenged by a user as unfair or simply wrong. One such example is the European Union's new General Data Protection Regulation (GDPR), where each consumer is protected by a right to question and obtain an explanation for any algorithm-based or machine-driven decision. Thus, there must be a guiding role of the human expertise required to make machines truly smart.

Assisting

Any AI system needs to work efficiently and safely, and responsibly, but to do that, and you need assistance in the form of employees who maintain the systems continuously. These are again experts in the field. Such experts may also be known as safety engineers (Wilson & Daugherty, 2018). Safety engineers sometimes provide reviews for the experts in the field, better known as explainers, essentially in the guiding role with analysis of specific events. For instance, safety engineers analyzing a self-driving car's fatal accident situation. Experts in assisting roles ensure that AI systems work and maintain all ethical norms (Wilson & Daugherty, 2018). An example, Apple's differential privacy team continuously works round the clock to ensure that no AI gathers unconstrained data, which may compromise a consumer's privacy and run afoul of the law.

Thus, humans play an integral part in how AI works efficiently. It is also essential to see why we say it is a complementarity since AI (Machines) also plays many roles in this Human and AI relationship.

Machines Expanding Human Potential

AI makes any machine truly a Smart Machine. Intelligent Machines have the capability of boosting human potential in many ways. Essentially AI does this in three ways:

Boosting Cognitive Capabilities

The most significant advantage which AI provides to human capability expansion is the ability to make better decisions. The robust data analysis helps in boosting an individual's creativity as well. An example is the use of AI in the design field. Designers use various AI-powered software to design exceptional products. Ai-powered tools such as Uizard, Khroma, Autodesk's Dreamcatcher, and many more are powering a designer's Imagination to the next level. The tools support the designer in developing a User Interface (UI), preparing protocepts and other assets, developing content, and personalizing the user experience.

Enhanced Human to Human Interactions

This is an area where AI bridges the gap in human-to-human interaction. In other words, a collaboration between human and machines enable organizations to interact in a far efficient way with its employees. Organizations are also adopting novel ways to connect with customers, especially in crises like the novel Covid-19 crisis. The advantage with AI-powered services for employees as well as customers is designed in such a way that they not only enhance the interaction but also can be scaled to meet the evolving customer responses and behavior. Like Siri by Apple and Cortona, we see AI assistants, by Microsoft personalizing their respective users' experience and evolving from their first generation to the next generations.

Personifying

In the age of Siri, Cortona, and many other digital entities of intelligent machines, it is now becoming more leisurely day by day to embody intelligence in physical machines like robots that augment work done by humans. Digital entities have kind of indirectly boosted how new physical machines are designed. Various sensors, motors, and actuators are now being created and used extensively to make AI-enabled machines not only innovative but more intelligent than before. An example of the same is how manufacturing companies in industries like Automobile, Steel, and many more can mimic human actions. The past industrial machines are now given a makeover and converted into what is known as context-aware 'cobot' (Colgate, Wannasuphoprasit, & Peshkin, 1996). Therefore, it is not just the digital entities but also the 'dumb' machines which can get a new life courtesy of AI.

In this transformation age where AI is now spreading like fire, human and AI collaboration is quintessential. However, for any organization's customer is supreme, it is essential to understand how this Human and AI complementarity transforms customer relationship management.

AI AND CRM CONFLUENCE

We understand from the investments being made in CRM that each organization leans towards information technology to deal with vast volumes of data. However, we have also observed that AI is one such technology that complements CRM very well. A review of literature, though limited, speaks volumes about the AI & CRM confluence. The table highlights how this confluence has been discussed in various contexts by various scholars in the recent past. The table describes the work's central theme and highlights some of the essential aspects of the confluence.

The table above clearly points out the synergies of AI & CRM and highlights certain essential aspects of the machine and human relationship. As supported by research, it is evident that CRM systems are destined to be integrated with AI systems. However, it is critical to understand how they are transforming. In other words, is AI able to transform CRM?

AI TRANSFORMING CRM

In times like today, we are at the cusp of change and chaos, where AI-CRM systems prove to be a resource for managers to make better decisions while dealing efficiently with large data sets (Agrawal, Gans, & Goldfarb, 2019). Better and effective decisions indicate that de facto the estimations towards future customer transactions (CLV) shall improve profits for the firm and reduce consumer surplus.

Undoubtedly, AI systems growth shall not overthrow or make relationship marketing redundant. Instead, it shall provide the right tools and techniques to make relationship-building more accurate, discriminating, and scalable (Libai et al., 2020). Such a betterment is bound to have an impact on customer equity as well. Therefore, we attempt to explore and discuss this AI-CRM system's capabilities and effects to transform CRM.

AI-Enabled Capabilities

Our understanding of human and AI collaboration provides us one clear picture that AI expands human capabilities. Similarly, AI has the potential to interrelate with CRM capabilities. It is better to term them as AI-CRM capabilities (Libai et al., 2020). The AI capabilities impact three essential activities of CRM – acquisition of customer, retention of the customer, and developing the relationship with the customer. Therefore, the AI-CRM capabilities which are primarily critical are:

Big Data Leverage

Big data is looked upon in three aspects – volume, variety, and velocity. Out of the three V's, variety happens to be the one that provides a competitive advantage to the firm implementing CRM practices to engage with customer success. In the context of AI-CRM capabilities, it is the scope and the breadth of customer data. Organizations need to spend a substantial amount of time building external partnerships to be perceived as trustworthy to achieve Big Data variety' (Libai et

Table 1. AI and CRM confluence

Authors	Main Theme	Important Aspects
(Galitsky, 2020)	This work presents a broad spectrum of application domains with a focus on solving customer problems.	• It is solving a customer problem through dialogue management. • Making Dumb CRM Intelligent – maintaining close customer interaction so that the problem can be clarified and multiple ways to fix the same can be sought.
(Zoltners, Sinha, Lorimer, & Shastri, 2019)	Identification of challenges and discovering simple, practical but often missed solutions.	• The potential of AI to transform selling in significant ways is highlighted. • Understanding new roles and skillsets are required to bring different AI models to life. • For CRM teams to work efficiently, what is required is a boundary spanner–a person who understands both sales and technology is crucial.
(Chatterjee, Nguyen, Ghosh, Bhattacharjee, & Chaudhuri, 2020)	The study is centered around Indian organizations where the attempt is to map how employees adopt CRM systems integrated with AI. It studies behavioral intention. .	• Identify different exogenous and endogenous factors to predict the adoption of AI integrated CRM system
(Paschen, Kietzmann, & Kietzmann, 2019) (Paschen et al., 2020)	The focus is on the building blocks of AI concerning market knowledge in B2B marketing.	• The lens adopted for this study is an input–processes–output lens along with the foundational building blocks of any AI system. • Illustrative use cases are used to demonstrate how AI can impact various B2B marketing functions.
(Libai et al., 2020)	Customer Prioritization as well as predicting customer lifetime value.	• Along with customer prioritization and service discrimination in markets, regulation of AI may not be easy, primarily for the definitional, ex-post, and ex-ante problems.
(Wilson & Daugherty, 2018)	Optimizing collaboration between humans and artificial intelligence.	• The goal of organizations should be about training people and reimagining or visualizing critical business processes that focus on optimizing the use of Ai to achieve more operational flexibility or speed, grander scale, and better decision-making or increased personalization of products and services.
(Iansiti & Lakhani, 2020)	Artificial Intelligence is the primary source of value creation and delivery.	• The AI-driven operating model has a revolutionary impact on operations, strategy, and competition.
(Dawar, 2018)	The role of AI assistants as trustworthy advisers is discussed.	• Organizations and brands will have to focus all their marketing activities towards AI platforms, looking to control platforms to get preferential placing on AI assistants.
(Brynjolfsson & Mcafee, 2017)	The article describes the real potential of AI, its practical implications, and the barriers to its adoption.	• Demand for AI skills is high. Not enough data scientists and ML experts. • As per the context, requisite algorithms and hardware for modern AI are either rented or bought. • There is a possibility that the machines develop hidden biases, resulting not from any objective of the Engineer/manager/designer but from the data provided to train the system. • Most AI systems (or neural network systems) work counter to explicit logic rules of traditional systems. Primarily dealing with statistical realities rather than literal facts. Thus, making the predictability sure across all cases -especially in situations that were not represented in the training data. • AI will not replace managers, but managers who use AI will replace those who does not?

al., 2020, p. 3). Compared to volume generating a variety of data is challenging, yet the AI-CRM relationship expands the scope of customer data types, leading to a more significant impact on firm performance.

Enhanced Communication and Understanding of Customers

In his seminal article, Turing (1950) talked about how machines (AI) could fool humans into believing that they were communicating with another human being on the other side of the machine. In the novel Covid-19 crisis, many organizations made changes to their interactions with customers by using chatbots. This adaptation to chatbots and AI-enabled automated assistance has lowered the cost for organizations in servicing their customers. We have already argued above that personifying the 'AI-CRM capabilities need not obtain full human empathy to complement human CRM judgment' (Libai et al., 2020, p. 4).

AI Effects on CRM Activities

The objective of any CRM activity is to develop a long-lasting relationship with its customers. The various activities involved in CRM can be classified under three categories:

Customer Acquisition

Basis the AI-CRM capabilities, a firm's ability is enhanced in predicting a prospect's CLV (Customer Lifetime Value), which uses the generated data better to manage the customer acquisition process through selective acquisition identify profitable customers (Libai et al., 2020). It is about identifying profitable customers and going deeper into this acquired customer's journey, in other words, going deeper and accumulating knowledge about a customer's decision-making and behavior, enabling the firm to craft new paths for not only retention but also about retention.

Customer Development

The AI-CRM systems are growing to be capable of creating personalized experiences for the customers. The complementarity of AI and human capabilities fuel how CRM systems work flexibly and build on the AI processes. The AI-CRM systems can soon perform tasks such as human communication at a personalized level. In various markets such as apparel, cars, travel, and banking (such as credit cards), many decisions are made concerning investment in customer development basis the expected Lifetime value of a customer. Given the profitability aspect attached to expected lifetime value, the AI-CRM systems shall enable a firm to be selective in customer development. However, with the growing technology and continued investment by firms in CRM systems, the question remains why customers persist to do what they do (Gurău, 2012; Libai et al., 2020)?

Customer Retention

To serve customers better to grow the relationship, managers and top leaders of the organizations continuously strive to adjust their thinking and strategy by paying attention to customer habits. Literature on Habits suggests that they are critical drivers of a customer's behavior (Wood & Rünger, 2016). It is a possible question that one may want to consider that when a customer's habit-forming behavior leads to less complexity in decision making, why would AI-driven systems be required. Interestingly, Internet-of-things (IoT) is just one example where numerous sensors work, and data inputs are processed to track habit-forming behavior. An example is Amazon's Alexa mechanism enabling customers to keep track of orders and reordering and managing stockouts of frequently used products. Once a habit-formation starts in retaining the customer, it is bound to happen that customers spend less amount of time in renewed decision-making. Besides, customer's past behavior enables firms to learn and update their knowledge about customers' wants and desires. Thus, due to this enhanced learning and the firm's investment towards retaining customers leads to higher switching costs for the customer. As AI-CRM systems will improve the customers' ease of making decisions with one organization, switching costs will increase, enabling firms to retain customers better.

CONCLUSION

In totality, the above discourse on AI-CRM System and the Machine-Human complementarity range between utopian and dystopian when it comes to effects on society at large. Across the domain, scholars, scientists, experts, and business leaders reference machines' intelligence as they improve individuals' quality of life overall. On the other side, some argue that there are more significant disadvantages that outweigh the advantages citing massive job losses, increase in disparity when it comes to equal benefits for all of such AI systems. It is believed that machines will undoubtedly take over the human race (Agrawal et al., 2019; Libai et al., 2020). However, when it comes to CRM, there is a positive wave. In respect of CRM, AI is specifically considered a boon. AI_CRM capabilities shall impact all facets of the CRM process, making both the customer and the firm benefit equally.

Despite the rosy picture, questions remain about the fate of customers in an AI-driven future.

REFERENCES

Agrawal, A., Gans, J., & Goldfarb, A. (2019). Economic policy for artificial intelligence. *Innovation Policy and the Economy*, *19*(1), 139–159. doi:10.1086/699935

Brynjolfsson, E., & Mcafee, A. (2017). The Business of Artificial Intelligence: what it can and cannot do for your organization. *Harvard Business Review Digital Articles*, 1–20.

Chatterjee, S., Nguyen, B., Ghosh, S. K., Bhattacharjee, K. K., & Chaudhuri, S. (2020). Adoption of artificial intelligence integrated CRM system: An empirical study of Indian organizations. *The Bottom Line (New York, N.Y.)*, *33*(4), 359–375. doi:10.1108/BL-08-2020-0057

Colgate, J. E., Wannasuphoprasit, W., & Peshkin, M. A. (1996). Cobots: robots for collaboration with human operators. In American Society of Mechanical Engineers, Dynamic Systems and Control Division (Publication) DSC (Vol. 58, pp. 433–439). Academic Press.

Daunt, K. L., & Harris, L. C. (2012). Exploring the forms of dysfunctional customer behaviour: A study of differences in servicescape and customer disaffection with service. *Journal of Marketing Management*, *28*(1–2), 129–153. doi:10.1080/0267257X.2011.619149

Davenport, T. H., & Ronanki, R. (2018, Feb.). Artificial intelligence for the real world. *Harvard Business Review*, 108–117.

Dawar, N. (2018, May). Marketing in the age of Alexa. *Harvard Business Review*, 80–87.

Foltean, F. S., Trif, S. M., & Tuleu, D. L. (2019). Customer relationship management capabilities and social media technology use: Consequences on firm performance. *Journal of Business Research*, *104*, 563–575. doi:10.1016/j.jbusres.2018.10.047

Frow, P., Payne, A., Wilkinson, I. F., & Young, L. (2011). Customer management and CRM: Addressing the dark side. *Journal of Services Marketing*, *25*(2), 79–89. doi:10.1108/08876041111119804

Galitsky, B. (2020). *Artificial Intelligence for Customer Relationship Management*. Retrieved from https://www.springer.com/series/6033

Gurău, C. (2012). A life-stage analysis of consumer loyalty profile: Comparing Generation X and Millennial consumers. *Journal of Consumer Marketing*, *29*(2), 103–113. doi:10.1108/07363761211206357

Haenlein, M. (2017). How to date your clients in the 21st century: Challenges in managing customer relationships in today's world. *Business Horizons*, *60*(5), 577–586. Advance online publication. doi:10.1016/j.bushor.2017.06.002

Hennig-Thurau, T., Malthouse, E. C., Friege, C., Gensler, S., Lobschat, L., Rangaswamy, A., & Skiera, B. (2010). The impact of new media on customer relationships. *Journal of Service Research*, *13*(3), 311–330. doi:10.1177/1094670510375460

Iansiti, M., & Lakhani, K. R. (2020). Competing in the age of AI: How machine intelligence changes the rules of business. *Harvard Business Review*, *2020*(January-February), 1–9.

Kaplan, A., & Haenlein, M. (2019). Siri, Siri, in my hand: Who's the fairest in the land? On the interpretations, illustrations, and implications of artificial intelligence. *Business Horizons*, *62*(1), 15–25. doi:10.1016/j.bushor.2018.08.004

Libai, B., Bart, Y., Gensler, S., Hofacker, C. F., Kaplan, A., Kötterheinrich, K., & Kroll, E. B. (2020). Brave New World? On AI and the Management of Customer Relationships. *Journal of Interactive Marketing*, *51*, 44–56. doi:10.1016/j.intmar.2020.04.002

Mangold, W. G., & Faulds, D. J. (2009). Social media: The new hybrid element of the promotion mix. *Business Horizons*, *52*(4), 357–365. doi:10.1016/j.bushor.2009.03.002

McGovern, G., & Moon, Y. (2007). Companies and the customers who hate them. *Harvard Business Review*, *85*(6). PMID:17580650

Nguyen, B., Jaber, F., & Simkin, L. (2020). A systematic review of the dark side of CRM: The need for a new research agenda. *Journal of Strategic Marketing*, *00*(00), 1–19. doi:10.1080/0965254X.2019.1642939

Nguyen, B., & Mutum, D. S. (2012). Customer relationship management: Advances, dark sides, exploitation, and unfairness. *International Journal of Electronic Customer Relationship Management*, *6*(1), 1–19. doi:10.1504/IJECRM.2012.046467

Paschen, J., Kietzmann, J., & Kietzmann, T. C. (2019). Artificial intelligence (AI) and its implications for market knowledge in B2B marketing. *Journal of Business and Industrial Marketing*, *34*(7), 1410–1419. doi:10.1108/JBIM-10-2018-0295

Paschen, J., Wilson, M., & Ferreira, J. J. (2020). Collaborative Intelligence: How human and artificial intelligence create value along the B2B sales funnel. *Business Horizons*, *63*(3), 403–414. doi:10.1016/j.bushor.2020.01.003

Payne, A., & Frow, P. (2005). A strategic framework for customer relationship management. *Journal of Marketing*, *69*(4), 167–176. doi:10.1509/jmkg.2005.69.4.167

Phan, D. D., & Vogel, D. R. (2010). A model of customer relationship management and business intelligence systems for catalogue and online retailers. *Information & Management*, *47*(2), 69–77. doi:10.1016/j.im.2009.09.001

Rigby, D. K. (2003). Management tools survey 2003: Usage up as companies strive to make headway in tough times. *Strategy and Leadership*, *31*(5), 4–11. doi:10.1108/10878570310492005

Rigby, D. K., & Ledingham, D. (2004). CRM done right. *Harvard Business Review*, *82*(11). PMID:15559450

Selden, L., & Macmillan, I. C. (2009). Manage Customer - Centric Innovation Systematically –. *Harvard Business Review*, (May), 108–117. PMID:16579418

Taylor, M. (2021). *18 CRM statistics you need to know for 2021 (and beyond)*. https://www.superoffice.com/blog/crm-software-statistics/#:~:text=The%20CRM%20industry%20has%20seen,with%2010%20employees%20or%20less

Turing, A. M. (1950). Computing machinery and intelligence. *MIND - A Quarterly Review of Psychology and Philosophy, 236*, 1–28. doi:10.1093/mind/LIX.236.433

Wilson, H. J., & Daugherty, P. R. (2018). Humans and AI Are Joining Forces. *Harvard Business Review, July-. Augus*, (August), 114–123.

Wood, W., & Rünger, D. (2016). Psychology of habit. *Annual Review of Psychology*, *67*(1), 289–314. doi:10.1146/annurev-psych-122414-033417 PMID:26361052

Zoltners, A. A., Sinha, P. K., Lorimer, S. E., & Shastri, A. (2019). Article Sales 4 Ways Sales Teams Could Get More Value Out of AI. *Harvard Business Review*, (February), 2–5.

Chapter 5
Fostering CRM Through Artificial Intelligence

Nidhi Shridhar Natrajan
https://orcid.org/0000-0001-8629-4799
Symbiosis Centre for Management Studies (SCMS), Symbiosis International University (Deemed), Noida, India

Sanjeev Kumar Singh
https://orcid.org/0000-0003-1152-2739
Apeejay Institute of Management and Engineering Technical Campus, Jalandhar, India

Rinku Sanjeev
https://orcid.org/0000-0003-4873-9982
Symbiosis Centre for Management Studies (SCMS), Symbiosis International University (Deemed), Noida, India

ABSTRACT

The use of technology has always provided competitive advantage to organizations. The current approach of adapting a new technology is the long-term planning. AI has become a new paradigm of enhancing organizational capabilities. AI is not a substitute of human intelligence but a strong support in terms of process automation. Apart from this, the decision-making process also gets streamlined. The success of business is when the customer is happy. To create and retain customer loyalty, effective CRM is required. The current chapter focuses on adoption of AI for efficient CRM and the factors for its successful implementation.

DOI: 10.4018/978-1-7998-7959-6.ch005

INTRODUCTION

The present competitive environment emphasizes liberalization and globalization of the economy. Presently, customer satisfaction has been focused as an important component towards the pursuit of corporate goals and objectives. Many companies organize their business focused to the rising customer expectation for quality, service and value. So, the Companies shift their focus towards the customer they serve instead of nearby product lines or geographic business units. In the early 1990, the term Customer Relationship management first gained importance. It states the holistic approach of the organisation. The organisation uses CRM to manage their relationships with the customer. It includes policies related to customer's contact, gather, store, analyse customer information, and the technology required to perform these jobs (Ngai, Xiu, & Chau, 2009; Scherer, 2015; Hofacker, 2019).

According to many authors (Bohling, et.al. 2006; Al-Ajlan, & Zairi, 2006; Frow & Payne, 2009; Filimonova, 2020; STATE, 2020) CRM is concerned to maximize customer loyalty by effectively managing the information about each customer and all customers 'touch point". In short, it may have defined to manage customers and all customer facing departments and partners with the alignment of related strategy, process and technology. CRM supports in developing effective customer relationships and provide better service to the customers. It includes company's sales, services and marketing teams to know about holistic view of a customer for customer relationship. The ultimate goal of CRM is to develop life time value of all the customer i.e. customer equity. By developing data warehouses and using data-mining technique CRM analyst try to maintain long term relationship with the valuable customers (Haenlein & Kaplan, 2019).

Artificial Intelligence plays a huge role in our routine life but still is unknown to many. While using different platforms like Uber, Alexa, Amazon or other voice assistants on our smartphones. . AI supports natural language processing and thus understand the audio data. There is also support to agricultural sector, this specifically becomes more important in Indian context. Monitoring crops till it ripens become easy with the help of drone and satellite system. Banking is another sector benefitting from AI. Risk analysis, fraud warning, credit reporting and audit trails become very efficient. Artificial Intelligence (AI) technology makes our work easier in different aspects (Luo, Tong, Fang & Qu,2019). Most of us must have used Netflix to find recommendations of which movie to watch, AI algorithms influence our decision on which movie to watch next. In Businesses also, AI influences the decision making process such as customer support, intelligent personal assistants, or process automation (Chatterjee, Nguyen, Ghosh, Bhattacharjee, & Chaudhuri, 2020). Businesses work for providing best services to consumers, which is revolving the use of Customer Relationship Management (CRM) software. It is important for companies to understand their customers; after realizing this importance companies are expected to grow their spending on CRM software by the year 2019. As per Medium.com, the trends of 2019 show that CRM systems have developed and integrated AI technology to progress the customer experience. AI is used by business to enhance the decision making process. Real time data has real value for the business, and CRM system connected to the ERP has many advantages for business. Data integration apps like Commercient SYNC, #1 platform for sales can accomplish many goals of business. Therefore, it will provide valuable information to business.

A question may arise in mind of many of us: Where does the need of using my current CRM with AI come from? A report of Statista.com; projected that in USA, additional revenue of $394 billion could be increased by 2021, from integrated use of Artificial intelligence with CRM. With the time CRM software has developed many tools such as face and voice recognition. Salesforce's Einstein and Zoho CRM's Zia are two examples of an AI-powered CRM that uses voice directions to access information. In addition, when an organisation grows, it becomes difficult to collect, store and provide data, and the clients won't get the information, they're looking for. Nowadays, Artificial Intelligence supports CRM to accomplish a more effective data management. Even more so when less than 0.5% of all data is being analysed and used, according to Forbes. But with digital transformation and improvements in technology, AI supports organisations to find new customers and keep the loyal ones pleased.

Integrated use of artificial intelligence and CRM provides more predictive and customized information in all fields of business. There are many reasons due to which we should be thoughtful about AI-driven CRM (Chatterjee, Ghosh & Chaudhuri, 2020).

1. Technology can be used to speed up the sales and interaction with customers on time. It is helpful to get rid from tedious workflows. Integrated use of AI into CRM leads to automatic preparation of client reports, emails, and gather information and so on, and this reduces the threat of human faults in the tasks.
2. An AI-powered CRM learns from historical decisions and predicts future customer behaviour by simply analysing behaviour on phone calls. AI helps in connecting with customers on a very new level as it gives them opportunity to have what they want, when and how they want.
3. AI helps in customer segmentation and also makes workers more productive by helping them in data entry. Workers are not required to entry data manually.
4. AI enabled CRM helps in image recognition and sentiment analysis that lead to better future of business. It increases customer engagement and understands customer satisfaction level, once a business gets insight of customers it becomes

easier to put actions and identify difficulties. Thus AI is helpful to know the client's intents.

5. AI enabled CRM tracks scenarios where sales are beneficial and where the deals have chance of rejection. AI algorithm can tell ideal discount rate and level of price-optimization. For example, an AI algorithm can help in price-optimization; it gathers data from historical information.

AI is something that is advantageous for companies to work in a more efficient and powerful manner. One should not choose the best tools as per needs. The application of AI in terms of effective CRM are due to the benefits it provides in the form of analysing sales call in a better manner, enhance overall customer experience, better engagement, recommendation in smart manner, reducing customer ticket, integrating social media for better consumer insights, automating service desk operations and applying predictive marketing analytics.

BACKGROUND

Customer loyalty through effective CRM is the key to success in this information age. The internet revolution has led to better awareness among customers and this makes them more empowered. On a click of the button variety of products and services are available for purchase decision making. With very less effort and time spent the comparison among various offerings is possible. Use of AI in CRM takes this a step ahead by providing suitable recommendations to the customer. Apart from this the manual aspect of CRM can be easily handled by AI based applications and thus providing the top management enough opportunity to focus on more strategic aspects.

Importance of CRM

CRM is significant now than ever for organisations as it helps in gaining new customers and retaining the existing ones. A study by Gartner stated that CRM software has undertaken multiple database management systems and became the major in the existing software markets.

In the current competitive market there are a number of products and services, consumers are too selective and behave in different manner. In these cases, CRM helps in prioritizing sales and marketing efforts while dealing with various customer groups. It helps in better understanding the customer's need to improve the product range that is to be offered to them. There are several reasons for which a business should invest in CRM system.

1. Sales can be enhanced by investing in the system of CRM

CRM helps in extracting the abundant data from the existing customers. This data is helpful for boosting the sales by targeting the right customers. Web forms are one of its examples. We can create our own customized forms and put columns like customer's name, age, address, preference, family member etc., and this make easy to send personalized gift.

2. CRM helps in generating leads

CRM is helpful in generating several leads. For example, if visitors provide email addresses in web forms, they can be offered with freebies. Another way of generating leads is through referrals, a company can ask its happy consumers to speak of the company's services to their friends and family.

3. To Improve customer services

Customers are important for any company, their time and satisfaction is valuable as the benefits of company rely on that. Customer service is essential to retain customers. CRM system helps in finding out the information about customer satisfaction and equip all the data in a central location and makes them available to the team or anyone from the company easily. Effective use of CRM helps in hearing complaints or negative experiences and resolves them effectively. The complaints may be related to defective products, false interpretation, and lack of guidance etc. through CRM valuable feedback of customer can also be obtained.

4. Improvement in efficiency in team's organisation

Through CRM system, all the interactions and communication between staff and customers are logged in one place for future references. CRM also helps in reminding the pending tasks as reply of customers' queries. CRM can be accessed from anywhere as it has the capacity to store huge data and documents, and a company can achieve access with effective team collaboration.

5. Daily task automation

In this competitive world if tasks will be done manually it will take a lot of time. Huge sales task is time- taking; CRM helps in reducing routine pressure of employees as the work becomes automated. CRM system also makes routine work less time consuming also reduces human error. Thus, CRM upkeep of all the details where sales representative can only focus on the closing sales and customer questions.

6. Employee accountability

When the organisation grows and its customer increases, more number of employees is needed. It makes difficult to handle the data and further results into losing the customers.

With the help of CRM, roles and responsibility can be divided among the employees and their working can be tracked. It gives transparency and along them to work on their weakness and grow along with the organisation's goal.

The Role of Technology: E-CRM and AI

In today's scenario, technology has a huge part in every aspect of business. Communication is a key to make the process easier and faster between the company and the customers. To know the latest trend in market effective communication with customers is essential as it helps in catering the needs of customers (Taylor & Hunter, 2002; Kımıloğlu & Zaralı, 2009; Dawn & Guha, 2010; Dehghanpouri, Soltani & Rostamzadeh, 2020). Use of integrated use of technology and CRM may result into benefit to the organisation. It is also needed to effectively face the competition and make their company successful. In this way, technology has crucial effects on improvement of CRM (Harrigan, Ramsey, & Ibbotson, 2009).

Customer Relationship Management (CRM) and Role of Technology

Databases help in collecting data and organizing it before use, it collects the information from internet which is helpful in making communication faster. Thus, the technology is an essential part of CRM, and it is impossible to use CRM without technology (Shaw & Hamilton, 2016; Chu, 2021).

1. Online services for the customers: While talking about technology, it makes the connection between the organisation and customer stronger even though they are far from each other, through the use of social media as a part of technology.
2. All time availability of services: With the help of gadgets like mobile phone and laptops customers can easily access the companies which suit their needs. They just need to have the application the company is using (Tian & Wang, 2016; Chatterjee, Chaudhuri, Vrontis, Thrassou & Ghosh, 2020).

3. Low-cost CRM: Advancement of technology has led to cost effective CRM. Now, Companies need not to spend a lot of money just for catering the needs of customer. CRM will continue to evolve with the advancement of technology.

Technology paves the great way for effective and efficient development of organisation. Now it is easy for the consumers to get directly what company is offering, CRM helps in keeping the existing customers and also adding the new one to survive in the rivalry of organisations. To make work better and more effective, integrated use of technology with CRM helps a lot (De Sutter, et.al. 2011; Blut,Frennea, Mittal& Mothersbaugh, 2015; Hummer, Muthusamy, Rausch, Dube, Maghraoui, Murthi & Oum, 2019 & Quyen, 2020). Electronic Customer Relationship Management (E-CRM) is an integrated strategy for online sales, marketing, and service which is used to keep organisation's consumers by identifying and attracting them. This improves and increases communication between company and its clients that enhances interaction. With E-CRM software profile and history of each communication can be obtained, which makes it a beneficial tool for small and medium enterprises (Akroush, Dahiyat, Gharaibeh & Abu-Lail, 2011).

All organizations need to educate themselves with the phenomenon of E-CRM as it is helpful for both B2B and B2C marketing companies. ECRM focuses on economically valued customers and eliminates economically invaluable ones. The author considers ECRM as a significant field of study in MIS as well as in Computer Science, Marketing and Psychology. There are number of reasons responsible for online purchasing. A research study of Forrester found that among 70 retailers, convenience was the biggest reason (84%) for making online purchases rather than off-line and in purchasing online customer service is ranked 7th on the list of reasons (11%), it recommends that consumers are eager to purchase online for the reason of convenience at online platform. Boston Consulting Group in its stated that 65% of on-line customers will never make second buy at a given web site. These facts show a need to understand the real service gap that should be addressed at time and companies who quickly bridge this gap benefitted. Organization should understand that marketing to an existing web customers cost less than that of attaining new one (Bawack, Fosso Wamba & Carillo, 2021). Investment in ECRM provides organisation with competitive advantages in their marketplace. The present study will look on the benefits of ECRM systems and talk over the five crucial points to reflect before applying an ECRM solution.

Technology Adoption With Respect to AI

The Technology Adoption (TA) life cycle is a sociological model that defines the receipt of a new produce or innovation, according to the demographic and emotional features of stated adopter groups. The TA model specifies that the people who first practice a new produce is called "innovators," followed by "early adopters". Next are the early majority and late majority, and the latter group who eventually adopt a product are called "laggards".

Innovators: Innovators are more informed, wealthier and are more risk-oriented.

- **Early Adopters:** This are younger generation, more informed, and tended to be public influential, less wealthy
- **Early Majority:** These are more traditional but exposed to novel thoughts, active in community and effect the neighbours.
- **Late Majority:** This group is older, less informed, fairly conservative and less socially active
- **Laggards:** These groups are very traditional, had less resources, oldest and are least informed.

Technology has made the communication between organization and the consumer. The internet plays an important role in making this smoother, user friendly and convenient for the consumers. The e-CRM is now an evitable aspect of marketing strategy (Rust, & Huang, 2014; Overgoor, Chica, Rand & Weishampel, 2019; Hoyer, Kroschke, Schmitt, Kraume & Shankar, 2020). The database of management information system, enterprise resource planning software and cloud based data storage provides a wide variety of support for storing and understanding customer behaviour. The services that are available online provide any time anywhere access to the CRM applications and thus results into better customer engagement. Web 2.0 technologies such as social media platforms further strengthen the customer loyalty. The smartphones have also added to the flexibility available to the customer. The low cost model is made available for the business due to the technology support. The internet based CRM applications brings down the process and logistics cost of reaching out to the customer.

The CRM software is integrated with email, social media, instant messengers, telephonic, and live chat options. This multidimensional connection gives a better experience to the customer. In order to enhance customer loyalty, the organization strategies and adopt new technology. Artificial Intelligence (AI) is a new technology trend in this area. According to Forbes (2019) and Pactera Technologies (2017) reports, there are a lot of AI-based sales activities in the organization and around fifty-one percent of organizations are adopting AI in this area during 2017-2019. The ERP based CRM has already contributed a lot in building customer loyalty however, AI has taken this to a new level altogether. AI has been in existence since the mid-20th century but recently it has been extensively integrated in the organizational working especially in the field of operations and marketing (Chatterjee, Ghosh, Chaudhuri & Chaudhuri, 2020).

The current age is of information overload and there is a need to derive meaningful analysis along with automating most of the manual processes. AI supports automation, fast decision making, better customer experience, research and data analysis and complex problem solving (Kumar, Rajan, Venkatesan & Lecinski, 2019; Quan & Sanderson, 2018). CRM and brand loyalty is all about providing improved customer experience. In the coming days the organization focusing on better customer experience will have a competitive edge. AI provides this opportunity to the companies taking them beyond conventional competition in the digital era.

Technology Adoption With Respect to AI

The technology adoption and expansion have become an important part of the organizational strategy. However, there is always a possibility of challenges during the adoption process. These challenges can be due to technological reasons or the cultural environment of the organization (Bradlow, Gangwar, Kopalle & Voleti, 2017). In fact, it is sometimes referred to as a sociological factor, which is governed by demographics and the psychological properties of the people adapting to the new innovation or technology. The innovators are always the first to use and get adapted to the new technology followed by the early adopters. Then the late adapters followed by the majority of the people fall under the category of laggards (Soni, Sharma, Singh & Kapoor, 2020).

In the current information age, the majority of organizations invest a lot in technology based business processes. If the technology adoption is carried out efficiently it results in huge success for the organizations (Van Doorn et. al., 2016). The current research work focuses on specific adoption of technology i.e. adoption of AI in the field of CRM. The generic parameters of technology adoption. The two important dimension of technology adoption are:

1. Perceived ease of use
2. Perceived usefulness

The perceived usefulness highlights the opinion of the users in terms of enhanced efficiency after deploying the new technology. The perceived ease of use is related to the user friendliness of the application/ technology (Marinchak, Forrest & Hoanca, 2018).

AI and Big Data

AI is also denoted as machine intelligence since the machine is supposed to show the human intelligence. The large amount of point of sales data helps in training the machine for problem solving. The current internet environment, increased online activities by the customer and the related social media content generates huge amount of data. This huge data known as Big data also supports success of AI in business specifically effective CRM.

E-Leadership

Digital evolution has changed many aspects of life especially in government and public interaction (e-participation) and administrative arrangements (e-administration). However, the study of changes in leader- follower interactions with the help of information and communication and Technologies (ICTs) and the theory construction in organizational studies and public administration are almost non-existing. A major reason for this lack of progress is the failure of producing functional definition of e-leadership that spans telework, team, and enterprise settings. "E" means electronic in this article (Gerbaudo, 2016; Gale & Aarons,2018; Liu, et.al.. 2018; Meffert & Swaminathan, 2018). The leadership of the new era is considered as E-leadership, namely the information age which is categorized by fast development of technology, where businesses continuously move across borders to wherever they can make a benefit. Many of the problems can only be fixed through Leadership (Gerbaudo, 2017).

Digital technology has changed organizations in an irretrievable way. Many technologies have change the historical way of working, digitalization is shaping organizations, work environment and processes, which creates new challenges leaders. Thus, Leaders are considered as key players in recognizing objectives, orienting followers, and providing uniqueness to organizations, by means of a mutual vision (Bakardjieva et al., 2018). Digitalisation in business environment force for strategic high level view on digital transformation and has a massive effect in competitive business surroundings, renovating markets, distribution channels, and relations with consumers. CEOs of company have huge role as digital change agents and digital enablers in this digital age, it gives them new responsibilities on the choice of digital technologies that make them work diligently to continue to be competitive in this highly digitized world (Lynn Pulley & Sessa, 2001; Avolio, Sosik, Kahai & Baker, 2014). E-business has expanded the worldwide connectivity and fast interchange of information which created a much more competitive environment for organisation, now E-business requires in dealing with speedy and uneven variations in demand, rivalry and technology (Gerth and Peppard, 2016). Leaders can only master if they succeed in inspiring and motivating employee. Where the digital tools provide autonomy to groups, it also drives them towards the isolation. Leaders have major role in creating positive environment in organisation that promotes a strong co-operation and harmony among employees. Yet, e-leaders' dependence on traditional social aids, such as the capabilities of vigorous listening and understanding others' feelings and opinions, may not be sufficient to permit accomplishment in developing such surroundings. Rather, they want to assimilate these societal skills with the capability to master a variety of virtual communication techniques. According to (Kahai, Avolio & Sosik, 2017; Bakardjieva, Felt & Dumitrica, 2018; Boe & Torgersen, 2018; Elkington, 2021) "while leadership in the more traditional face-to-face context may emerge using a variety of mechanisms, in the virtual context it likely relies largely on the communication effectiveness of the leader." Greater want for speed is one of the aspects which changed the organisation with introduction of technology. This seems to suggest that decisiveness, and problem-solving abilities keep being extremely relevant for e-leaders, and may become even more prominent in the future. Everlasting urgency can force leaders to make decisions without having proper information and time to analyse the problems, which may result into usual responses instead of new and innovative ideas. To face such situations leaders, have to be creative besides being able to help navigate such situations, leaders need to be able to tolerate ambiguity, while being creative at the same time. If it is true that the digital world forces leaders to examine problems and provide innovative answers at a faster peace, the use of information technology also allows them to make more informed decisions. Highly developing technological advancement leads to great demands on organizations' capability to work with constantly varying situations and players (Gerth & Peppard, 2016); Kahai, S.Avolio, & Sosik, 2017.; Cecilia, 2020; Graham, Daniel & Doore, 2021). Lynn highlighted that there is continuous requirement for companies and other institutes to adjust, forecast chances, and sometimes make improvement to keep their competitiveness in the market. As there is increasing innovativeness in every aspect, leaders should carry out vigorous role in recognizing the need for change and also initiating this change in their teams and organisation (Schwarzmüller et al., 2018). As innovation is becoming a main concern, leaders should to know how to take benefit of networking prospects. Leaders operate in hyper-connected environment, the omnipresent social media and other digital platforms usage offers novel interacting chances due to both an easy access to large groups of persons, and the opportunity to found networks with the help of more instant communications. It is important for individual to be both the people-oriented and of technically in to order to lead in this digital transformation era. The stated two skills are important for people in an organisation to implement digital transformation in their organisation. The case study presented by, for cross-functional and cross-skill contamination, there is a need create a lucrative exchange association between people-oriented leaders (e.g., sales), and IT functions. The most efficient method to feast information and knowledge across the business is the organized knowledge distribution from an individual to the groups (Boe and Torgersen, 2018).

Trends in AI Based CRM

Managing customer has transformed to engaging customer and enhancing customer experience. As per the Salesforce Survey, around eighty percent of the customers chose better experience as par with the product or the service offered. Similarly, in a report of State of Marketing the companies using AI for CRM increased to 84% in 2020 as compared to 29% in 2018. This clearly indicates the popularity and benefit of AI (Totah, 2020).

Issues in Adopting AI

Technology adoption has always been a concern for the organizations. Same is applicable for AI based applications. The role of top management is very crucial in such implementations. The customers are very important and AI based CRM is the need of the hour but at the same time the employees in the organization must be aligned with the new technology adoption process. It should be part of strategic planning to keep employees aware about the technology change and must be suitably trained in use of AI based application. They should be made aware that such adoption will lead to efficiency due to automation of manual processes (Chatterjee et al, 2020).

RESEARCH QUESTIONS

RQ1. What is the current trend in CRM based on AI? (Answered though Background section)

RQ2. How to make AI adoption in CRM successful? (Answered through Proposed model)

DISCUSSION AND PROPOSED MODEL

The current age is of information overload and there is a need to derive meaningful analysis along with automating most of the manual processes. AI supports automation, fast decision making, better customer experience, research and data analysis and complex problem solving. CRM and brand loyalty is all about providing improved customer experience. AI is the future of effective CRM since it has two-fold benefit.

On one hand it supports automation of routine work and on the other hand provides support for taking effective decision. In this digital era the customer service has become very proactive. Earlier the customer would endlessly wait for phone call for query resolution. But now with AI based CRM there is social media, review sites and customer communities to have a better connect. In the coming days the organization focusing on better customer experience will have a competitive edge (Stieninger, Nedbal, Wetzlinger, Wagner & Erskine, 2014; Rai, Sahoo & Mehfuz, 2015; Garg & Stiller, 2015; Ali, Shrestha, Osmanaj & Muhammed, 2020). AI provides this opportunity to the companies taking them beyond conventional competition in the digital era (Marinchak, Forrest & Hoanca, 2018).

Proposed Model

AI is the simulation of the human mind through programming which highlights the self-learning of the machine. Since there is a large volume of data due to the internet, social media and ecommerce there is a need to take support of analytics and AI to manage it (Fotiadis and Vassiliadis, 2017). There are many ways in which AI can be leveraged to enhance customer experience. The way the customer queries are being handled by the AI based system is completely different from the traditional virtual response system. The AI based model understands the customer's accent and dialects and does not require the customer to repeat the queries multiple times (Sterne, 2017; Chatterjee, Ghosh, Chaudhuri & Nguyen, 2019)). This minimizes the time consumed and the inconvenience caused. Since AI is based on automatic learning of the machine even the mistakes lead to learning of AI based systems. The facility of personalized emails through machines is possible by using algorithms, based on initial emails sent by the customers and the blogs read by them. The personalized experience can be provided through the website visit pattern. The chatbots work in the proactive way and help in streamlining the sales process (Venkatesh, Thong, & Xu. 2012; Lechman, 2015); Azam, 2015; Priyadarshinee, 2020; Sarea & Taufiq-Hail, 2021). AI fosters productivity of the customer care team by managing routine issues and involving the human team only for the complex queries. AI and advanced machine learning algorithms help in identifying the customer segment to be added or removed from a particular campaign. There is an added advantage of cost and task optimization (Sakunthala, 2020; Talwar & Koury, 2017).

The adoption of technology has always been a pivot in enhancing technological capabilities of the organization. This is very much applicable to the adoption of AI (Agrawal, Gans & Goldfarb, 2019). The parameters of technology adoption model; perceived usefulness & perceived ease of use are the basis of the current study to understand the adoption of AI with special reference to Indian context (Wu & Wang,2005; de Graaf et.al. 2019). These variables are important in managing the adoption of the AI based CRM, however with the better strategic approach and technology leadership the process of adoption becomes more effective. Following model portrays the essence of the current paper.

Figure 1. Conceptual Model (Proposed)

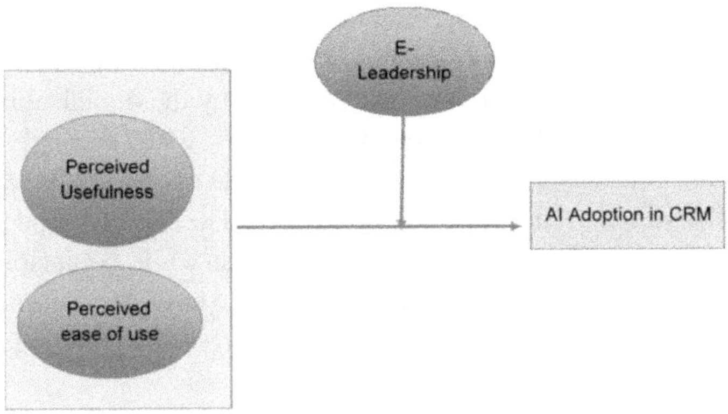

The need to create a digital environment and E-leadership is very essential for the organizations apart from establishing the usefulness and ease of use for any AI based process. The current paper attempts to elaborate the successful adoption of AI for CRM under the influence of e-leadership with special reference to Indian context.

The proposed model is based on the concept of adopting new technology namely AI for making CRM effective (André et.al.2017; Huang & Rust, 2018; Kumar, Rajan, Venkatesan, & Lecinski, 2019). Since AI is a new technology the factors that are associated with its adoption must be taken into account. The perceived usefulness and the perceived ease of use from the customer's perspective is important. However, before the technology reaches to the customer the application based on this technology has to be successfully created. And at this level also the adoption of technology is an important aspect. The digital culture of the organization plays an important role in technology adoption (Swinton & Casey,1999; Florenthal, 2019; Alzahrani & Daim, 2021; Yildiz, O. (Ed.), 2021). The leadership of the organization acts as a catalyst in motivating and aligning the people in exhibiting a positive attitude while adopting AI. Thus the proposed model suggested that the importance of AI in effective CRM is undeniable and the factors affecting the adoption must be taken into account well. Also, the moderating role of e-leadership makes the process of adoption speedy and positive. AI possesses a lot of scope for engaging and having loyal customers thus leading to the overall success of the business.

CONCLUSION

AI have become the new buzz word and have started showing benefits for business world as well. Although it is still in its early stage of implementation in various spheres of organization, big organizations like Amazon, Netflix and Uber have already started using it for their competitive advantage. The importance of AI for effective CRM is evident and is supported through better decision making, strong online customer support, personalized support and process automation. While implementing AI, the technology adoption aspect has to be taken care by the organization. The most vital parameters for successful adoption of technology, with special reference to AI are perceived usefulness & perceived ease of use. The overall digital culture of the organization also supports successful adoption of AI. The role of digital leadership or e-Leadership also acts as facilitator in smooth transition while expansion or adoption of the new technology. Thus the current chapter tries to emphasise the application of AI in the business arena while having a strategic approach in planning its adoption.

REFERENCES

Agrawal, A., Gans, J., & Goldfarb, A. (2019). Economic Policy for Artificial Intelligence. *Innovation Policy and the Economy*, *19*, 139–159. doi:10.1086/699935

Akroush, M. N., Dahiyat, S. E., Gharaibeh, H. S., & Abu-Lail, B. N. (2011). Customer relationship management implementation. *International Journal of Commerce and Management*, *21*(2), 158–190. doi:10.1108/10569211111144355

Al-Ajlan, M., & Zairi, M. (2006). Critical Success Factors in CRM Implementation: Some Research Issues. Metamorphosis. *Journal of Management Research*, *5*(1), 19–30. doi:10.1177/0972622520060103

Ali, O., Shrestha, A., Osmanaj, V., & Muhammed, S. (2020). Cloud computing technology adoption: An evaluation of key factors in local governments. *Information Technology & People*, *34*(2), 666–703. doi:10.1108/ITP-03-2019-0119

Alzahrani, S., & Daim, T. U. (2021). *Technology Adoption. Recent Developments in Individual and Organizational Adoption of ICTs*. doi:10.4018/978-1-7998-3045-0.ch006

André, Q., Carmon, Z., Wertenbroch, K., Crum, A., Frank, D., Goldstein, W., Huber, J., van Boven, L., Weber, B., & Yang, H. (2017). Consumer Choice and Autonomy in the Age of Artificial Intelligence and Big Data. *Customer Needs and Solutions*, *5*(1-2), 28–37. doi:10.100740547-017-0085-8

Avolio, B. J., Sosik, J. J., Kahai, S. S., & Baker, B. (2014). E-leadership: Re-examining transformations in leadership source and transmission. *The Leadership Quarterly*, *25*(1), 105–131. doi:10.1016/j.leaqua.2013.11.003

Azam, M. S. (2015). *Diffusion of ICT and SME Performance. E-Services Adoption: Processes by Firms in Developing Nations*. doi:10.1108/S1069-096420150000023005

Bakardjieva, M., Felt, M., & Dumitrica, D. (2018). The mediatization of leadership: Grassroots digital facilitators as organic intellectuals, sociometric stars and caretakers. *Information Communication and Society*, *21*(6), 899–914. doi:10.1080/1369118X.2018.1434556

Bawack, R. E., Fosso Wamba, S., & Carillo, K. D. A. (2021). A framework for understanding artificial intelligence research: Insights from practice. *Journal of Enterprise Information Management*, *34*(2), 645–678. doi:10.1108/JEIM-07-2020-0284

Blut, M., Frennea, C. M., Mittal, V., & Mothersbaugh, D. L. (2015). How procedural, financial and relational switching costs affect customer satisfaction, repurchase intentions, and repurchase behavior: A meta-analysis. *International Journal of Research in Marketing*, *32*(2), 226–229. doi:10.1016/j.ijresmar.2015.01.001

Boe, O., & Torgersen, G.-E. (2018). Norwegian "Digital Border Defense" and Competence for the Unforeseen: A Grounded Theory Approach. *Frontiers in Psychology*, *9*, 555. Advance online publication. doi:10.3389/fpsyg.2018.00555 PMID:29725314

Bohling, T., Bowman, D., LaValle, S., Mittal, V., Narayandas, D., Ramani, G., & Varadarajan, R. (2006). CRM Implementation. *Journal of Service Research*, *9*(2), 184–194. doi:10.1177/1094670506293573

Bradlow, E. T., Gangwar, M., Kopalle, P., & Voleti, S. (2017). The Role of Big Data and Predictive Analytics in Retailing. *Journal of Retailing*, *93*(1), 79–95. doi:10.1016/j.jretai.2016.12.004

Cecilia, F. (2020). E-Leadership: The Implication of Digital Transformation for Leadership in Organizations in Africa. doi:10.31219/osf.io/sj6zf

Chatterjee, S., Chaudhuri, R., Vrontis, D., Thrassou, A., & Ghosh, S. K. (2020). ICT-enabled CRM system adoption: a dual Indian qualitative case study and conceptual framework development. *Journal of Asia Business Studies*. doi:10.1108/JABS-05-2020-0198

Chatterjee, S., Ghosh, S. K., & Chaudhuri, R. (2020). Knowledge management in improving business process: An interpretative framework for successful implementation of AI–CRM–KM system in organizations. *Business Process Management Journal*, *26*(6), 1261–1281. doi:10.1108/BPMJ-05-2019-0183

Chatterjee, S., Ghosh, S. K., Chaudhuri, R., & Chaudhuri, S. (2020). Adoption of AI-integrated CRM system by Indian industry: from security and privacy perspective. *Information & Computer Security*. doi:10.1108/ICS-02-2019-0029

Chatterjee, S., Ghosh, S. K., Chaudhuri, R., & Nguyen, B. (2019). Are CRM systems ready for AI integration? *The Bottom Line (New York, N.Y.)*, *32*(2), 144–157. doi:10.1108/BL-02-2019-0069

Chatterjee, S., Nguyen, B., Ghosh, S. K., Bhattacharjee, K. K., & Chaudhuri, S. (2020). Adoption of artificial intelligence integrated CRM system: An empirical study of Indian organizations. *The Bottom Line (New York, N.Y.)*, *33*(4), 359–375. doi:10.1108/BL-08-2020-0057

Chu, K.-M. (2021). Measuring Customer Service Experience in Offline and Online Retail Environments. doi:10.20944/preprints202102.0250.v1

Dawn, S. K., & Guha, A. (2010). E-CRM: A Critical Analysis by Developing an Effective Model. *Asia Pacific Business Review*, *6*(3), 106–114. doi:10.1177/097324701000600309

de Graaf, M. M., Ben Allouch, S., & van Dijk, J. A. (2019). Why would I use this in My home? A model of domestic social robot acceptance. *Human-Computer Interaction*, *34*(2), 115–173. doi:10.1080/07370024.2017.1312406

De Sutter, R., Matton, M., Laukens, N., Van Rijsselbergen, D., & Van de Walle, R. (2011). MediaCRM: Enabling Customer Relationship Management in the Broadcast. *Lecture Notes in Computer Science*, *6987*, 19–26. doi:10.1007/978-3-642-23971-7_3

Dehghanpouri, H., Soltani, Z., & Rostamzadeh, R. (2020). The impact of trust, privacy and quality of service on the success of E-CRM: The mediating role of customer satisfaction. *Journal of Business and Industrial Marketing*, *35*(11), 1831–1847. doi:10.1108/JBIM-07-2019-0325

Elkington, R. (2021). E-Leadership as Enabling Function for Technology-enriched Learning. *Effective Leadership for Overcoming ICT Challenges in Higher Education: What Faculty, Staff and Administrators Can Do to Thrive Amidst the Chaos*, 59–71. doi:10.1108/978-1-83982-306-020211007

Filimonova, V. (2020). CRM Systems as a Tool for Improving Business Efficiency. *Bulletin of Science and Practice*, *6*(2), 235–240. doi:10.33619/2414-2948/51/25

Florenthal, B. (2019). Young consumers' motivational drivers of brand engagement behavior on social media sites. *Journal of Research in Interactive Marketing*, *13*(3), 351–391. doi:10.1108/JRIM-05-2018-0064

Forbes. (2019). Retrieved from: https://www.forbes.com/sites/falonfatemi/2019/08/10/5-ways-artificial-intelligence-is-transforming-crms/?sh=6a8dd2ba5354

Fotiadis, A. K., & Vassiliadis, C. (2017). Being customer-centric through CRM metrics in the B2B market: The case of maritime shipping. *Journal of Business and Industrial Marketing*, *32*(3), 347–356. doi:10.1108/JBIM-11-2014-0226

Frow, P. E., & Payne, A. F. (2009). Customer Relationship Management: A Strategic Perspective. *Journal of Business Market Management*, *3*(1), 7–27. doi:10.100712087-008-0035-8

Gale, M., & Aarons, C. (2018). Digital Transformation. *Leader to Leader*, *2018*(90), 30–36. doi:10.1002/ltl.20390

Gangwar, H., Date, H., & Raoot, A. D. (2014). Review on IT adoption: Insights from recent technologies. *Journal of Enterprise Information Management*, *27*(4), 488–502. doi:10.1108/JEIM-08-2012-0047

Garg, R., & Stiller, B. (2015). Factors Affecting Cloud Adoption and Their Interrelations. *Proceedings of the 5th International Conference on Cloud Computing and Services Science*. 10.5220/0005412300870094

Gerbaudo, P. (2016). Social media teams as digital vanguards: The question of leadership in the management of key Facebook and Twitter accounts of Occupy Wall Street, Indignados and UK Uncut. *Information Communication and Society*, *20*(2), 185–202. doi:10.1080/1369118X.2016.1161817

Gerth, A. B., & Peppard, J. (2016). The dynamics of CIO derailment: How CIOs come undone and how to avoid it. *Business Horizons*, *59*(1), 61–70. doi:10.1016/j.bushor.2015.09.001

Graham, C., Daniel, H., & Doore, B. (2021). Virtual Leadership. *Research Anthology on Digital Transformation, Organizational Change, and the Impact of Remote Work*, 1678–1691. doi:10.4018/978-1-7998-7297-9.ch082

Grewal, D., Kroschke, M., Mende, M., Roggeveen, A. L., & Scott, M. L. (2020). Frontline Cyborgs at Your Service: How Human Enhancement Technologies Affect Customer Experiences in Retail, Sales, and Service Settings. *Journal of Interactive Marketing*, *51*, 9–25. doi:10.1016/j.intmar.2020.03.001

Haenlein, M., & Kaplan, A. (2019). A Brief History of Artificial Intelligence: On the Past, Present, and Future of Artificial Intelligence. *California Management Review*, *61*(4), 5–14. doi:10.1177/0008125619864925

Harrigan, P., Ramsey, E., & Ibbotson, P. (2009). Investigating the e-CRM activities of Irish SMEs. *Journal of Small Business and Enterprise Development*, *16*(3), 443–465. doi:10.1108/14626000910977161

Hofacker, C. F. (2019). The Growing Importance of Software as a Driver of Value Exchange. *Marketing in a Digital World*, 85–95. doi:10.1108/S1548-643520190000016007

Hoyer, W. D., Kroschke, M., Schmitt, B., Kraume, K., & Shankar, V. (2020). Transforming the Customer Experience Through New Technologies. *Journal of Interactive Marketing*, *51*, 57–71. doi:10.1016/j.intmar.2020.04.001

Huang, M.-H., & Rust, R. T. (2018). Artificial Intelligence in Service. *Journal of Service Research*, *21*(2), 155–172. doi:10.1177/1094670517752459

Hummer, W., Muthusamy, V., Rausch, T., Dube, P., El Maghraoui, K., Murthi, A., & Oum, P. (2019). ModelOps: Cloud-Based Lifecycle Management for Reliable and Trusted AI. *2019 IEEE International Conference on Cloud Engineering (IC2E)*. 10.1109/IC2E.2019.00025

Kahai, S., Avolio, B. J., & Sosik, J. J. (2017). E-Leadership. The Wiley Blackwell Handbook of the Psychology of the Internet at Work, 285–314. doi:10.1002/9781119256151.ch14

Kımıloğlu, H., & Zaralı, H. (2009). What signifies success in e-CRM? *Marketing Intelligence & Planning*, *27*(2), 246–267. doi:10.1108/02634500910945011

Kumar, V., Rajan, B., Venkatesan, R., & Lecinski, J. (2019). Understanding the Role of Artificial Intelligence in Personalized Engagement Marketing. *California Management Review*, *61*(4), 135–155. doi:10.1177/0008125619859317

Lechman, E. (2015). What Matters for ICT Diffusion? *ICT Diffusion in Developing Countries*, 167–222. doi:10.1007/978-3-319-18254-4_5

Liu, C., Ready, D., Roman, A., Van Wart, M., Wang, X., McCarthy, A., & Kim, S. (2018). E-leadership: An empirical study of organizational leaders' virtual communication adoption. *Leadership and Organization Development Journal, 39*(7), 826–843. doi:10.1108/LODJ-10-2017-0297

Lok, C. K. (2015). Adoption of Smart Card-Based E-Payment System for Retailing in Hong Kong Using an Extended Technology Acceptance Model. *Advances in Business Marketing and Purchasing*, 255–466. doi:10.1108/S1069-09642015000023B003

Luo, X., Tong, S., Fang, Z., & Qu, Z. (2019). Frontiers: Machines vs. Humans: The Impact of Artificial Intelligence Chatbot Disclosure on Customer Purchases. *Marketing Science*, mksc.2019.1192. Advance online publication. doi:10.1287/mksc.2019.1192

Lynn Pulley, M., & Sessa, V. I. (2001). E-leadership: Tackling complex challenges. *Industrial and Commercial Training, 33*(6), 225–230. doi:10.1108/00197850110405379

Marinchak, C. M., Forrest, E., & Hoanca, B. (2018). Artificial Intelligence. *International Journal of E-Entrepreneurship and Innovation, 8*(2), 14–24. doi:10.4018/IJEEI.2018070102 PMID:30145103

Meffert, J., & Swaminathan, A. (2018). Leadership and the urgency for digital transformation. *Leader to Leader, 2018*(88), 44–49. doi:10.1002/ltl.20357

Ngai, E. W. T., Xiu, L., & Chau, D. C. K. (2009). Application of data mining techniques in customer relationship management: A literature review and classification. *Expert Systems with Applications, 36*(2), 2592–2602. doi:10.1016/j.eswa.2008.02.021

Overgoor, G., Chica, M., Rand, W., & Weishampel, A. (2019). Letting the Computers Take Over: Using AI to Solve Marketing Problems. *California Management Review, 61*(4), 156–185. doi:10.1177/0008125619859318

Pactera Technologies & Nimdizi. (2017). Retrieved from:https://www.nimdzi.com/wp-content/uploads/2019/06/Nimdzi-AI-whitepaper.pdf

Priyadarshinee, P. (2020). Examining Critical Success Factors of Cloud Computing Adoption. *International Journal of Decision Support System Technology, 12*(2), 80–96. doi:10.4018/IJDSST.2020040105

Quan, X. I., & Sanderson, J. (2018). Understanding the Artificial Intelligence Business Ecosystem. *IEEE Engineering Management Review, 46*(4), 22–25. doi:10.1109/EMR.2018.2882430

Quyen, D. (2020). Efficiency Evaluation of e-CRM System in Banking Sector under Digitalization. *Journal of Advanced Research in Dynamical and Control Systems, 12*(SP4), 1800–1807. doi:10.5373/JARDCS/V12SP4/20201665

Rai, R., Sahoo, G., & Mehfuz, S. (2015). Exploring the factors influencing the cloud computing adoption: A systematic study on cloud migration. *SpringerPlus, 4*(1), 197. Advance online publication. doi:10.118640064-015-0962-2 PMID:25977891

Ramzaev, V. M., Khaimovich, I. N., & Chumak, V. G. (2017). *Big Data Analysis for Demand Segmentation of Small Business Services by Activity in Region.* Data Science. doi:10.18287/1613-0073-2017-1903-48-53

ReportG. (2019). https://www.gartner.com/smarterwithgartner/3-barriers-to-ai-adoption/#:~:text=More%20organizations%20are%20adopting%20artificial,the%20business%20impact%20and%20benefits

ReportG. (2020). Retrieved from:https://www.gartner.com/smarterwithgartner/2-megatrends-dominate-the-gartner-hype-cycle-for-artificial-intelligence-2020/

Rust, R. T., & Huang, M.-H. (2014). The Service Revolution and the Transformation of Marketing Science. *Marketing Science, 33*(2), 206–221. doi:10.1287/mksc.2013.0836

Sakunthala, A. (2020). Role of information technology on CRM implementation in selected industries. *Asian Journal of Management, 11*(4), 413–418. doi:10.5958/2321-5763.2020.00063.3

Sarea, A., & Taufiq-Hail, G. A.-M. (2021). Evaluation of Compatibility of Cloud-based Applications, Credibility, and Trust Perceptions on the Adoption of Cloud Technology: A Review. *Advanced Machine Learning Technologies and Applications*, 889–907. doi:10.1007/978-3-030-69717-4_83

Scherer, M. U. (2015). Regulating Artificial Intelligence Systems: Risks, Challenges, Competencies, and Strategies. SSRN *Electronic Journal*. doi:10.2139/ssrn.2609777

Schwarzmüller, T., Brosi, P., Duman, D., & Welpe, I. M. (2018). How Does the Digital Transformation Affect Organizations? Key Themes of Change in Work Design and Leadership. *Management Review, 29*(2), 114–138. doi:10.5771/0935-9915-2018-2-114

Shaw, C., & Hamilton, R. (2016). How to Move to the Next Level of Customer Experience. *The Intuitive Customer*, 161–191. doi:10.1057/978-1-137-53430-9_10

Soni, N., Sharma, E. K., Singh, N., & Kapoor, A. (2020). Artificial Intelligence in Business: From Research and Innovation to Market Deployment. *Procedia Computer Science, 167*, 2200–2210. doi:10.1016/j.procs.2020.03.272

State, M. (2020). A statistical perspective of ERP and CRM using in EU enterprises. *Journal of Applied Computer Science & Mathematics*, *14*(1), 37–42. doi:10.4316/JACSM.202001006

Sterne, J. (2017). *Artificial Intelligence for Marketing*. doi:10.1002/9781119406341

Stieninger, M., Nedbal, D., Wetzlinger, W., Wagner, G., & Erskine, M. A. (2014). Impacts on the Organizational Adoption of Cloud Computing: A Reconceptualization of Influencing Factors. *Procedia Technology*, *16*, 85–93. doi:10.1016/j.protcy.2014.10.071

Swinton, S. M., & Casey, F. (1999). From Adoption to Innovation of Environmental Technologies. *Flexible Incentives for the Adoption of Environmental Technologies in Agriculture,* 351–359. doi:10.1007/978-94-011-4395-0_22

Talwar, R., & Koury, A. (2017). Artificial intelligence – the next frontier in IT security? *Network Security*, *2017*(4), 14–17. doi:10.1016/S1353-4858(17)30039-9

Taylor, S. A., & Hunter, G. L. (2002). The impact of loyalty with e-CRM software and e-services. *International Journal of Service Industry Management*, *13*(5), 452–474. doi:10.1108/09564230210447931

Tian, J., & Wang, S. (2016). Signaling Service Quality via Website e-CRM Features. *Journal of Hospitality & Tourism Research (Washington, D.C.)*, *41*(2), 211–245. doi:10.1177/1096348014525634

Totah, Z. (2020). *9 Critical CRM Trends to Keep an Eye on for 2021*. Retrieved from https://www.selecthub.com/customer-relationship-management/crm-trends/

Van Doorn, J., Mende, M., Noble, S. M., Hulland, J., Ostrom, A. L., Grewal, D., & Petersen, J. A. (2016). Domo Arigato Mr. Roboto. *Journal of Service Research*, *20*(1), 43–58. doi:10.1177/1094670516679272

Venkatesh, T., Thong, & Xu. (2012). Consumer Acceptance and Use of Information Technology: Extending the Unified Theory of Acceptance and Use of Technology. *Management Information Systems Quarterly*, *36*(1), 157. doi:10.2307/41410412

Wu, J., & Wang, S. (2005). What drives mobile commerce? An empirical evaluation of the revised technology acceptance model. *Information & Management*, *42*(5), 719–729. doi:10.1016/j.im.2004.07.001

Yildiz, O. (Ed.). (2021). Advances in Wireless Technologies and Telecommunication *Recent Developments in Individual and Organizational Adoption of ICTs*. doi:10.4018/978-1-7998-3045-0

Chapter 6
Artifical Intelligence and CRM:
A Case of Telecom Industry

Shailja Dixit
https://orcid.org/0000-0001-8123-6872
Amity University, Lucknow, India

ABSTRACT

Disruptive technologies such as IoT, big data analytics, blockchain, and AI have changed the ways businesses operate, with AI holding immense marketing transformation potential. AI is influencing marketing strategies, business models, sales processes, customer service options, and customer behaviors. AI-CRM's improving ability to predict customer lifetime value will generate an inevitable rise in implementing adapted treatment of customers, leading to greater customer prioritization and service discrimination in markets. CSPs are working through the challenging process of digital transformation, driven by the need to compete with fast-moving OTT and consumer tech players. CSPs need to move quickly and can advance digital transformation with solutions that leverage AI which can drive value across the business from network optimization and data analytics through to customer care and marketing engagement. The chapter tries to identify how AI is impacting the CRM in the telecom industry and leveraging the benefits of this technology for better customer management and growth.

INTRODUCTION

AI technology is evolving faster than expected and is already surpassing human decision making in certain instances. While many are alarmed by this, AI is producing some of the most effective and dramatic results in business today. On the contrary,

DOI: 10.4018/978-1-7998-7959-6.ch006

using uncontrolled AI for certain business functions may cause regulatory and ethical issues that could lead to liability, thus optimizing AI for maximum benefit requires a new approach.

Telecommunications service providers face a handful of daunting market conditions. To combat profit erosion, most communications service providers (CSPs) are struggling through a process to become digital service providers more akin to web companies that offer rapidly evolving and highly customized services. According to reports, a central element of this transformation is the adoption of artificial intelligence (AI) technologies for network automation and management, customer experience management (CEM) and service delivery, virtual assistants for customer service and marketing, intelligent customer relationship management (CRM), and other key applications.

The digital revolution over the past few decades has enabled companies to collect an impressive amount of customer data and digitise many of their existing processes. Companies are now trying to leverage these assets to create improved sales engagement strategies geared at target audiences and to streamline their processes.

Artificial Intelligence in telecom isn't a new phenomenon. Adopting AI and ML just doesn't drive differentiation but has become essential for survival. Businesses are competing fiercely for every customer these days, meaning providing a good product is no longer enough. Companies are constantly finding new and innovative ways to attract new customers, deliver excellent services and retain customer loyalty.

The Telecommunications Industry is Ripe for Artificial-Intelligence Driven Solutions, with Service Providers Expected to Spend $11.2 Billion by 2025. It is forecasted that CSPs will spend $11.2 billion annually on AI-driven software solutions by 2025, up from $419.0 million in 2018. Telecom operators have begun to experiment and deploy AI-driven solutions that leverage fast, scalable interpretation, analytics, and prediction to generate revenue or reduce costs. According to a survey by Deloitte, 40% of Telecom, Media and Tech executives say they have garnered "substantial" benefits from cognitive technologies, with 25% having invested $10 million or more. More than three-quarters expect cognitive computing to "substantially transform" their companies in years to come.

UNDERSTANDING THE CONCEPTS

Customer Relationship Management (CRM)

CRM as defined by Paul Greenberg: "CRM is study of fundamental nature of knowledge, reality and a business strategy, supported by the system and technology, designed to improve human interactions to that of the business environment. It is a continuing business process which demands a dynamic, ongoing plan of action for customer agreement." Due to the customer aligned view of the market, the business needs to concentrate on the needs of the customers. To customize their products according to the customers liking, every organization should study their customers closely and observe their activities. CRM mainly indicate business practices taking place across the enterprise to set-up the assets, aggregate and analyze the customer profiles Amoako, et.al 2012.

Components of CRM

Customer Relationship Management (CRM) aims to get a "single integrated view of customers" and a „customer centric approach". There are three components of CRM Maheshwari, 2014:

1. Customer
2. Relationship
3. Management

Types of CRM

There are three types of CRM (Rababah, et. al. 2011, Haridasan, & S. Venkatesh, 2011):

1. Operational CRM: commonly refers to services targeted towards the customers to solve their problem.
2. Collaborative CRM: is a very efficient method of communication since it includes feed-backs and issue reports directly from the customers.
3. Analytical CRM: takes into consideration product and service decision-making as well as pricing and new product development.

The main targets of CRM are to achieve higher profits and increased sales by the means of customer satisfaction and reducing buying and delivery costs. The basic steps to accomplish the targets are (Maheshwari et. al. 2014).

1. Customer Identification: Getting to label the customer overtime via different websites marketing medium, surveys and communications.
2. Customer Differentiation: Differentiate each and every customer depending on their individual unique demands and requirement.
3. Customer Interaction: Interact with the customers to keep track of their behavior and needs and the changes in demand over time.

4. Customization: Customize the product in such a way that the customers are treated uniquely and they're each and every demands are fulfilled.

Artificial Intelligence (AI)

The father of Artificial Intelligence, John McCarthy states a definition for AI which says that "Artificial Intelligence is the science and engineering of making intelligent machines, especially intelligent computer programs". Artificial Intelligence (AI) is intelligence exhibited by machines. In computer science the field of AI defines itself as the study of "intelligent agents". Generally, the term "AI" is used when a machine simulates functions that human's associate with other human minds such as learning and problem solving. Subfields of AI such as Machine Learning, Natural Language processing, Image Processing and Data mining have become an important topic for today's tech giants. Machine Learning is actively being used in Google's predictive search bar, in the Gmail spam filer, in Netflix's show suggestions. Natural Language Processing exists in Apple's Siri and Google voice. Image Processing is necessary for facebook's facial recognition tagging software and in Google's self driving cars. Data Mining

has become a slang for software industry due to the mass amounts of data being collected every day. Companies like Facebook and Google collect large amounts of statistics from users every second and need a way to interpret the data they receive. Artificial Intelligence has already proven to be useful new tool in today's technology heavy culture.Artificial Intelligence can automate the business process, learn insights from past data, and generate consumer and market insights through the program-based algorithm (Davenport et al 2020). Technologies like Machine Learning (ML), Deep Learning, and Natural Language Processing (NLP) train machines to handle big data for the generation of market intelligence (Davenport et al 2020).

In simpler terms Artificial intelligence (AI) is a wide-ranging branch of computer science concerned with building smart machines capable of performing tasks that typically require human intelligence. AI is an interdisciplinary science with multiple approaches, but advancements in machine learning and deep learning are creating a paradigm shift in virtually every sector of the tech industry.

In their ground breaking textbook Artificial Intelligence: A Modern Approach, authors Stuart Russell and Peter Norvig approach the question by unifying their work around the theme of intelligent agents in machines. With this in mind, AI is "the study of agents that receive percepts from the environment and perform actions." (Russel and Norvig viii)

Norvig and Russell go on to explore four different approaches that have historically defined the field of AI:

- Thinking humanly
- Thinking rationally
- Acting humanly
- Acting rationally

The first two ideas concern thought processes and reasoning, while the others deal with behavior.

Types of Artificial Intelligence—Weak AI vs. Strong AI

Weak AI—also called Narrow AI or Artificial Narrow Intelligence (ANI)—is AI trained and focused to perform specific tasks. Weak AI drives most of the AI that surrounds us today. 'Narrow' might be a more accurate descriptor for this type of AI as it is anything but weak; it enables some very robust applications, such as Apple's Siri, Amazon's Alexa, IBM Watson, and autonomous vehicles.

Strong AI is made up of Artificial General Intelligence (AGI) and Artificial Super Intelligence (ASI). Artificial general intelligence (AGI), or general AI, is a theoretical form of AI where a machine would have an intelligence equaled to humans; it would have a self-aware consciousness that has the ability to solve problems, learn, and plan for the future. Artificial Super Intelligence (ASI)—also known as superintelligence—would surpass the intelligence and ability of the human brain. While strong AI is still entirely theoretical with no practical examples in use today, that doesn't mean AI researchers aren't also exploring its development.

Deep Learning vs. Machine Learning

Since deep learning and machine learning tend to be used interchangeably, it's worth noting the nuances between the two. Both deep learning and machine learning are sub-fields of artificial intelligence, and deep learning is actually a sub-field of machine learning.

Deep learning is actually comprised of neural networks. "Deep" in deep learning refers to a neural network comprised of more than three layers—which would be inclusive of the inputs and the output—can be considered a deep learning algorithm. This is generally represented using the following diagram:

The way in which deep learning and machine learning differ is in how each algorithm learns. Deep learning automates much of the feature extraction piece of the process, eliminating some of the manual human intervention required and enabling the use of larger data sets. Classical, or "non-deep", machine learning is more dependent on human intervention to learn. Human experts determine the

Figure 1. Visual representation of how AI, ML and DL relate to one another

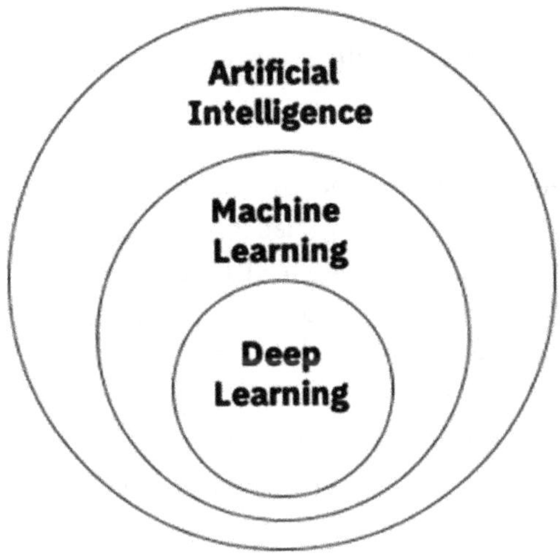

hierarchy of features to understand the differences between data inputs, usually requiring more structured data to learn.

"Deep" machine learning can leverage labeled datasets, also known as supervised learning, to inform its algorithm, but it doesn't necessarily require a labeled dataset. It can ingest unstructured data in its raw form (e.g. text, images), and it can automatically determine the hierarchy of features which distinguish different categories of data from one another. Unlike machine learning, it doesn't require human intervention to process data, allowing us to scale machine learning in more interesting ways.

Figure 2. Diagram of deep neural network

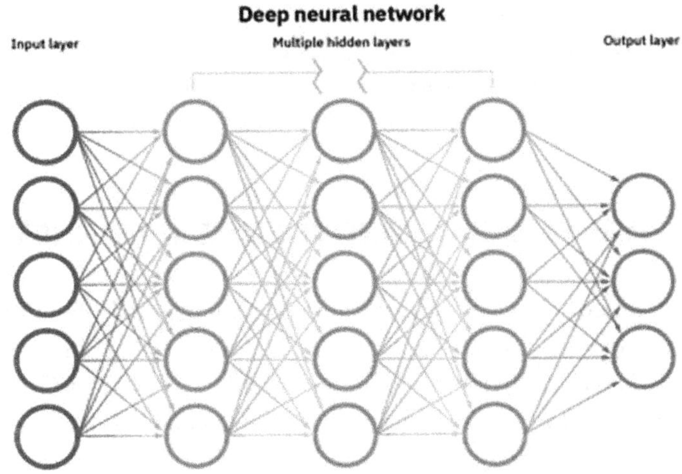

Artificial Intelligence Applications

There are numerous, real-world applications of AI systems today. Below are some of the most common examples:

- Speech Recognition: It is also known as automatic speech recognition (ASR), computer speech recognition, or speech-to-text, and it is a capability which uses natural language processing (NLP) to process human speech into a written format. Many mobile devices incorporate speech recognition into their systems to conduct voice search—e.g. Siri—or provide more accessibility around texting.
- Customer Service: Online chatbots are replacing human agents along the customer journey. They answer frequently asked questions (FAQs) around topics, like shipping, or provide personalized advice, cross-selling products or suggesting sizes for users, changing the way we think about customer engagement across websites and social media platforms. Examples include messaging bots on e-commerce sites with virtual agents, messaging apps, such as Slack and Facebook Messenger, and tasks usually done by virtual assistants and voice assistants.
- Computer Vision: This AI technology enables computers and systems to derive meaningful information from digital images, videos and other visual inputs, and based on those inputs, it can take action. This ability to provide recommendations distinguishes it from image recognition tasks. Powered by convolutional neural networks, computer vision has applications within photo tagging in social media, radiology imaging in healthcare, and self-driving cars within the automotive industry.
- Recommendation Engines: Using past consumption behavior data, AI algorithms can help to discover data trends that can be used to develop more effective cross-selling strategies. This is used to make relevant add-on recommendations to customers during the checkout process for online retailers.

ARTIFICIAL INTELLIGENCE AND ITS USE IN MARKETING

Artificial intelligence can support marketers in strategy and planning marketing activities by helping in segmentation, targeting, and positioning (STP). Besides STP, AI can help marketers in visioning strategic orientation of firm (Huang & Rust, 2017). Text mining and machine learning algorithms can be applied in sectors like banking and finance, art marketing, retail and tourism for identification of profitable customer segments (Dekimpe, 2020; Netzer et al., 2019; Pitt et al., 2020; Valls et al., 2018). A combination of data optimization techniques, machine learning and causal forests can narrow down the targeted customers also (Chen et al., 2020; Simester et al., 2020).

Use of Artificial Intelligence in Product Management

Artificial intelligence-based marketing analytics tool can gauge the suitability of product design to the customer needs and resultant customer satisfaction (Dekimpe, 2020). Topic modeling adds to the system capabilities to service innovation and designs (Antons & Breidbach, 2018). Preference weight assigned to product attributes during product search help the marketers to understand product recommender system and align marketing strategies for meaningful product management (Dzyabura & Hauser, 2019). Deep learning can personalize the point of interest recommendation and helps to explore new places (Guo et al., 2018). Artificial intelligence offers capabilities to customize offerings to suit to the customer needs (Kumar et al., 2019).

Use of Artificial Intelligence in Pricing Management

Pricing involves factoring of multiple aspects in finalization of price and it is a calculation intensive job. Real time price variation based on fluctuating demand adds to the complexity of pricing task. Artificial intelligence based multiarmed bandit algorithm can dynamically adjust price in real time scenario (Misra et al., 2019). In the frequently changing pricing scenario like e-commerce portal, Bayesian inference in machine learning algorithm can quickly adjust the price points to match the competitor's price (Bauer & Jannach, 2018). According to Dekimpe (2020), best response pricing algorithms encapsulate customer choices, competitor strategies and supply network to optimize dynamic pricing.

Use of Artificial Intelligence in Place Management

Product access and product availability are essential component of marketing mix for heightened customer satisfaction. Product distribution relies on networked relationship, logistics, inventory management, warehousing and transportation problems, which is largely mechanical and repetitive in nature. Artificial intelligence is the perfect solution in the case of place management by offering cobots for packaging, drones for delivery, IoT for order tracking and order refilling (Huang & Rust, 2020). Standardization and mechanization of distribution process adds convenience to both suppliers and customers. Besides utility in distribution management, AI also offers customer engagement opportunities in service context. Service robots programmed with emotional AI codes are handy in surface acting (Wirtz et al., 2018). Embodied robots greet and engage with customers, but human elements need to complement the service environment for customer delight. Automation of service process with AI offers additional opportunity for performance and productivity improvement (Huang & Rust, 2018).

Use of Artificial Intelligence in Promotion Management

Promotion management entail media planning, media scheduling, advertising campaign management, search engine optimization etc. Promotion tactics are transforming from physical to phygital. Digital marketing and social media campaigns made an inroad due to digital transformation across the globe. In the changed technological world, customer decide the content, place, and timing. AI offers personalization and customization of message as per the customer profile and likings (Huang & Rust, 2020). Content analytics can optimize value and message effectiveness. Customer likings and disliking can be tracked in real time with emotive AI algorithms. Netnography on social media content offers new avenues for marketers to align their marketing strategies as per the customer likings (Tripathi & Verma, 2018; Verma, 2014; Verma & Yadav, 2020).

CRM AND ARTIFICIAL INTELLIGENCE

It is evident from above discussion that AI can offer competitive advantage to companies in all aspects of Marketing. It has been especially useful for CRM where the data is huge and real time solutions are need of the hour. Technological disruptions such as artificial intelligence (AI), internet of things (IoT), big data analytics (BDA) have offered digital solutions for attracting and maintaining the customer base (Anshari, Almunawar, Lim, & Al-Mudimigh, 2018; Bolton et al., 2018). Emerging technologies provide a competitive advantage (Rouhani et al., 2016; Spring et al., 2017) by facilitating the customers' product and service offerings (Balaji & Roy, 2017; Khanagha et al., 2017; Liao, 2015). In the current business scenario, the cut-throat competition and technological disruptions have changed the way organizations operate (Gans, 2016). Globally customer-centric approach focused on customer needs plays a pivotal role in organizational growth (Vetterli, Uebernickel, Brenner, Petrie, & Stermann, 2016). Artificial intelligence (AI) is a widely used emerging technology that helps organizations track real-time data to analyze and respond swiftly to customer requirements (Wirth, 2018). AI offers consumer insight on consumer behavior essential for customer attraction and customer retention. AI incites the customer's next move and redefines the overall experience (Tjepkema,

2019). AI tools are useful to deduce customer expectations and navigate the future path (Shabbir, 2015).CRMs that can extract, analyse and interpret data in real-time, can help businesses face this challenge head-on; allowing them to forge deeper, long-lasting relationships with their customers based on tailored communication and data-driven insights. More than this, advanced automation systems are capable of learning as they are provided with more data, effectively improving their ability to analyse and process data over time leading more useful and valuable solutions for sales teams.

Automation similarly offers a lot of value to the average salesperson by minimising the repetitive but necessary processes involved in the sales process - such as updating forecasts and data retrieval - they are given far more time to focus on closing deals and reaching targets. A recent study revealed that three in four sales professionals find prospecting as "extremely" important to convert sales. Yet, 40 per cent admit they find prospecting a struggle. With automation, much of the heavy lifting is taken away from the individual salesperson and instead were able to dedicate more time to calling and having face-to-face meetings with interested prospects. Automation helps sales professionals become more granular in their segmentation approach. With the help of intelligent algorithms, companies segment customers effortlessly based on demographics purchase behaviour, likes and dislikes.

Considering the volume of information available online about each prospect, these activities typically consume a large portion of salespeople's time and resources. With AI, sales professionals can access all these powerful insights with the click of a button, to understand specific customer's needs, predict future behaviour and create the personalised strategies to close the deal.

Furthermore, with a smart lead qualification system in place, salespeople can quickly understand which the high value are leads with good chances of closing a deal and which are not worth pursuing because those prospects will never buy their product. When dealing with a high volume of leads, some of them are bound to slip through the cracks. But every lost opportunity is lost business. To tackle this challenge, automation can actively monitor customers' status, automatically trigger events and notify salespeople when they need to take action.

Gacanin and Wagner (2019) described the implementation challenges of autonomous customer experience management (CEM). The paper also narrated how the intelligence network and critical business value driver were established through AI and ML. Customer experience improved through AI-driven chatbot with Natural Language Processing (NLP) (Nguyen and Sidorova, 2018). AI and ML algorithms enabled efficient data processing, which allows us to formulate the correct decision (Maxwell et al., 2011). Application of AI is required to analyze customer habits, purchases, likings, disliking, etc. (Chatterjee et al., 2019). Customer Relationship Management (CRM) functions benefited through Artificial Intelligence User Interface

(AIUI) (Seranmadevi & Kumar, 2019). AI and IoT converted traditional retail stores to smart retail stores. The smart retail stores elevated customer experience and ease of shopping, and better supply chain (Sujata et al., 2019). Besides brick-and-mortar stores, AI guides the online businesses also. Sha and Rajeswari (2019) described the advancement of AI and demonstrated the AI-supported machine, which can track the five senses (sight, hearing, taste, smell and touch) of humans. The result showed a better consumer-brand association and product-brand association in the e-commerce business.

LINK BETWEEN AI, CRM AND DATA ANALYTICS

Data Analytics and CRM together is mostly known as CRM analytics or analytical CRM. Every customer-centric enterprise uses various CRM tools to analyze the customer profile. These CRM application uses Online Analytical Processing (OLAP) Carmilovic, 2008. CRM lets an organization to modify business operations depending on the information obtained by analyzing the data. CRM makes it easier to choose the appropriate customers from a set of promising customers and Data Analytics helps the organization to propose the most tempting products to the current customers (Maheshwari et. al. 2014). CRM analytics cater customer segmentation grouping (For example, grouping up customers based on most and least likely to repurchase a product), profitability analysis (an analysis which gives an idea of the most profit incurred over time with respect to individual customer), personalization/ customization (the action of modifying products for individual customers depending on the information collected about them), event monitoring (for example, the event of reaching a particular dollar volume of purchases of a customer), what-if scenario (what are the chances of a customer buying a product which is similar to the previously bought product), and predictive modelling (for example, a comparative study of different product development plans as par their probable future success based on the customer profile).

Collecting data and analyzing them are continuous are repetitive process and with time decisions are taken depending on the feedback from previous analysis and respective decisions (Milovic, 2012) Perks of CRM analytics are not only better and more beneficial customer relations with respect to sales and service but also enhancement in supply chain management (lower inventory and speedier delivery) and therefore lower costs and more competitive pricing (Kasthuri, 2016).

From Basic Automation to Artificial Intelligence

AI built on machine learning adds another dimension to automation, helping to complete complex tasks that require capabilities that used to be considered exclusive to humans. These capabilities include understanding and interacting using human speech, interpreting and matching images, recognizing patterns in data, making recommendations, predicting outcomes, and learning from experience instead of being explicitly programmed.

From a sales perspective, AI-based CRMs could combine information from a variety of inputs, analysing information rapidly, acting on insights and adjusting based on successes and failures. This means that as the AI continues to analyse data and to determine the best course of action, it will grow and evolve alongside the salesperson, creating a seamless partnership that almost guarantees success.

With the emergence of AI-powered tools, such as sales assistants, CRMs continues to become more like personal sales coaches, able to motivate and offer human-like advice to guide salespeople to take the right actions at the right time to move the most promising deals forward more efficiently and quicker. Beyond this, AI-powered CRMs improves forecasting and identify new market opportunities, help close deals faster and ultimately, help salespeople perform at their best, day in day out. While automation doesn't require AI, deploying both these solutions in tandem allows for these processes to be optimised over time and reap further benefits.

CRMs that can extract, analyse and interpret data in real-time, helps businesses face this challenge head-on; allowing them to forge deeper, long-lasting relationships with their customers based on tailored communication and data-driven insights. More than this, advanced automation systems are capable of learning as they are provided with more data, effectively improving their ability to analyse and process data over time meaning more useful and valuable solutions are available for sales teams

Automation similarly offers a lot of value to the average salesperson. By minimising the repetitive but necessary processes involved in the sales process - such as updating forecasts and data retrieval - they are given far more time to focus on closing deals and reaching targets.

WHY APPLY CRM ANALYTICS IN TELECOM INDUSTRY

The application of machine learning to mining CSPs' big data makes possible automated personalized services that serve millions of customers at a time. This is the breakthrough to automated personalization at scale. Consumers are interacting with AI-powered applications on a regular basis without even being aware of it: personalized recommendations, online translation services, and fraud detection systems that protect their online transactions, for example. AI is already manifest as incremental improvements to internet services that consumers use and benefit from on a daily basis, and this will accelerate going forward. AI can take network optimization to new levels, bringing advanced intelligence to data analytics while making customer-facing operations and services more effective than ever before. The latter includes personalized plans and service bundles, more interactive marketing engagement, and proactive, efficient customercare operations.

AI solutions can extract data from one part of the business to feed other areas of the business, with self-learning capabilities constantly improving over time. By injecting intelligence across multiple areas of the business, AI can create cross-domain value. For example, it can leverage the customer behavior and engagement data to automatically fine-tune the product catalogue offerings. AI can propose the optimal price, content, size, validity, or other parameters of a product catalogue entry and configure it based on deep learning of the competition from available data such as advertising, voice of the customer feedback, and BSS data.

CRM analytics in telecommunication industry is a rising but partially explored area. In today's competitive market, service providers always need to give something „extra"- as in customized offers, own a predictive tool to identify the needs of the customer, make some offers which the customers cannot turn down, and so on. Telecommunication industry should not only be able to increase profit but also hold on to the existing customers. This industry contains a huge pile data but they are not being used properly. Lots of customer information in the form of network data, customer data, location, etc lies unused in the industry. In the coming years, telecommunication industry is going to be an important data source for innumerable other industries. There are more than one reasons for applying CRM analytics in telecommunication (Carmilovic, 2008).

Competitive Market

After years of unchanging market due to monopoly, now it is changing continuously rise in competition. Due to a large no of options in service providers, customers can switch any time. Hence telecommunication companies are using CRM analytics to gain reasonable dominance. By studying the statistical features and customers" actions, telecommunication industry can profitably modify their marketing strategies (Kamalraj, and A. Malathi, 2013, Dahiya, and Bhatia, 2015).

High Churn Rates

Churn rate relates to the monthly or annual percentage rate of customers leaving the service provider. Due to a competitive market the churn rates are also high.

At the beginning, when the telecommunication market was going through a rapid change, new customers were subscribing everyday and hence the churn rate was not a matter of concern. But with time as the market have matured, the churn rate has also increased.

This high competition is making the telecommunication companies pay attention to their current customers and to find a way to make them stay. CRM analytics can be used to analyze the customer behavior to predict if a particular customer will leave and the reason behind it (Kamalraj, and A. Malathi, 2013).

Massive Data Collection

The amount of data available in the telecommunication is massive, with the main product of the companies being the call. The thousands of calls created by the customer per day, per hour is one of the reasons for this huge data. Each call details record containing the time records, the details about the source and the destination, network details, and so on are stored in the database which is a very large one. Telecommunication enterprise also collect data about their customer and network data containing the status of the network components (Routray, 2015).

THE AI IN THE TELECOM INDUSTRY

Artificial Intelligence applications in the telecommunications industry are increasingly helps CSPs manage, optimize and maintain not only infrastructure, but also customer support operations. Network optimization, predictive maintenance, virtual assistants and RPA are all examples of use cases where AI has impacted the telecom industry, delivering enhanced CX and added value for enterprises.

As Big Data tools and applications become more available and sophisticated, AI can be expected to continue to accelerate growth in this highly competitive space.

The telecommunications industry is leading the adoption of artificial intelligence-based technologies ,confirmed by the launch of Siri, Alexa, Augmented Reality (AR), object recognition, and many similar features. Telecoms are not just communication service providers (CSPs) anymore, but digital service providers. With users doubling up as content creators, there is an ever-increasing appetite for faster, better, and more reliable connections. This unique aspect pitches the need for more efficient networks, better bandwidth handling, improved media content management, etc. All while, telecoms navigate the tricky waves of 5G, security, and connected things.

How Does AI Make a Real Impact?

AI-based solutions provide immediate feedback, enabling telecoms to make decisions in real-time. User consumption patterns hold the key to many deep insights that telecoms can gather using AI.

Figure 3. The AI-CRM effect in Telecom

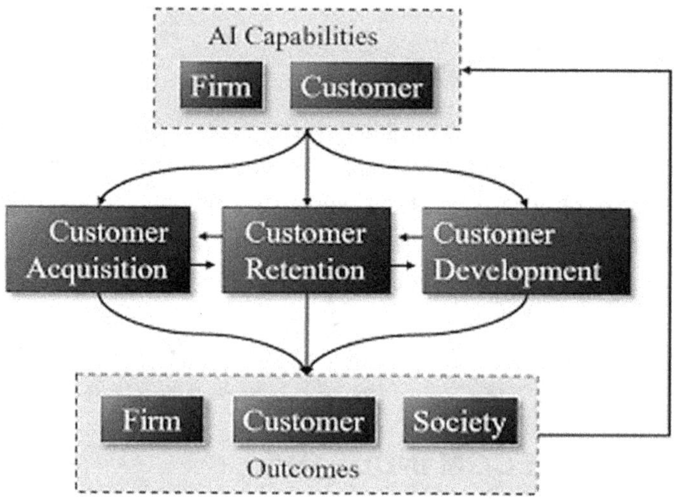

The five key areas where AI can make a difference in telecoms operations are:

1. Network Operations Monitoring

With the adoption of Network Functions Virtualization (NFV) and Software-Defined Networking (SDN) along with AI, intelligent network operations and control to a different level has been excuted. Analyzing traffic in real-time gives plenty of opportunities to plan and react for capacity demands, predict network congestion, and design better network capabilities, thereby enhancing the customer experience.

From a networking perspective, NFV and SDN provides a common place for network configuration and a programmable interface for integrating AI. AI integration at this central place helps detect, predict, and take control. Network statistics is collected, and the information then used for continuous network improvement and developing an AI-optimized network strategy is done.

AI and Machine Learning (ML) based automation tools leverage NFV/SDN network infrastructure metrics to monitor unusual activity. These metrics are processed to provide practical insights and solutions within the ambit of operator-defined policies. Network events are predicted. Their impact on infrastructure is constantly assessed and automatically responded to with preventive and/or corrective actions before the issue reaches the customer. Hereby, "closing the loop," without any human intervention.

A network management platform with a built-in AI engine perform:

- *Multi-layer fault correlation*
- *Real-time network fault positioning*
- *Real-time prediction*
- *Fault diagnostics*
- *Anomaly detection*
- *Predict capacity demands*
- *Predict network congestion*
- *Root cause analysis*

2. Predictive Maintenance

With the help of AI, the monitoring of the condition of network equipment and infrastructure becomes easy. By analyzing historical patterns, telecoms are able to accurately predict network outages and work out pre-emptive remedial action. This makes it much more cost and time-efficient in comparison to corrective maintenance.

AI-based solutions helps in monitoring the network health and infrastructure to predict network incidences and predict equipment failure and faults. Real-time and historical data from power lines, cell towers, data center services, and user consumption are used for such insights.

3. Network Security and Fraud Mitigation

Telecom is the most vulnerable among other industries, suffering the largest financial losses due to breaches in their cybersecurity systems. Conventional telecom security systems only identify commonly occurring issues but fail in detecting or predicting potential future threats.

Telecom fraud happens in various forms such as subscription, voicemail fraud, identity theft, international revenue sharing fraud and vishing or voice phishing calls.

Telecommunications data includes highly sensitive information such as source number, destination number, call duration, call type, geography, region, and account billing information. AI helps in monitoring this large volume of streaming data and instantly identify scams that appear in the garb of anomalies.

AI and ML helps in fraud prevention and detection by identifying transactions that are likely to be fraudulent, distinguishing them from legitimate ones, and detecting false positives. ML algorithms and neural networks are used to identify fraud patterns by monitoring subscriber behavior. AI is used on data to learn patterns that best reflect legitimate behaviors or to discover outliers that show previously undetected forms of fraud.

4. Customer Service, Chatbots and Virtual Assistants (VAs)

Although AI cannot replace actual human interaction in contact centres, it helps telecoms identify issues sooner, resolve them faster, and prevent cases from recurring. It offers many opportunities for telecoms focusing on contact centre optimization.

Chatbots and VAs though are not new but backed by AI, their usability has increased. They are much more intelligent now and go beyond responding to basic queries. They take on tasks related to FAQs, know your customer (KYC) updates, grievance redressal and complaint registration, etc. This effectively free up first line support and be a huge cost savings for telecoms.

A step further are chatbots with natural language processing (NLP) capabilities that helps interpret customer sentiment. By applying sentiment analytics, these bots offer an appropriate response based on the customer's tone or choice of words. With AI, network operation centers (NOCs) turning into service operation centers (SOCs), branching out with not only support and administrative functions but has analytical capabilities to proactively advise rather than reactively resolve.

5. Intelligent Customer Relationship Management (CRM) Systems

AI in CRM is bringing a high level of analytics-driven insights and predictive accuracy to marketing strategies that were previously not present.

Some of the popular ones are Salesforce's (AI tool is Einstein,) SugarCRM's Hint, and Zoho's Zia assistant. These solutions tackle:

- *Customized promotions*
- *Sentiment analysis*
- *Cross sell/upsell*
- *Sale opportunity identification*
- *Conversational AI assistants*
- *Predict customer segmentation*
- *Customer churn prevention*

Other applications include calculating customer lifetime value, strategizing new product offerings, and statistics that help formulate customer service and retention policies.

These intelligent, integrated, and data-driven capabilities help make smart recommendations about a customer or a prospect based on user data collected over time. The customer experience leads to higher lifetime customer value.

CONCLUSION: HOWEVER, TECH CAN'T REPLACE TALENT

AI is the future of automation, providing new efficiencies and streamlining at a massive scale of millions of data points, whether they be performance metrics from the networks or customers. However,

- CSPs need to avoid the twin dangers of becoming a laggard in the market as a reaction to AI hype or of being too visionary and ending up with products for which the market is not ready.
- For a CSP AI strategy, take a three-step approach: identify and assess your opportunity; build the capability, with AI expert partners where you lack in-house expertise; and follow through with a managed lifecycle.
- Data fuels AI automation. Successful use of AI is dependent on access to data to build, train, and constantly improve the algorithms that power it.
- Customer personalization at scale, made possible through AI, is a prime differentiator for CSPs in a highly competitive market.
- AI applications must be introduced carefully and responsibly. AI applications need to be robustly tested to ensure that they perform as intended and to avoid any negative outcomes. Some users can be malicious and attempt to subvert a well-intentioned AI system. All these capabilities aim to help sales teams elevate their processes, understand customers and their needs better and close more deals, faster: from analysing various data points and client interactions to enable sales teams to build efficient road maps for leads and deals, to informing strategies to drive better results in any given situation.

Though world over the CSPs are making best use of AI for CRM, it should always be kept in mind that however capable the technology is and will become, AI-driven CRMs or automation won't replace talented salespeople who make connections human to human. While customers may appreciate automation and speed for small everyday purchases, when it comes to big items and B2B transactions, buyers still need salespeople to guide them through a purchase decision. Great salespeople understand the needs of the customer and create a relationship that solves the customer's problem. The sale then becomes inevitable. By leveraging an AI-powered CRM with automation, the path to meaningful interactions between salesperson and buyer can be accelerated.

REFERENCES

Amoako, G. K., Arthur, E., Bandoh, C., & Katah, R. K. (2012, January). The impact of effective customer relationship management (CRM) on repurchase: A case study of (GOLDEN TULIP) hotel (ACCRA-GHANA). *African Journal of Marketing Management*, *4*(1), 17–29.

Anshari, Almunawar, Lim, & Al-Mudimigh. (2018). Customer relationship management and big data-enabled: Personalization & customization of services. *Applied Computing and Informatics, 15*(2), 94-101.

Antons, D., & Breidbach, C. F. (2018). Big data, big insights? Advancing service innovation and design with machine learning. *Journal of Service Research*, *21*(1), 17–39. doi:10.1177/1094670517738373

Arumawadu, H. I., Rathnayaka, R. M. K. T., & Illangarathne, S. K. (2015, August). Mining Profitability of Telecommunication Customers Using K-Means Clustering. *Journal of Data Analysis and Information Processing*, *3*(03), 63–71. doi:10.4236/jdaip.2015.33008

Balaji, M. S., & Roy, S. K. (2017). Value co-creation with the Internet of things technology in the retail industry. *Journal of Marketing Management*, *33*(1–2), 7–31. doi:10.1080/0267257X.2016.1217914

Bauer, J., & Jannach, D. (2018). Optimal pricing in e-commerce based on sparse and noisy data. *Decision Support Systems*, *106*, 53–63. doi:10.1016/j.dss.2017.12.002

Bolton, R. N., McColl-Kennedy, J. R., Cheung, L., Gallan, A., Orsingher, C., Witell, L., & Zaki, M. (2018). Customer experience challenges: Bringing together digital, physical, and social realms. *Journal of Service Management*, *29*(5), 776–808. doi:10.1108/JOSM-04-2018-0113

Cambria, E. (2016). Affective computing and sentiment analysis. *IEEE Intelligent Systems*, *31*(2), 102–107. doi:10.1109/MIS.2016.31

Carmilovic, D. (2008). Data Mining and CRM in Telecommunications. *Serbian Journal of Management*, *3*(1), 61–72.

Chatterjee, S., Ghosh, S. K., Chaudhuri, R., & Nguyen, B. (2019). Are CRM systems ready for AI integration? A conceptual framework of organizational readiness for effective AI-CRM integration. *The Bottom Line (New York, N.Y.), 32*(2), 144–157. doi:10.1108/BL-02-2019-0069

Chen, C., Ibekwe-SanJuan, F., & How, J. (2010). The Structure and Dynamics of Cocitation Clusters: A Multiple-Perspective Cocitation analysis. *Journal of the American Society for Information Science and Technology, 61*(7), 1386–1409. doi:10.1002/asi.21309

Chen, Y., Lee, J. Y., Sridhar, S., Mittal, V., McCallister, K., & Singal, A. G. (2020). Improving cancer outreach effectiveness through targeting and economic assessments: Insights from a randomized field experiment. *Journal of Marketing, 84*(3), 1–27. doi:10.1177/0022242920913025

Costa, P. B., Neto, G. M., & Bertolde, A. I. (2017). Urban mobility indexes: A brief review of the literature. *Transportation Research Procedia, 25*, 3645–3655. doi:10.1016/j.trpro.2017.05.330

Dahiya, K., & Bhatia, S. (2015). *Customer Churn Analysis in Telecom Industry*. IEEE. doi:10.1109/ICRITO.2015.7359318

Davenport, T., Guha, A., Grewal, D., & Bressgott, T. (2020). How artificial intelligence will change the future of marketing. *Journal of the Academy of Marketing Science, 48*(1), 24–42. doi:10.100711747-019-00696-0

Davenport, T., & Kalakota, R. (2019). The potential for artificial intelligence in healthcare. *Future Healthcare Journal, 6*(2), 94–98. doi:10.7861/futurehosp.6-2-94 PMID:31363513

Day, G. S. (2011). Closing the marketing capabilities gap. *Journal of Marketing, 75*(4), 183–195. doi:10.1509/jmkg.75.4.183

Dekimpe, M. (2020). Retailing and retailing research in the age of big data analytics. *International Journal of Research in Marketing, 37*(1), 3–14. doi:10.1016/j.ijresmar.2019.09.001

Giatsoglou, M., Vozalis, M. G., Diamantaras, K., Vakali, A., Sarigiannidis, G., & Chatzisavvas, K. C. (2017). Sentiment analysis leveraging emotions and word embeddings. *Expert Systems with Applications, 69*, 214–224. doi:10.1016/j.eswa.2016.10.043

Guo, J., Zhang, W., Fan, W., & Li, W. (2018). Combining geographical and social influences with deep learning for personalized point-of interest recommendation. *Journal of Management Information Systems, 35*(4), 1121–1153. doi:10.1080/07421222.2018.1523564

Han, J., Kamber, M., & Pei, J. (2014). *Data Mining Concepts and echniques* (3rd ed.). Morgan Kaufmann.

Haridasan, V., & Venkatesh, S. (2011). CRM Implementation in Indian Telecom Industry- Evaluating the Effectiveness of Mobile Service Providers Using Data Envelopment Analysis. *IJBRM, 2*(3), 110–127.

Hilas, C. S., Mastorocostas, P. A., & Rekanos, I. T. (2015). Clustering of Telecommunications User Profiles for Fraud Detection and Security Enhancement in Large Corporate Networks: A case Study. *Applied Mathematics & Information Sciences, 9*(4), 1709–1718.

Huang, M. H., & Rust, R. T. (2017). Technology-driven service strategy. *Journal of the Academy of Marketing Science, 45*(6), 906–924. doi:10.100711747-017-0545-6

Huang, M. H., & Rust, R. T. (2018). Artificial intelligence in service. *Journal of Service Research, 21*(2), 155–172. doi:10.1177/1094670517752459

Kamalraj & Malathi. (2013). Apply Data Mining Techniques in Telecom Churn Prediction. *International Journal of Advanced Research in Computer Science and Software Engineering, 3*(10), 363-370.

Kasthuri, Shanthi, & Manigandan. (2016). Customizing Clustering algorithm for Data mining in CRM. *International Journal of Computer Science and Information Technology & Security, 6*(2).

Maheshwari, R. U., & Mahesan, S. S. (2014, February). Tamilarasan, and A. K.Subramani, "Role of Data Mining in CRM. *International Journal of Engine Research, 3*(2), 75–78. doi:10.17950/ijer/v3s2/208

Milovic, B. (2012). Application of Customer Relationship Management Strategy (CRM) in Different Business Areas. Economics and Organization, 9(3), 341-354.

Mujawar, S., & Joshi, A. (2015, February). Data Analytics Types, Tools and their Comparison. *IJARCCE, 4*(2), 488–491.

Nadaf & Kadam. (2013). Data Mining in Telecommunication. *International Journal on Advanced Computer Theory and Engineering, 2*(3).

Nagarajan, Minu, Vedanarayanan, Sundersingh Jebaseelan, & Vasanth. (2015). CIMTELMining Algorithm for Big Data in Telecommunication. *International Journal of Engineering and Technology*, 7(5), 1709-1715.

Rababah, K., Mohd, H., & Ibrahim, H. (2011, April). Customer Relationship Management (CRM) Processes from Theory to Practice: The Pre-implementation Plan of CRM System. *International Journal of e-Education, e-Business, e- Management Learning*, *1*(1).

Rouhani, S., Ashrafi, A., Zare Ravasan, A., & Afshari, S. (2016). The impact model of business intelligence on decision support and organizational benefits. *Journal of Enterprise Information Management*, *29*(1), 19–50. doi:10.1108/JEIM-12-2014-0126

Routray, Mishra, & Sahoo. (2015). Adaptation of Fast Modified Frequent Pattern Growth approach for frequent item sets mining in Telecommunication Industry. *American Journal of Engineering Research, 4*(12), 126-133.

Sha Nazim, S., & Rajeswari, M. (2019). Creating a Brand Value and Consumer Satisfaction in E-Commerce Business Using Artificial Intelligence with the Help of Vosag Technology. *International Journal of Innovative Technology and Exploring Engineering*, *8*(8), 1510–1515.

Simester, D., Timoshenko, A., & Zoumpoulis, S. I. (2020). Targeting prospective customers: Robustness of machine-learning methods to typical data challenges. *Management Science*, *66*(6), 2495–2522. doi:10.1287/mnsc.2019.3308

Spring, M., Hughes, A., Mason, K., & McCaffrey, P. (2017). Creating a competitive edge: A new relationship between operations management and industrial policy. *Journal of Operations Management*, *49*(1), 6–19. doi:10.1016/j.jom.2016.12.003

Weiss. (2005). Data Mining in Telecommunications. Springer.

Wirth. (2018). Hello marketing, what can artificial intelligence help you with. *International Journal of Market Research, 60*(5), 435-438.

Wirtz, J., Patterson, P. G., Kunz, W. H., Gruber, T., Lu, V. N., Paluch, S., & Martins, A. (2018). Brave new world: Service robots in the frontline. *Journal of Service Management*, *29*(5), 907–931. doi:10.1108/JOSM-04-2018-0119

Wunderlich, N. V., Heinonen, K., Ostrom, A. L., Patricio, L., Sousa, R., Voss, C., & Lemmink, J. (2015). "Futurizing" smart service: Implications for service researchers and managers. *Journal of Services Marketing*, *29*(6/7), 442–447. doi:10.1108/JSM-01-2015-0040

Yong-Hak, J. (2013). *2013. Web of science*. Thomson Reuters.

Zhang, H., Cao, X., Ho, J. K., & Chow, T. W. (2016). Object-level video advertising: An optimization framework. *IEEE Transactions on Industrial Informatics*, *13*(2), 520–531. doi:10.1109/TII.2016.2605629

Zhang, T., Huang, X., Tang, J., & Luo, X. (2011). *Case Study on Cluster Analysis of The Telecom Customers Based on Consumers' Behavior*. IEEE. doi:10.1109/ICIEEM.2011.6035407

Chapter 7
Investigating the Critical Success Factors of Artificial Intelligence-Driven CRM in J. K. Tyres:
A B2B Context

Surabhi Singh
https://orcid.org/0000-0002-8565-7348
IMS Ghaziabad, India

José Duarte Santos
https://orcid.org/0000-0001-5815-4983
Polytechnic Institute of Gaya, Portugal

ABSTRACT

AI-powered technologies allow online B2B companies to serve their customers with accurate and relevant information, 24/7. For example, they experience an increase in requests for information from customers on such aspects as product availability, features, or other services. The chapter aims to explore artificial intelligence in B2B business. The study employed qualitative research, and the data was collected through a focus group for data collection. An AI-powered chatbot enhanced with natural language processing and understanding conversationally-worded requests could instantaneously provide this information without a human representative. This is vital as the added uncertainty around the pandemic means business customers seek real answers and ways to adapt and fast. The findings suggest the critical success factors of AI-driven CRM in B2B markets. The limitations of the study include the data collection being restricted to one B2B company. The implications are that further study can be extended for exploring AI-based CRM in B2B markets.

DOI: 10.4018/978-1-7998-7959-6.ch007

INTRODUCTION

Artificial intelligence (AI) is changing the customer experience (Deb et al., 2018; Verma et al., 2021), emerging as disruptive technology with potential in various areas of services, industry, but also in the primary sector (Verma et al., 2021).

AI offers the potential to create intelligent assistants that perform tasks on our behalf. As companies learn to use smart machines for improving revenue, reduce costs, and increase customer contentment, AI will become the valuable emerging resource. The adoption ofAIin B2Bmarketinghelps businesses, but it also touches customers.

AI and machine learning (ML) are tools that manufacturers and distributors can give with their e-commerce experiences. The effortsimprove their work with AI-powered tools automation and run faster than their human counterparts. These tools visualize large groupings of data sets, run tests, understand the context, change based on results, understand human languages, examine digital images, make predictions, and continually updated based on more use of the tool. AI helps in having a better understanding of the customer in driving the personalized customer experiences. The increased data has the better the experience for the customer and the possible return on investment. The B2B eCommerceplatformswith AI are still in the early days, but future-readiness reports that it should be a top tool on your roadmap to prepare to implement.

The use of AI by e-commerce allows a better consumer experience with AI assistants and chatbots, but the company will also be able to know better customers, providing specific product recommendations who generate more leads (Girdher, 2019), that is, feed the entire CRM.Customer service chatbots use natural language processing and customer service data. Thus, they answer common questions, improving the quality of these answers over time.Most examples of AI rely on deep learning and natural language processing.

This is where marketers can reap insights from theirintelligentsoftware and transform it into smart purchase decisions for customers.AI offers the ability to formbuyer-enabled B2B customer journeys that are just as personalized as the superior consumer experiences provided by B2C leaders like Netflix and Amazon. AI addresses to provide highly customized experiences to hundreds of thousands or millions of prospects and customers. The elements are: scaling operations, outsourcing the right decisions, analyzing large volumes of data.

THEORETICAL BACKGROUND

Relationship marketing includes affinity marketing, loyalty marketing, cross-selling, up-selling, co-branding, co-marketing, and customer-supplier partnering as per the pioneer study (Sheth&Parvatiyar,2000).90% of the B2B professional services sector marketersrefer that AI is advantageousover competitors (Ransbotham et al., 2019). Gartner (2018) predicted that one-third of all B2B marketers would AI-powered technologies, such as virtual customer assistants and Chatbots, and drive marketing automation by 2020. Siemens AG, an industrial manufacturing company in Europe, uses machine learning to analyze supplierinvitations to support decision-making. 20-30% acceleration of the tendering process resulted from the efforts (Ransbotham et al., 2019).

Marketing has become increasingly interested in AI's capabilities in imitating humans (Vlačić et al., 2021).Academics and practitioners recognize various benefits of using AI techniques in B2B settings. These entail increasing sales(Syam& Sharma, 2018), improve the buyer and supplier relationship (Gordini &Veglio, 2017), target B2B marketing campaigns (Liu, 2019), and deliver support in managers'decisions (Jabbar et al., 2019). The transformative benefits of AI adoption arelimited to a limited number group of B2B marketers. The majority of the intensive literature focuses on the technological understanding of AI (Dwivedi et al., 2021), the knowledge of the implications of AI for B2B is far from conclusive.

The research topics are driven by the challenges of AI implementation. Artificial intelligence's economic value depends on having access to high-quality and quantity data and data management properly. However, data for B2B marketing are scarce, and value extraction is difficult (Lilien, 2016). With the lack of precious data and the fact that collected datawith less essential and poorly managed, B2B marketers miss out on actionable insight, leading to nonreal marketing and sales strategies. The lack of data management is a priority for AI use in B2B marketing.

Second, AI use for robust B2B sales is still in the initial stage and has not significantly impacted. The studies have sought to explore the potential impact of AI on B2B sales management (Kietzmann, &Kietzmann, 2019);no research examines how artificial intelligence processes communication and involvement or how AI-fostered new product development can be attained with regulations of AI linkedsystems and capabilities. These issues have amore in-depth investigation, and many firms have been found to invest in AI for maintaining competitiveness (Ransbotham et al., 2019) continuously.

Third, customer data processing customer using biased AI algorithms leads to severe issues related to privacy concerns, absence of transparency and useless marketing communication (Davenport et al., 2019). The persistent and intense advertising circulated by automatic email and social media marketing with AI often annoy B2B customers. Such inapt marketing initiatives developed by AI result in brand reputation harm. Therefore, it is compulsory that B2B marketers rethink how to minimize ethical concerns when designing AI solutions for B2B marketing.

Artificial intelligence management is not only a technical issue. It requires a consistent balance between human beings' abilities, knowledge, and AI technologies to work together (Duan et al., 2019).B2B firms aim to achieve AI,explain the abilityto makehealthy marketing decisions by maintaining the collaboration between humans and AI (Wang, Xiong, &Olya, 2020). The firms have a clear goal;they may consider it tricky to combinethe marketing professionals' work and AI algorithms/robots.

AI is exploited to improve the economic impact of B2B marketing and explore ways to tackle the technologicaland governance challenges that AI might face in the B2B marketing context. The four key ways AI platforms and technologies are changing the game for B2B marketers right now.Artificial intelligenceis useful to businesses in the B2C space. The B2C companies have more customers; they have more data and make AI impactful. However, the truth is somewhat different. AI is as significant to a B2B companyasit is for a B2C company.It'sessential for every B2B company for examining the ways AI help them produce better products, provide better services, and improve business processes. There are some ways of B2B companies that use artificial intelligence today. The author focused on machine learning and artificial intelligence (AI) and their impact on personal selling and sales management.

Communication is the ability for intelligent systems to interact with human users. Natural Language Processing (NLP) is vital communication technology. For example, service agents in the hospitality sector can support multi-lingual communication with guests at a reduced cost compared to employing multi-lingual staff 24/7 (Ivanov & Webster, 2017). Web 2.0 functionality as social interaction and social media receive more attention from marketing researchers as tools and allow customers to collaborate, communicate, share and connect (Kaplan &Haenlein, 2010).

AI enables companies to applymarketing strategy and CRM vision supported by knowledge-based (Vlaˇci´c et al., 2021)which optimize big data analytics and that also allows machine learning (Verma et al., 2021).AI and machine learning are readily available, and these technologies can be used to automate many of the repetitive tasks and processes humans perform. The CRM use machine learning to predict what the sales team should do from these records. Consequently, it proactively remembers, without any manual data entry.It's possible to get customer profiles more accurately by inferring changes in customer journeys over time and adjusting service strategies using AI and machine learning. So, it'sfeasible learning help predict which customer profiles prefer to talk to a human agent rather than using self-service, for example, and also to see how customer expectations meet services in terms of speed and flexibility, reliability and transparency, interaction and service.

AI can capture and transcribe customer interactions through emails, chats, phone conversations, chatbots and provide better customer knowledge. The service and support can be more effective with incorporating AI into CRM Systems (Deb et al., 2018).

CRM System with AI, can help fill gaps or overcome the existence of outdated elements in customer information (Vladimirovich, 2020), can make suggestions about the customers to the sales force, and suggestions to the customer, for example about products or services (Girdher, 2019). Purchase history, product viewing time, social media behavior, purchases made by customers with identical profiles (Deb et al., 2020), can also generate more opportunities for up-selling, cross-selling and deep-selling (Ali & Lee, 2018).When is the right time to do the upsell? What other products can the customer benefit from? So, it's possible identify opportunities to expand relationships with existing customers.

With AI software its possible analyze the most important customers based on certain data points and then compare them with new potential customers and predict their value. Predicting customer behavior, customized actions can be developed avoiding invasive tools, relying on permission marketing, offering value propositions to the customer.This also allows sales managers to refocus resources more appropriately, based on customer value.

Sales prediction is supported not only in interactions recorded in CRM, but also with algorithms that incorporate AI technology that select attributes that can influence the predicted values obtained (Ali & Lee, 2018). With AI it is possible to identify characteristics in leads that lead to a higher conversion. Engagement in emails, websites, social channels, along with profile data, are factors that can help predict the likelihood of conversion.It'sfeasible to get more reliable predictions by applying machine learning models that consider all commitments related to a transaction and that can influence its outcome.Knowing what generates the most Marketing Qualified Leads and Sales Qualified Leads is one of the many benefits machine learning brings.The lead score also contains these elements (Ali & Lee, 2018).The predictive score of each sales lead, including the omnichannel link, becomes a better indicator of potential new sales, helping sales teams prioritize time, efforts, and sales strategies.

AI detects irregularities or duplicates that could compromise CRM data and is possible more easily eliminate redundant data.CRM systems using AI have increased their capacity from 50% to 90% and in addition to volume, they also increase data quality, with increasing data accuracy and reliability by 80% (Vladimirovich, 2020).

CRM systems with AI can increase marketing and sales team productivity by increasing automation, which enables faster response. More efficient self-service and more effective in human care. Also, the accuracy of the company based on a more exhaustive analysis of information is further strengthened. All these elements contribute to customer satisfaction, thus increasing the likelihood of keeping them loyal.

CONCEPTUAL FRAMEWORK

Intelligent design softwaredrives how to design and build things. With machine learning, the B2B e-commerce companies providetheir customers in manufacturing, architecture, engineering, and construction automated generative design technology. Artificial intelligence is also behind a CRM framework that includes machine learning features, natural language processing, and predictive analytics. This can further increase the sales and marketing services of businesses. The study's conceptual framework is brought by the idea that it is a critical success factor that led to the adoption and execution of technology in any market setting. The paper has formulated the framework for the success of AI-driven CRM in B2B markets (Figure 1).

Figure 1. Framework for the success of AI-driven CRM in B2B markets.
Source: authors

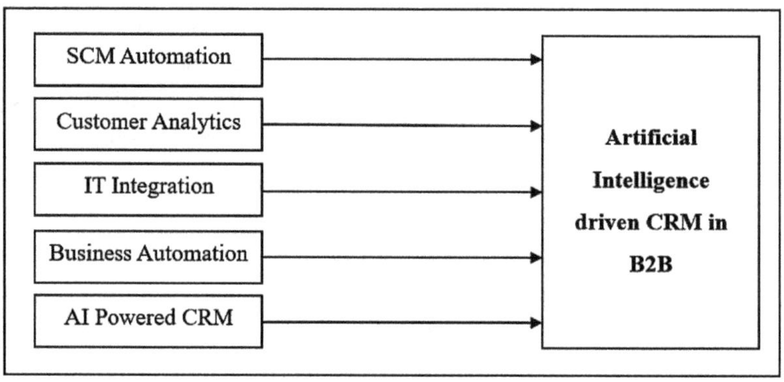

The techniques of SCM and prediction of maintenance were improved or resulted fromIndustry 4.0manufacturing innovations. With the adoption of machine learning, McKinsey forecasted a drop in forecasting errors by 50 percent, samecost and time savings in every stage of the SCM Automation- SCM automation united many siloed processes and departments. The integration of AI into many business sectors has proved to reduce costs, increase revenue, and enhance asset utilization (Kar et al., 2019).

Customer analyticsis increasingly employed for Customer Relationship Management (CRM). It lacks the value of marketing knowledge available from the

Marketing Research (MR) function due to inadequate inter-functional knowledge integration (Lichtenstein et al., 2008).Analytical CRM analyzes data that will then be monetized by operational software (Zaby& Wilde, 2018).

IT integrationuses computing devices such as desktop computers, laptops, tablets, software, or the Internet for educational purposes (Hew & Brush, 2007). The integration of the various devices through the different CRM functions – marketing, sales, service – must be ensured to feed the information repository (Kampani&Jhamb, 2020).

Business automation it is the software-based solution to automate rules-based business processes that involve routine tasks, structured data, and deterministic outcomes (Aquirre et al., 2017).CRM processes to be more productive must be automated, including claims management,which is very important to relationship construct (Zaby& Wilde, 2018).

AI-powered CRM: with the advancement in Artificial Intelligence (AI) technologies, these interactions are becoming more sophisticated in CRM (Van Doorn et al., 2017).

With the maximum amount of transactions, the size of customer data also increases. This increase help businesses understand their customers better, as they can process more information about them. It also means that they require to work much to extract relevant information because most of the data remain unstructured. It is challenging to understand unstructured data that covers around90%of the total data, and AI tools can convert raw data to polished data.

OBJECTIVES

The gaps found in the literature led to the objectives of the study. The paper aims to examine the impact AI is making on J K Tyres B2B businesses and the customer experience. Further, the research would state how to tackle the technological and governance challenges faced in the B2B context.

METHODOLOGY

The paper carried out Qualitative research, and the focus group is used for data collection. The open-ended questions were asked from the five employees of J K Tyresand their five industrial customers through an online focus group.The goal in collecting data from practice was to research the alignment between theory and practice. The literaturewas examined B2B and AI support. The online focus group enabled the data collection on practice from two groups: 1) employees of J K Tyres, and 2) industrial customers. The online focus group went one hour long and was connected through video conferencing.

DATA ANALYSIS

AI and Automation

The AI has enabled automation, and so has the workforce is reduced. The company use TensorFlow as an AI tool and on the Azure platform. The tool helps in getting the cognitive aspect of our customers and our processes. AI impacts the customer satisfaction and improves the interactivity. More customers contact us and praise our products. AI helps in connecting with customers in less time. Suppose a defect comes in the tyre, the message with the picture goes to the AI model. By this, 70-80% fault gets detected, and deep learning happens.AI works by means of its more data in a fast manner. It has repeated processing and intelligent algorithms. It learns automatically from patterns or features in the data.The tyres sales are consistently owing to AI support. The demand is more for J K Tyres as compared to other competitors like CEAT and MRF.

AI in CRM in J K Tyres

With 12manufacturingplants (9 in India and 3 in Mexico) producing 30 million types per annum,JK Tyresranks among India's top tyre manufacturers. The tire industry's first CRM program, JK Baadshah, is a Customer Relationship Program and is point-based for transporters buying JK Truck/Bus Radial & Bias Tyres. The initiative has entered its 9th year and is committed to deliver enthusiasm and rewards at each stage. The members acquire points on the purchase of both Truck/Bus Radial and Bias Tyres. It is our effort to build strong bonds with our end customers and their families through this initiative.Another programme is J K Advantage 2.0. for dealers.

Findings

The study implies the framework for AI-based CRM in B2B Markets (Figure 2).

The paper implies that customer data and market data, acceptance of cloud, workforce support, and customer-centric processes are significant for AI-based CRM in B2B markets. The employees get immense help from AI for acquiring customers and retaining customers in the organization.Gartner predicts CRM as the single largest revenue spending area on enterprise software by 2021. From SMEs to big banks and consultancies, most companies employ a CRM system to track their sales.The

Figure 2. Framework for AI-based CRM in B2B markets
Source: authors

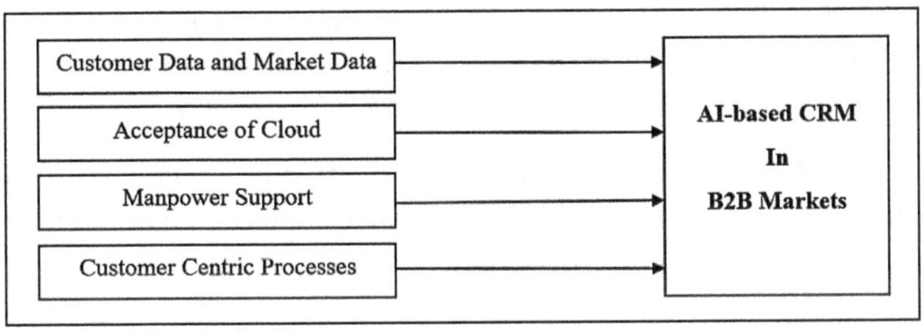

growing AI enables this technology to be combined into the CRM tools, and these tools are getting more preferred by businesses. The impact of AI in CRM tools is observed better as processes become more complex and customer data increases.

CRMsystems withartificial intelligencecan enableB2Bbusinesses to analyze data across a wide range of sources, namely from emails, submission forms, transcribed phone calls, and even more, to gain tremendous insight into each lead's corresponding value likeliness of securing a sale.The companies with more than 11 employees use a Customer Relationship Management (CRM) system in a maximum manner. The tools have become an essential part of businesses' sales processes, and the advances in AI technology impact this solution.

As CRM tools are getting more intelligent, they provide more accurate sales insights and help companies make better sales processes. With therising volume of unstructured data and the increasing complexity of customer relations processes, AI technology is becoming a necessity in CRM systems. As per the study, only 12% of CRM users infact use an AI-powered CRM tool in their processes. Many users think that AI-powered tools are expensive and are not much useful. Thus, it may take time to observe AI's actual impact on sales processes.

Implications

The study implies that academia can extend their studies for other B2B companies to execute AI-based CRM in their systems. The industry may use the study's insightsto smooth direct their use of AI-based CRM systems and processes for customers. The AI-based CRM is the future of today's dynamic organizations.

REFERENCES

Aguirre, S., & Rodriguez, A. (2017, September). Automation of a business process using robotic process automation (RPA): A case study. In *Workshop on engineering applications* (pp. 65-71). Springer. 10.1007/978-3-319-66963-2_7

Ali, M., & Lee, Y. (2018, April). Crm sales prediction using continuous time-evolving classification. *Proceedings of the AAAI Conference on Artificial Intelligence, 32*(1), 7727–7734.

Dash, R., McMurtrey, M., Rebman, C., & Kar, U. K. (2019). Application of artificial intelligence in automation of supply chain management. *Journal of Strategic Innovation and Sustainability, 14*(3), 43–53. doi:10.33423/jsis.v14i3.2105

Davenport, T., Guha, A., Grewal, D., & Bressgott, T. (2019). How artificial intelligence will change the future of marketing. *Journal of the Academy of Marketing Science*. Advance online publication. doi:10.100711747-019-00696-0

Deb, S. K., Jain, R., & Deb, V. (2018, January). Artificial Intelligence—Creating Automated Insights for Customer Relationship Management. In *2018 8th International Conference on Cloud Computing, Data Science & Engineering (Confluence)* (pp. 758-764). IEEE.

Duan, Y., Edwards, J. S., & Dwivedi, Y. K. (2019). Artificial intelligence for decision making in the era of Big Data–evolution, challenges, and research agenda. *International Journal of Information Management, 48*, 63–71. doi:10.1016/j.ijinfomgt.2019.01.021

Dwivedi, Y. K., Hughes, L., Ismagilova, E., Aarts, G., Coombs, C., Crick, T., ... Galanos, V. (2021). Artificial Intelligence (AI): Multidisciplinary perspectives on emerging challenges, opportunities, and agenda for research, practice and policy. *International Journal of Information Management, 57*, 101994. Advance online publication. doi:10.1016/j.ijinfomgt.2019.08.002

Gartner. (2018). *Gartner Says 25 Percent of Customer Service Operations Will Use Virtual Customer Assistants by 2020*. https://www.gartner.com/en/newsroom/press-releases/2018-02-19-gartner-says-25-percent-of-customer-service-operations-will-use-virtual-customer-assistants-by-2020

Girdher, S. (2019). Role of Artificial Intelligence in Transforming E-commerce Sector. *Research Review International Journal of Multidisciplinary, 4*(6), 282–284.

Gordini, N., & Veglio, V. (2017). Customers churn prediction and marketing retention strategies. An application of support vector machines based on the AUC parameter-selection technique in B2B e-commerce industry. *Industrial Marketing Management, 62*, 100–107. doi:10.1016/j.indmarman.2016.08.003

Hew, K. F., & Brush, T. (2007). Integrating technology into K-12 teaching: Current knowledge gaps and recommendations for future research. *Educational Technology Research and Development, 55*(3), 223–252. doi:10.100711423-006-9022-5

Ivanov, S., & Webster, C. (2017). Adoption of robots, artificial intelligence and service automation by travel, tourism and hospitality companies – a cost-benefit analysis. *Proceedings of the International Scientific Conference "Contemporary tourism – traditions and innovations"*.

Jabbar, A., Akhtar, P., & Dani, S. (2019). Real-time big data processing for instantaneous marketing decisions: A problematization approach. *Industrial Marketing Management, 90*, 558-569. doi:10.1016/j.indmarman.2019.09.001

Kampani, N., & Jhamb, D. (2020). Analyzing the role of e-crm in managing customer relations: A critical review of the literature. *Journal of Critical Review, 7*(4), 221–226.

Kaplan, A. M., & Haenlein, M. (2010). Users of the world, unite! the challenges and opportunities of social media. *Business Horizons, 53*(1), 59–68. doi:10.1016/j.bushor.2009.09.003

Lichtenstein, S., Bednall, D. H., & Adam, S. (2008). Marketing research and customer analytics: Interfunctional knowledge integration. *International Journal of Technology Marketing, 3*(1), 81–96. doi:10.1504/IJTMKT.2008.017341

Lilien, G. L. (2016). The B2B knowledge gap. *International Journal of Research in Marketing, 33*(3), 543–556. doi:10.1016/j.ijresmar.2016.01.003

Liu, X. (2019). Analyzing the impact of user-generated content on B2B firms' stock performance: Big data analysis with machine learning methods. *Industrial Marketing Management, 86*, 30-39. doi:10.1016/j.indmarman.2019.02.021

Parvatiyar, A., & Sheth, J. N. (2000). The Domain and Conceptual Foundations of Relationship Marketing. In J. N. Sheth & A. Parvatiyar (Eds.), *Handbook of Relationship Marketing* (pp. 3–38). Sage Publications. doi:10.4135/9781452231310.n1

Paschen, J., Kietzmann, J., & Kietzmann, T. C. (2019). Artificial intelligence (AI) and its implications for market knowledge in B2B marketing. *Journal of Business and Industrial Marketing, 34*(7), 1410–1419. doi:10.1108/JBIM-10-2018-0295

Ransbotham, S., Khodabandeh, S., Fehling, R., LaFountain, B., & Kiron, D. (2019). Winning With AI. *Sloan Management Review, 10*. https://sloanreview.mit.edu/projects/winning-with-ai

Syam, N., & Sharma, A. (2018). Waiting for a sales renaissance in the fourth industrial revolution: Machine learning and artificial intelligence in sales research and practice. *Industrial Marketing Management, 69*, 135–146. doi:10.1016/j.indmarman.2017.12.019

Van Doorn, J., Mende, M., Noble, S. M., Hulland, J., Ostrom, A. L., Grewal, D., & Petersen, J. A. (2017). Domo arigato Mr. Roboto: Emergence of automated social presence in organizational frontlines and customers' service experiences. *Journal of Service Research, 20*(1), 43–58. doi:10.1177/1094670516679272

Verma, S., Sharma, R., Deb, S., & Maitra, D. (2021). Artificial intelligence in marketing: Systematic review and future research direction. *International Journal of Information Management Data Insights, 100002.*

Vlačić, B., Corbo, L., Silva, S. C., & Dabić, M. (2021). The evolving role of artificial intelligence in marketing: A review and research agenda. *Journal of Business Research, 128*, 187–203. doi:10.1016/j.jbusres.2021.01.055

Vladimirovich, K. M. (2020). Future Marketing in B2B Segment: Integrating Artificial Intelligence into Sales Management. *International Journal of Innovative Technologies in Economy, 4*(31).

Wang, Y., Xiong, M., & Olya, H. G. (2020). Toward an Understanding of Responsible Artificial Intelligence Practices. *Proceedings of the 53rd Hawaii International Conference on System Sciences*. 10.24251/HICSS.2020.610

Zaby, C., & Wilde, K. D. (2018). Intelligent business processes in CRM. *Business & Information Systems Engineering, 60*(4), 289–304. doi:10.100712599-017-0480-6

Chapter 8
AI and Customer Experience in the Fashion Industry

Jasmandeep Kaur
https://orcid.org/0000-0002-7454-7338
Ideal Institute of Management and Technology, Delhi, India

Surabhi Singh
https://orcid.org/0000-0002-8565-7348
IMS Ghaziabad, India

Ramanjeet Singh
Amity University, Noida, India

ABSTRACT

This chapter portrays artificial intelligence with the improvement of customer experience on online and offline fashion purchases. The presence of AI in the retail business is turning into a vital part of the customer experience. AI attempts to disclose approaches to interpret with the end goal for organizations to make a genuine use out of them, either online or offline. Thus, with this research, the authors additionally give knowledge on how this experience of AI could be improved in later fashion purchases and how it will undoubtedly be part of the everyday customer experience.

INTRODUCTION

The Fourth industrial revolution introduced by the digital transformation is allowing the fashion industry, like many other sectors, to increase its capacity to produce and use data that was not previously technically or financially feasible. The most important impact on production and distribution is yet to come. In a recent interview (March

DOI: 10.4018/978-1-7998-7959-6.ch008

6, 2019) Federico Marchetti, CIO and founder of YOOX talks about how Artificial Intelligence (AI) is not only helping to revolutionize the production - the brand “8” is produced by YOOX through AI-but also in selling and marketing, since big data and AI will allow each customer to have his/her own homepage.

Artificial Intelligence has been around since 1956 and has made massive rise: beating the best human at chess, beating the best human at complex strategy game. Recently brands have started to adopt this technology for the core service. There is no doubt that the relationship between machine and human has changed. AI covers computing technology that can do things typically requiring human intelligence, from understanding language and recognizing visuals to making plans and solving problems. Artificial Intelligence has been gaining lots of attention in the recent months, and is a growing technology used in different fields. Through the collection of organized data, AI and its algorithm has the ability to take out useful, meaningful information. Providing a full customer experience is the goal of every brand, and AI is more and more incorporated in it. It is believed that “By 2020, 85% of the customer interactions will be managed without human” – Gartner and we can already notice that AI has been more than present in our past shopping experiences, either online or offline. The main objectives in its use for customer experience are to improve it, by time and efficiency, it allows us to answer easy questions that doesn’t need to be asked anymore, just by the use of specific information.

According to the Artificial Intelligence High Level Group of the European Commission (2019): “Artificial intelligence (AI) refers to systems that display intelligent behaviour by analysing their environment and taking actions with some degree of autonomy to achieve specific goals. AI-based systems can be purely software-based, acting in the virtual world (e.g. voice assistants, image analysis software, search engines, speech and face recognition systems) or AI can be embedded in hardware devices (e.g. Advanced robots, autonomous cars, drones or Internet of Things applications) “.

Due to the online antagonism, many e-stores give to customer the opportunity to personalize the pages so that they can use it more easily. This is very expensive process as it needs several employees to work on this kind of system implementation. This is the reason that many researchers are working in finding and evaluating customer aids in their shopping. Different studies allow an imitation of the virtual shopping of users. Many experiments used a behavioural approach, and the results has shown that a personalized page is not always the best customer aid function for all the users in comparison with simpler ones(Saponaro, M., Le Gal, D., Gao, M., Guisiano, M., & Maniere, 2018).

The time has come to restyle the fashion industry business which has been the embodiment of styling for quite a long time. It is the circumstance of the pandemic which causes such changes inescapable. The progressing pandemic (COVID) has constrained the style business to vamp up the advances which can make individuals more secure just as give the client's an enhancing experience. Fashion Industry is viewed as perhaps the most serious business sectors where something which is moving today may end up in the corner the following day. In the background of the pandemic, the AI can be utilized as of the most brilliant instrument to help the interests of the clients. At the present time, it has been utilized to expand the efficiency of the assembling of the garments and the smooth working of ventures. We have just seen the "recommendations dependent on what you have seen" on different OTT stages like Netflix, Amazon, and a plenty of others. The current climate esteems individual experience as the most noteworthy. The steadily expanding request of shoppers for profoundly customized design style, the requirement for improved stock administration, the expanding impact of advanced media on style decision, and the need to recognize significant purchasing patterns have been not many key drivers of AI in style.

The AI in the Fashion Industry is anticipated to grow at a CAGR of ~39.17% during the forecast period 2020–2026(Research, 2020).This report endows comprehensive research about the current and the competitive trends following the usage of AI in the fashion industry. There has been aenormous demand for AI in the fashion industry and this is major because of the escalating influence of social media on the fashionistas industry. The increasing popularity of tailor made experience is the driving force behind the demand for AI.

AI proposes tremendous potentials for better services to customers and energize profits to the fashion, but getting into the area like customer service is not that important, which could very well be the thing that saves fashion brands and retailers from the ambush of Amazon etc. But success for offline stores now depends on how sales events are arranged and managed — and that means accurately predicting discounts to drive in-store shoppers. This is just one area where AI can shine: not only enhancing discounts, concessions etc, but also shaping territorial allocation of stock, taking in consideration the supply chain and its distribution. Behind many fashion brands is a highly complex supply chain. The infamously fast-to-fabricate H&M hit a drop in sales last quarter, and told shareholders that it was sitting on $4.3 billion in unsold merchandise. This is a problem that AI can solve(Boss Chris, 2018). The choice of channel is especially influenced by the kind of product (Puccinelli, et.al, 2019) and moreover, within the case of fashion, the consumer's mood may be a key determinative element (Nicholson, et.al, 2002). Hence, customers square measure additional seemingly to pick out a physical store once they buy epicurean fashion product as a result of sturdy physical environments elevate the mood through opportunities for social interaction, product analysis, and sensory stimulation . However, recent information show that customers consider on-line fashion as a style of diversion, devoting their leisure to search for garments on-line.

CUSTOMER EXPERIENCE IN SHOPPING THROUGH AI

The increasing concentrate on client expertise arises as a result of customers currently move with corporations through myriad touch points in multiple channels and media, leading to more advanced client journeys Understanding client expertise, experiences and therefore the client journey over time is essential for companies. Customers currently move with companies through myriad bit points in multiple channels and media, and client experiences a lot of social in nature. These changes need companies to integrate multiple business functions, and even external partners, in making and delivering positive client experiences. Online fashion searching as associate amusing and gratifying activity, it would be valuable to research however the amount of expertise in shopping for wear online will influence consumers' perceptions and motivations to shop for in numerous channels. In marketing practice, we observe a strong use of such customer feedback metrics as an easy measurement of the customer experience.

In Schmitt's framework, customer experience management consists of five steps: (1) analyzing the experiential world of the customers, (2) building the experiential platform, (3) designing the brand experience, (4) structuring the customer experience, and (5) engaging in continuous innovation. In this discussion, customer touch points do not have a prominent position. Herhausen et al. (2015) report that online–offline channel integration reduces perceived risk of the online store and increases perceived quality of the online channel, resulting in positive choice effects for the online channel and reduced cannibalization in the offline channel.

- **Chatbots or AI Smart Assistants**: The increasing scale and granularity of personalization in online fashion would be impossible to manage without AI applications. The most popular services for personalized online shopping use chatbots or AI smart assistants. These are virtual machines that interact with customers via chat, responding to customer service inquiries, helping users navigate ranges online and in-store, recommending clothing and accessories that best suit a specific customer as if they were human shopping assistants working 24 hours a day.

Chatbots can be divided in two categories: scripted and artificially intelligent. Scripted chatbots are able to follow only a predetermined set of rules. It means that they are only able to answer the questions they are programmed for. Artificially intelligent chatbots are instead able to interpret human language and are capable of coming up with answers to question that have not been predefined.Furthermore, there are specialized chatbots specifically for retail applications (Luce 2019 p.23).

Figure 1.
Source: https://botpublication.com/fashion-code-5-chatbots-to-try-to-look-effortless-and-chic-this-holiday-season-202912af1eaa

Figure 2. FifyWorld's first fashion shopping botfriend
Source: https://botpublication.com/fashion-code-5-chatbots-to-try-to-look-effortless-and-chic-this-holiday-season-202912af1eaa

- **Image Search:** Personalized shopping is also achieved using AI applications based on computer vision and augmented and virtual reality. Indeed, fashion is probably one of the industries that relies the most on images. Image search usually refers to the process of finding images using a text input. Search engines as Google introduced this possibility since 2001.

- **Personal AI Stylist:** Having a Personal stylist would represent the top of personalization, but for an average citizen it would be unaffordable. AI is making this possible by creating personal virtual AI stylist. This product is the culmination of the technologies presented so far: natural language processing, natural language understanding, computer visions, neural networks and various types of machine learning.

Applications of AI to Fashion

Fashion is one of the most valuable sectors in the world. Its estimated worth is about $3 trillion, representing 2% of Global Domestic Product (Sennaar 2019). However, this industry has remained quite traditional for decades. As the digital transformation progresses, it is also imposing profound transformations on the fashion industry. In particular, the abundance of data made available by the use of digital technologies has enabled the diffusion of many applications of AI in this industry. The most widespread applications are in the domain of customer services, bringing the ability to capture the trend of customer personalization by enhancing customer experience online and in stores. Schneider (2017) estimates that AI will manage up to 85% of all B2C interactions by 2020.

Research Questions

- How does a further conceptualized Customer Experience construct relate to other major constructs in customer management and shopping?
- How should organizations be structured in order to successfully manage the customer experience?
- How AI is affecting the purchase behaviour of customer (Online or Offline)

AI IN ONLINE FASHION INDUSTRY

AI has been mostly used on online platforms, such as online shopping malls. AI is changing jobs (not replacing them) and augmenting human tasks in consumer goods, manufacturing, customer service and many more verticals. In retail and fashion, the biggest opportunities are in trend forecasting and better supply chain management (Boss Chris, 2018).Chatbots are very well implemented, they can answer questions, and guide the customer through his online shopping experience, by helping him and even recommending items that could be liked or matching the already purchased ones. This can be done thanks to the data collected during the time the customer was browsing the website, his past shopping experiences and matching other users' data. By doing so, the AI can provide a personalized experience to each customer, which is similar to offline shopping experience with an assistant but provided at distance. Furthermore, Artificial Intelligence is closely linked with shopping applications using Augmented Reality as well as computer vision-driven image recognition and predictive inventory. Augmented Reality, or AR, can be defined by a virtual interface adding to the real-world complementary elements, such as texts, sounds, animations, and virtual objects that can be clothes. It works thanks to a camera, jointed to another device which can be a smartphone, glasses, a helmet or a screen. The real world and the virtual information are connected together through geo-localization and captors put inside the device, so that the user is well situated in the field he is standing in.As an example of AR used in fashion retail, Alibaba is a multichannel application, that is to say that many brands items are sold through its virtual wardrobe, allowing customers to recall what they have tried on in-store while they also can read other buyers' or sellers' recommendations, so that customers are able to make one piece of clothes matching with other brands' ones(Alibaba Group, 2019). In few words, Fashion AI innovation allows us to acquire a very wide sight of the trendy products in a well personalized way.

Ecommerce firms in the service aspects that motivate customer satisfaction, belief,and loyalty. Customer service is an important feature that should be built with proper applications. Customer Engagement Services, Website interface properties, and other reliable services leads to customer satisfaction(Sobihah et al., 2015). (Sujata et al., 2019) portrays the role of innovation in gaining customer satisfaction. The researcher states that Virtual Reality, Augmented Reality, and Artificial Intelligence play a key innovation role in providing unique service for customers and thereby they get satisfied. Customer satisfaction leads to customer delight and customer retention that values customer experience.

AI IN OFFLINE FASHION INDUSTRY

Several are the innovation technologies that stores are trying to introduce as a new way of customer experience. Nowadays Fashion AI is growing as a system used to accurately observe and learn how to help the consumers in their style choices depending on what clothes they have tried in a store. One of these Fashion innovative devices consists in a screen able to recognize the clothes chosen and worn by a customer, and to suggest him or her other items matching with the tried one. Some of these screens are called smart mirrors, installed into stores' changing rooms. There use is mostly oriented in the help for consumers to find the articles in the boutique. This is called the customer experience improvement. E-commerce is more and more developing; offline stores are still going to stay sustainable thanks to the new technologies' investments. However, we could be asking if this kind of technical innovations in offline retail will continue to preserve this movement to keep being modern and attractive. Indeed, despite technologies being a precious help for both customers and retailers, the constant evolution endangers the offline area to be quickly out of fashion. So, what could be able to save this sector? The winning recipe may consist in the alliance of humanity and technology.AI in Fashion: CRM & Marketing business has proven benefits throughout the value chain: Reduction in the Operational Costs, Increase in Operational Efficiency, Support more Sustainable Practices, Omni channel Brand Experience.

AI AS TRUE OMNICHANNEL SHOPPING FOR FASHION INDUSTRY

AI renders new fashion designs complete with sewing patterns using a powerful algorithm that studies past designs and future trends. Retailers may opt to directly submit AI-designed apparel to production or integrate this as an additional step to automate the process of pattern making and fitting.

Human designers can then make alterations on these pre-designed garments to significantly speed up design to market time. By automating fabric quality control, pattern checks, colour matching and defect identification, AI scales the manufacturing process in fashion. Manual production processes are completed with improved precision by AI at a fraction of the time.

AI acts as a Predictive analyst as it analyses business success at a per-attribute level by means of automated product labelling. Buyers are not only told about the goods that perform well, but also about detailed features such as color, prints, sleeves, necklines, and more. In addition, instead of looking at patterns and product results at the end of each season as a snapshot, AI offers real-time information to observe changing trends and stock performance as they occur. Buying and merchandising teams should also follow a constructive approach to combat customer demand as it emerges and remain relevant at all times.

AI helps a retailer to consider returning consumers at any point of interaction, irrespective of the platforms in which they have interacted in the past, completely breaking the limits of conventional retail. Connecting data from both digital and traditional retail outlets under one umbrella ensures that a loyal customer will obtain for the first time in the physical store of a retailer or at another venue.

Smart Mirrors at the online stores turn their store into an experience centre, they incorporate AI technology into a range of customer touch points on the shop floor. In order to make personalised product and outfit suggestions, AI-powered smart mirrors directly communicate with the consumer. This encourages the exploration of goods and decreases fatigue from an abundance of options. AI uses visual detection and key product attributes to acclaim visually alike alternatives for each product on a fashion retailer's online store. When a product goes out of stock or size, customers are redirected to multiple relevant product pages on the retailer's website. They can easily find what they are looking for without the hassle of restarting product search, which often leads to frustration and site abandonment. Using similarity recommendations increases customer engagement and reduces sales opportunities lost to competitors.

Key Technologies for the Future of Fashion

How is the fashion industry interacting with digital technologies? And in particular, what are the most relevant technologies for the future of fashion? Alcimed (2017), a French consulting company, identifies the following 11 technologies as key to ensure the agility and competitiveness of the French fashion industry:

- Cloud
- Big Data
- Artificial Intelligence
- Cybersecurity
- Tags
- RFID
- IoT
- Robots/Cobots
- Drones
- Additive manufacturing
- Immersive technologies

ARTIFICIAL INTELLIGENCE AND FASHION

Artificial Intelligence as a Game Changer

The fashion industry is at a turning point. The McKinsey Global Fashion Index (2018) forecasts that industry sales growth will triple from 2016 to 2018, from 1.5% to between 3.5% to 4.5%. This growth is characterized by two phenomena: 1) the West will no longer play the major role in fashion sales and more than half of apparel sales will come from emerging market countries across Asia-Pacific, Latin America and other regions; 2) the adoption of digital technologies such as mobile internet, advanced analytics, virtual and augmented reality, advanced robotics and artificial intelligence are profoundly changing the industry and setting the stage for a strong trend towards a decisive phase of digital adoption by mainstream consumers; these processes are geared to match some specific trends in customer and enterprise behavior

FUTURE RESEARCH AND CONCLUSION

"Fashion is not a winner of the pandemic," he said. "As a category we are a loser, but as an online channel we are a winner from Covid-19."(Weiss,2021). Online platforms are also strengthening their position in the fashion sector. Platforms such as Amazon, Zalando and Myntra are promoting their own private label fashion offerings. They are also differentiating their offering in specific sectors such as sportswear or premium and luxury segments. At the same time, fashion brands have to figure out how to collaborate in a mutually convenient way with platforms to avoid that not only their fashion brand but also their customers' data could be used by platforms to build their own label-collections.AI provides multiple solutions for fashion retailers to more effectively address each pain point in the omnichannel customer journey and deliver a better brand experience that sets them apart from the competition. However, integrating AI into a fashion business is like finding the right suit: one size does not fit all and the best fit will be achieved through a tailored application.

Fashion retailers who leverage AI as Augmentative Intelligence to supercharge their existing business model will scale their resources, amplify their core strengths, be empowered by data-driven insight to overcome their weaknesses and maximise their market penetration as a brand. Growing market share and revenue while cutting down operational costs means an increasingly profitable business.

For fashion and product designers, machine learning techniques may be beneficial. Based on historical and real-time data, they may take advantage of predictive analysis of future patterns. In improving the existing recommendation engines, which currently rely on collaborative or content-based filtering, this can also prove promising. These engines can be improved by integrating with consumer data from social media and real-time trends from fashion blogs, magazines and other social networks such as Pinterest, Instagram.

AI is starting to be used extensively in the fashion industry, in particular to improve customer experience both online and off. Trend forecasting, supply chain management and price optimizations are also widely employed applications in the industry. Additional and more tailored applications are exploited by some companies of a larger size or with also a particularly strong presence in the online or off-line markets.

The "datafication of fashion" – the capacity to create digital data in relation to fashion products and production processes – that is making the fashion sector both an important consumer and supplier of data, which proves very useful in informing production decisions, improving planning and logistics and customizing products. Moreover, fashion data are also used to feed into the rest of the value chain: wholesalers, retailers, finance and product input sectors such as textiles and leather.

REFERENCES

Alibaba Group. (2019). https://www.alibabagroup.com/en/about/overview

Chris, B. (2018, April 27). *How Fashion Should (and Shouldn't) Embrace Artificial Intelligence | Opinion, Op Ed | BoF*. https://www.businessoffashion.com/opinions/news-analysis/how-fashion-should-and-shouldnt-embrace-artificial-intelligence

Herhausen, D., Binder, J., Schoegel, M., & Herrman, A. (2015). Integrating Bricks with Clicks: Retailer-Level and Channel-Level Outcomes of Online-Offline Channel Integration. *Journal of Retailing*, *91*(2), 309–325. doi:10.1016/j.jretai.2014.12.009

Luce, L. (2019). *Artificial Intelligence for Fashion*. Apress - Springer Nature. doi:10.1007/978-1-4842-3931-5

Nicholson, M., Clarke, J., & Blakemore, M. (2002). One brand, three ways to shop: Situational variables and multichannel consumer behaviour. Review of Retail. *Distribution and Consumer Research*, *12*(2), 131–148. doi:10.1080/09593960210127691

Nwaizugbo, I. C., & Ifeanyichukwu, C. D. (2016). Understanding Consumers' Behaviour Towards Online Shopping: A Study of Online Shoppers in Anambra State. *International Journal of Sales. Retailing & Marketing*, *5*(2), 28–37. doi:10.6007/ijarafms.v1i2.8

Puccinelli, N., Goodstein, R., Grewal, D., Price, R., Raghubir, P., & Stewart, D. (2019). Customer experience management in retailing: Understanding the buying process. *Journal of Retailing*, *85*(1), 15–30. doi:10.1016/j.jretai.2008.11.003

Research, I. (2020, July 31). *AI in Fashion market worth $ 2.42 billion in 2026*. https://www.prnewswire.com/news-releases/ai-in-fashion-market-worth--2-42-billion-in-2026--301103837.html

Saponaro, M., Le Gal, D., Gao, M., Guisiano, M., & Maniere, I. C. (2018). Challenges and Opportunities of Artificial Intelligence in the Fashion World. *International Conference on Intelligent and Innovative Computing Applications (ICONIC)*, 1–5. 10.1109/ICONIC.2018.8601258

Sobihah, M., Mohamad, M., Ali, N. A. M., & Wan Ismail, W. Z. (2015). E-commerce service quality on customer satisfaction, belief and loyalty: A proposal. *Mediterranean Journal of Social Sciences*, *6*(2), 260–266. doi:10.5901/mjss.2015.v6n2p260

Sujata, J., Aniket, D., & Mahasingh, M. (2019). Artificial intelligence tools for enhancing customer experience. *International Journal of Recent Technology and Engineering, 8*(2), 700–706. doi:10.35940/ijrte.B1130.0782S319

KEY TERMS AND DEFINITIONS

Artificial Intelligence (AI): Is a wide-ranging branch of computer science concerned with building smart machines capable of performing tasks that typically require human intelligence.

Dress: According to Tortora (2015), dress is first and foremost an element of culture whose visibility makes it immediately perceptible, even to the most inattentive observer; it is the identity card of the wearer since it carries a social message, signals a status, and signifies particular activities and specializations.

Offline Shopping: Offline shopping is a traditional way of purchasing services or products by directly visiting to the store/shop/ or vendor.

Online Shopping: Online shopping occurs when a customer buys through a digital platform.

Chapter 9
Zero Customer Defection

Renu Yadav
Ideal Institute of Management and Technology, India

ABSTRACT

AI-oriented CRM has a bright future in business transformation. We're living in the age of the customer. Due to the proliferation of data, customers are more informed than ever. Armed with empowerment, customers are demanding that customer experience be put on a pedestal. According to research by Walker, customer experience is slated to overtake price and product as the key brand differentiator by the end of 2020. Quality is a buzz word. In this sharp, opportunistic, and calculating world, one can survive only if it is having not only good quality but a unique quality. As it is very well explained by Darwin that the mantra for success is "survival of fittest." Every organization has its own procedure of achieving its best quality and to sustain in this tough world. This chapter will not only discuss about the zero customer defection but also emphasize on the issues, problems, and trends of artificial intelligence in CRM and in turn zero customer defection.

INTRODUCTION

Technology blending into relationship management continues at a very rapid rate: Information technology and advanced analytics support omnipresent customer communication and increasing availability of customer data, in turn enabling firms to offer personalized services and crating customer relationships to grow more profitable customers (Rust and Huang, 2014, Gupta et al., 2020). At the heart of marketers' attention in this regard are the emerging technologies of *artificial intelligence (AI),* which refer to "a system's ability to *correctly interpret external data, to learn from such data, and to use those learnings to achieve specific goals and tasks through*

DOI: 10.4018/978-1-7998-7959-6.ch009

Figure 1. The AI-CRM effect.
Source: Journal of Interactive Marketing, Volume 51,August 2020,Page 44-56

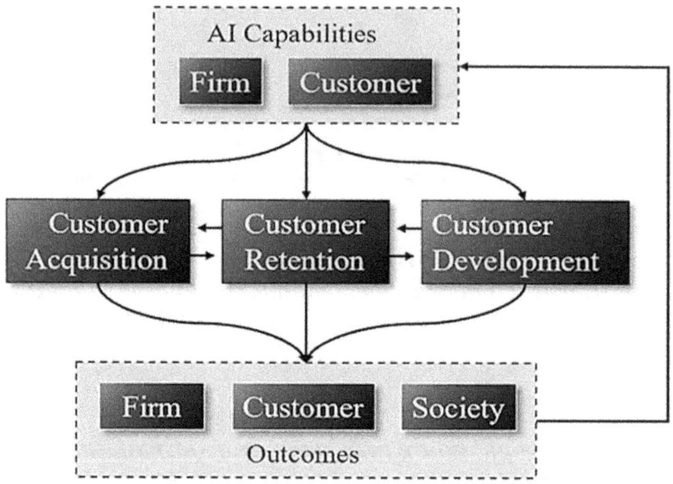

flexible adaptation" (Kaplan & Haenlein, 2019, p. 15). In the context of customer relationship management, these technologies enable firms to analyze data and interact with consumers faster and on a larger scale. In the longer term, enabling human-like interactions between AI-driven systems and customers will allow the provision of widespread personalized services at low cost, possibly altering the nature of customer service as they do so (Kaplan and Haenlein, 2019, Hoyer et al., 2020; Grewal, Kroschke, Mende, Roggeveen, & Scott, 2020). Combining the two notions of AI and CRM, we suggest that *any CRM system exhibiting sufficiently flexible adaptation can be labeled an artificially intelligent CRM system or AI-CRM.*

Our aim in this article is to examine AI systems' fundamental effects on how firms manage their relationships with their customers and how it affects the overall iteration rate of customers. There has been escalating discussion, in a of recent publications, of the expected progress of AI systems, their future ability to replace humans, and the specifics of the technologies that fall under the rubric "AI" (Agrawal et al., 2018, Haenlein and Kaplan, 2019, Kaplan and Haenlein, 2019). Some of this work is customer-related and has focused on the expected change in the nature of customer service (Huang and Rust, 2018, Kumar et al., 2015). While we handle on some of these areas. Our aim here is not to conduct another review of this topic. Instead, our focus is on the broader implications of the effects of AI-CRM on Zero customer defection, and in particular, the outcomes for customers and other stakeholders. Following diagram shows the scope of Artificial Intelligence'

As the diagram itself shows the relationship of AI in customer retention or customer churn or Zero Customer Defection. Before taking the relationship in detail one should understand the concept and other related things about Zero Customer defections.

STATEMENT OF THE PROBLEM AND RESEARCH QUESTION

Artificial Intelligence will adapt to changing customer landscapes and get smarter. When applied optimally in CRM tools, it will make a business provide predictable service to its customers. In turn, this will help the business generate predictable revenue. AI will be essential to deliver high-quality personalized experiences for customers. And it is the next step in the modern execution of CRM.

Main Objective

The main objective of this chapter is to have deep insights in to the role of AI in CRM and in turn to Zero Customer Defection.

Secondary Objectives

- To understand the significance of the term Zero Customer Defection
- To understand the extended relationship of AI and Zero Customer Defection
- To explore newer ways of AI advancements in service sectors.

Research Questions

- **Q1:** What role AI is playing in Customer Relationship Management?
- **Q2:** How Customer Zero Defection or Customer churn or Customer Iteration rate is getting affected with Artificial Intelligence Technologies?

Research Model of the Proposed Work

See Figure 2.

Concept of Zero Customer Defection

A common term used for the loss of a customer to rivals is customer defection. Companies that require "zero defections" (keeping any customer they can service profitably) can maximize profits. Defection levels are both an indicator of the standard of service and a guide to achieving it. Managers know exactly where the business is falling short and by listening to the reasons why customers defect. Yet customer

Figure 2. Research model

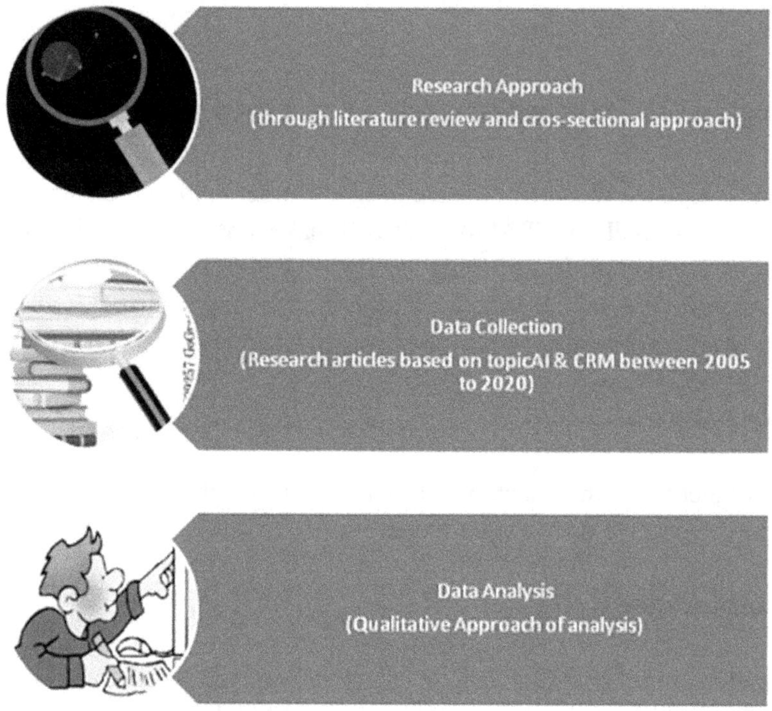

defection is one among the foremost illuminating measures in business. First, it's the clearest possible sign that customers see a deteriorating stream useful from the corporate . Second, a climbing defection rate may be a sure predictor of a diminishing flow of money from customers to the corporate —even if the company replaces the lost customers—because new customers cost money to accumulate and since older customers tend to supply greater income and profits than newer ones. By checking out the basis causes of customer departures, companies with the will and capacity to find out can identify business practices that require fixing and, sometimes, can win the customer back and reestablish the relationship on firmer ground.

BACKGROUND

The phrase of zero defects was coined by Philip Crosby in his 1979 book titled " Quality is free". It is defined as a way of thinking and doing things in a right manner and reinforces this phrase more importantly that defects are not acceptable. This will ultimately leads to decrease in cost of failure and increasing revenues trough increased customer satisfaction.

According to Shashwat Sharma, chief marketing officer, Bharti Airtel, the connection between Airtel and its customers has never been more important, and to serve them even better the corporate has decided to require the customer care to subsequent level. "We know that "ZERO questions" is an impossible utopian thought especially for a telecom brand, but that won't stop us from trying because we all know that the closer we get to ZERO,the happier our customers are going to be.

Zero customer defection is not a single concept .It is an umbrella which will cover a lot many processes in it. For example for its campaign of "Zero questions" by Bharti Airtel the company is now re-engineering the entire organisation towards this goal and are obsessed with building a culture of consumer centricity.

THE COST OF LOSING A CUSTOMER

If companies knew what proportion it really costs to lose a customer, they might be ready to make accurate evaluations of investments designed to retain customers. Its a pity that today's accounting systems do not capture the value of a loyal customer. Most systems specialize in current period costs and revenues and ignore expected cash flows over a customer's life-time. Served correctly, customers generate increasingly more profits annually they stick with a corporation . Across a good range of companies, the pattern is that the same: the longer a corporation keeps a customer, the extra money it stands to for. For one auto-service company, the expected take advantage of a fourth-year customer is quite triple the profit that very same customer generates within the first year. When customers defect, they take all that profit-making potential with them.

According to latest survey it was found that if we work on Zero Customer Defection the change occurs. Although the magnitude of the change varies by company and industry, the pattern holds: profits rise sharply. Reducing the defection rate just 5% generates 85% more profits in one bank's branch system, 50% more in an insurance brokerage, and 30% more in an auto-service chain. Quality revolution is just now coming to services. As quality improved, fewer customers had reason to go away.

Types of Customer Defection

1. **Brand Value**: A decline in brand value leads to decline in consumer as well.
2. **Customer Relationships**: If the company does not value their customer than also it leads to customer defection.

3. **Customer Service**: Poor customer service experiences frequently result in a customer defection.
4. **Ease of Use**: Making the things easier for customers also make the thr customers loyal towards the company.
5. **Fairness**: People that tend to have a strong sense of justice. They may defect thanks to perceptions that practices like legal terms, conditions, rules or practices.
6. **Innovation**: A new technology or approach makes your product less competitive in the market.
7. **Involuntary Chun**: Factors that are unrelated with your business ie customers moving to different countries.
8. **Price Need**: Firms that charge higher prices to their loyal customers or that face intense price competition.
9. **Quality**: Deteriorating quality is also one of the factor of customer defection
10. **Reputation**: The product should be positioned in the mind of customer well enough so that its reputation should not go down such as financial, environmental or social wrongdoing
11. **Risk**: A perception that you present a risk. For example customers may defect in large numbers if they think that you may go out of business.
12. **Trends**: Changing preferences such as fashion trends
13. **Unpopular features**: features that customers find invasive, annoying and cumbersome.

FACTS ABOUT CUSTOMER DEFECTION

The concern for reducing and eliminating customer attrition emerged from studies that indicate the following:

- Across industries, profits can increase by 35 to 85% by increasing customer retention by only 5%.
- About 70% of customers switch to competitive offerings due to perceived indifference of the current provider.
- About !4% of customers switch due to product dissatisfaction
- About 9% of customer left the particular brand due to friendship
- 96% of unhappy customers never bother to complain.
- 71% of the customers fee their complaint has been handled satisfactorily if they only need to deal with one individual.
- If a customer complaint was handled well, 95% of customers will return to do business with the organization.

Figure 3.

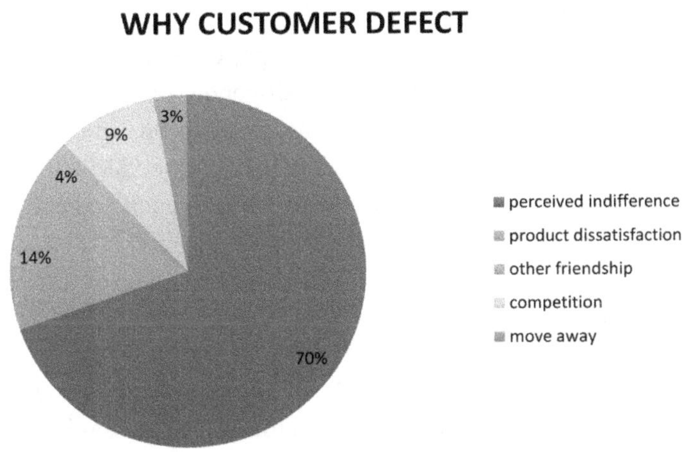

ISSUES PROBLEMS AND TRENDS OF CRM AND ZERO CUSTOMER DEFECTION

Issues and Trends

- **Intelligent CRM Automation**

Intelligent automation – the combination of AI and robotic process automation (RPA) – is having a profound impact on CRM. With intelligent automation, bots can not only automate manual, time-consuming tasks like data entry, they can automate more complex processes like customer segmentation, predictive lead scoring, and sales forecasting.

Lead scoring, for example, used to be based on salesperson intuition and educated guesses. With AI, machine learning algorithms can study massive data sets, understand how deals are won and lost, recognize patterns, and identify triggers in the customer's journey. The algorithm can then automatically apply its learning to the entire sales pipeline and score each lead based on fact, not instinct.

By automating key CRM processes, sales, service, and marketing teams can free up their time to focus on more valuable activities – like meeting customer needs and improving their experiences. Automation can also help you widen your net as it gives you the bandwidth to nurture more relationships through the buyer's journey, identify cross and up-sell opportunities, and increase your overall revenue.

- **Hyper-Personalization**.

Hyper-personalization takes everything into account about customer profiles and transaction history, online behavior, social media posts, conversational styles, timing and context of past purchases, device type, GPS data, and so much more. Using this Big Data along with artificial intelligence, hyper-personalization can more accurately interpret customer intentions, pick up on subtleties, and deliver highly tailored customer experiences. It can display specially curated products, services, promotions, content, and recommendations to each and every customer – automatically and at scale.

- **CRM Chatbots**

Chatbots are a game changer for CRM. These AI-powered programs simulate conversations with customers via websites, text messages, messaging apps, and over the phone in a natural, increasingly human way.

Chatbots are used for customer service, marketing, e-commerce, and sales. They can answer basic questions much faster than a rep can – no cheesy hold music required – and they work 24×7. Chatbots can follow-up post-purchase, offer support, collect feedback and conduct surveys, and recommend personalized products and content based on past interactions.

They can also act as virtual assistants for the sellers, marketers, and customer service agents who use CRM – making their jobs easier and improving their productivity and effectiveness. CRM chatbots can empower users with in-the-moment insights, prompts and alerts, recommendations, and next-best actions. During live interactions, chatbots can even determine the next likely question, suggest resolutions, and help the employee strike the right conversational tone.

- **AI-Powered Customer Analytics**

Too often there is a mismatch between what customers want and what companies think they want. AI-powered CRM analytics can fix this issue – analyzing an ocean of data from all sorts of sources to uncover customer insights that would otherwise remain hidden. The technology has the power to research and analyze thousands, even millions, of customers to pinpoint their needs, preferences, and interests and help customer-facing teams deliver the products, services, content, and experiences they actually want – in real time. AI customer analytics can also dramatically improve sales forecasting, enhance behavior and sentiment analysis, predict potential churn and retention issues, and power one-to-one marketing initiatives.

- **Creating Immersive Customer Experiences with Virtual and Augmented Reality**

AR and VR are beginning to play a larger role in CRM and CX. The immersive technology – and low-cost hardware – have moved beyond the gaming industry and into the realm of marketing, sales, e-commerce, and customer service. Many forward-looking companies are connecting AR and VR apps to their CRM systems to deliver delightful – and differentiated – experiences throughout the customer journey.

- **IoT: Getting More Personal – and Proactive – with IoT Data**

In customer service and field service, if there was an issue or product malfunction pre-IoT, the customer would have to explain the problem as best they could to a service rep, the rep would try to troubleshoot, and, failing that, the rep would dispatch a technician. By connecting IoT device feeds to CRM, service departments can monitor product data, detect lapses in performance, and identify the cause of the problem before the customer even notices there's an issue. The CRM system can automatically create a service ticket, order the right part, and schedule a field service technician with minimal involvement from the customer – if any.

This proactive approach to maintenance and service increases customer satisfaction – as well as rep and technician efficiency. It's a win-win.

- **IoT in Marketing and Sales**

In marketing and sales, sensor data flowing into your CRM system can let you know how, when, and where your products are being used by individual customers. Using this insight, marketers can deliver hyper-personalized content and offers at just the right time. And sales teams can identify highly relevant cross and up-sell opportunities – and encourage repeat sales.

With IoT data, sales and marketing people can get to know customer needs, wants, and behaviors on a much deeper level – and deliver the types of experiences that make them feel valued and understood.

- **Mobile CRM: Putting CRM into Employee Pockets and Improving Their Responsiveness**

Mobile CRM – apps that let sales, service, and marketing teams access their most important tools on the go – has been on every major CRM technology list for a decade. But it's not a bygone trend. Mobile usage has only continued to grow, along with employee expectations for intuitive CRM apps, remote work, and flexible hours.

PROBLEMS OF AI POWERED ZERO CUSTOMER DEFECTION

- **The Economic Hurdle**: Demonstrating improvements to the bottom line.

A company that is growing its earnings or reducing its costs is said to be improving its bottom line. So its very important that through virtual agents company should be in the condition of increasing thr profits.

- **The Technical Hurdle**: Ensuring that systems are ready.

Virtual agents need to know when IT agrees on priorities with the lines of the business directly implementing virtual agents

- **The Cultural Hurdle**: Getting past human-centric prejudices.

Virtual agents can affect multiple parts of the company, including its brand. As a result, the decision to commit to virtual agents typically involves not just the head of customer service, but an array of C-level decision makers, including the chief operating officer, the CIO, some of the CIO's direct reports, the head of sales, and often the chief experience officer (assuming the company has one). Because the virtual agent can become a highly visible part of the brand, chief marking officers and heads of product management may also become involved.

- **The Political Hurdle**: Winning over management

In the end, much of the resistance to virtual agents comes down to the company in the manner that whether company is willing to let machines talk to customers, or is it a job that only people can handle?

MANAGERIAL IMPLICATIONS

- Managers can improve lead generation by having more accurate marketing campaigns. Integrating AI into CRM can also automate customer reports, emails, data capture, and more. This helps to avoid the risk of human errors in everyday tasks and administrative duties.
- An AI-powered CRM will be able to learn from past decisions and historical patterns to score the best leads for sales. Artificial Intelligence will also be able to predict future customer behavior. AI is very helpful when it comes to analyzing customer's emotions by a simple phone call, in order to establish

strategies that will increase the engagement. Thus you can connect to your customers in an altogether different way.

- Another very important aspect of AI is in segmentation. Segmenting customers becomes easier. AI won't take away jobs, but will actually help team workers to be more productive. For example: Having intelligent algorithms will help in segmenting customers easily.
- Increase customer engagement with AI-driven CRM. This technology can help in getting an emotional insight from the customer. Image recognition and sentiment analysis are two powerful tools which make AI-enabled CRM as the future of business.
- AI can help to understand a customer's satisfaction in real time. Once managers have this valuable insight, it's easy to take action and identify problems. Essentially, AI will be able to better read the customers intentions.
- Artificial intelligence is coming, heavy research is being carried out in the field and parties are investing to make A.I a reality. However, the bright side is that there are research groups focused on preventing an uncontrollable A.I and they are making sure we do not create our own destruction.

CONCLUSION

AI-powered CRM is the road ahead to future business transformation. However, enterprises have doubts about the implementation and security of AI-enabled CRM systems.

Research and further advancements are very much possible before it is implemented in every aspect of the organization, but there is a long way to go. AI-powered CRM will make enterprises future-ready and boost efficiency, speed, and productivity.

Industry experts estimate that by 2020, 85% of global businesses will implement AI-enabled CRM solutions. Now this future emerging technology will become a necessity for every business in the coming years.

The need of the hour is for enterprises to evaluate their current engagement model and see if it is still relevant in the present scenario and if it will work in the long term or not. Consequently, companies must come up with marketing campaigns which are ultra-personalized for each individual customer in order to optimize customer engagements. At the same time, they must empower their salespeople with insights on customers so that zero customer defection target can be achieved. Customer support agents should be equipped with the business intelligence required to delight customers during every interaction. The integration of AI into various processes like sales, marketing, and customer relationship management is imperative for enterprises to ensure smarter, proactive, and delightful engagement with customers. AI-driven technologies using smart data sources can help companies and their teams understand where each customer is in their unique journey. As a result, businesses can easily identify the gaps in customer experience and present relevant actionable insights and solutions to retain customer interest, while ensuring their overall satisfaction with the brand.

Artificial intelligence is a buzz word now a days. Profound research is being carried out in the field and companies are investing to make A.I a reality. However, the dazzling side is that there are research groups focused on preventing an abandoned A.I and they are making sure that it should be used for human wealth and creation and not for destruction.

REFERENCES

Agrawal, Gans, & Goldfarb. (2019). Economic policy for artificial intelligence. Innovation Policy and the Economy, 19(1), 139–159.

Aguiar, M., & Bils, M. (2015). Has consumption inequality mirrored income inequality? *The American Economic Review*, *105*(9), 2725–2756. doi:10.1257/aer.20120599

André, Q., Carmon, Z., Wertenbroch, K., Crum, A., Frank, D., Goldstein, W., Huber, J., van Boven, L., Weber, B., & Yang, H. (2018). Consumer choice and autonomy in the age of artificial intelligence and big data. *Customer Needs and Solutions*, *5*(1–2), 28–37. doi:10.100740547-017-0085-8

Andrews, M., Goehring, J., Hui, S., Pancras, J., & Thornswood, L. (2016). Mobile promotions: A framework and research priorities. *Journal of Interactive Marketing*, *34*, 15–24. doi:10.1016/j.intmar.2016.03.004

Arbel, Y. A., & Shapira, R. (2020). Theory of the nudnik: The future of consumer activism and what we can do to stop it. *Vanderbilt Law Review*.

Arts, J. W. C., Frambach, R. T., & Bijmolt, T. H. A. (2011). Generalizations on consumer innovation adoption: A meta-analysis on drivers of intention and behavior. *International Journal of Research in Marketing*, *28*(2), 134–144. doi:10.1016/j.ijresmar.2010.11.002

Ascarza, E. (2018). Retention futility: Targeting high-risk customers might be ineffective. *JMR, Journal of Marketing Research*, *55*(1), 80–98. doi:10.1509/jmr.16.0163

Audretsch, D. B., & Feldma, M. P. (1996). R&D spillovers and the geography of innovation and production. *The American Economic Review*, *86*(3), 630–640.

Barney, J. (1991). Firm resources and sustained competitive advantage. *Journal of Management*, *17*(1), 99–120. doi:10.1177/014920639101700108

Bart, Y., Shankar, V., Sultan, F., & Urban, G. L. (2005). Are the drivers and role of online trust the same for all web sites and consumers? A large-scale exploratory empirical study. *Journal of Marketing*, *69*(4), 133–152. doi:10.1509/jmkg.2005.69.4.133

Batra, R., & Keller, K. L. (2016). Integrating marketing communications: New findings, new lessons, and new ideas. *Journal of Marketing*, *80*(6), 122–145. doi:10.1509/jm.15.0419

Blut, M., Wang, C., & Schoefer, K. (2016). Factors influencing the acceptance of self-service technologies: A meta-analysis. *Journal of Service Research*, *19*(4), 396–416. doi:10.1177/1094670516662352

Cao, Y., & Gruca, T. S. (2005). Reducing adverse selection through customer relationship management. *Journal of Marketing*, *69*(4), 219–229.

Chung, T. S., Wedel, M., & Rust, R. T. (2016). Adaptive personalization using social networks. *Journal of the Academy of Marketing Science*, *44*(1), 66–87.

(2006). CRM implementation: Effectiveness issues and insights. *Journal of Service Research*, *9*(2), 184–194.

De Keyser, S. K. (2019). Frontline service technology infusion: Conceptual archetypes and future research directions. *Journal of Service Management*, *30*(1), 156–183.

Decker, R., & Trusov, M. (2010). Estimating aggregate consumer preferences from online product reviews. *International Journal of Research in Marketing*, *27*(4), 293–307.

Deighton, J. (2019). Big Data. *Consumption Markets & Culture*, *22*(1), 68–73.

Du, R. Y., Hu, Y., & Damangir, S. (2015). Leveraging trends in online searches for product features in market response modeling. *Journal of Marketing*, *79*(1), 29–43.

Eagle, N., Pentland, A. S., & Lazer, D. (2009). Inferring friendship network structure by using mobile phone data. *Proceedings of the National Academy of Sciences of the United States of America*, *106*(36), 15274–15278.

Eyal, N. (2014). *Hooked: How to Build Habit-Forming Products*. Penguin.

Fader, P. (2012). *Customer Centricity: Focus on the Right Customers for Strategic Advantage*. Wharton Digital Press.

Fader, P., & Toms, S. E. (2018). *The Customer Centricity Playbook: Implement a Winning Strategy Driven by Customer Lifetime Value*. Wharton Digital Press.

Gensler, S., Völckner, F., Egger, M., Fischbach, K., & Schoder, D. (2015). Listen to your customers: Insights into brand image using online consumer-generated product reviews. *International Journal of Electronic Commerce*, *20*(1), 112–141.

Grewal, D., Kroschke, M., Mende, M., Roggeveen, A. L., & Scott, M. L. (2020). Customer experiences in retail, sales, and service settings. *Journal of Interactive Marketing*, *51*, 9–25.

Guerrero, M., Montoya, F. G., Baños, R., Alcayde, A., & Gil, C. (2017). Adaptive community detection in complex networks using genetic algorithms. *Neurocomputing*, *266*, 101–113.

Gupta, S., & Lehmann, D. R. (2003). Customers as assets. *Journal of Interactive Marketing*, *17*(1), 9–24.

Gupta, S., & Lehmann, D. R. (2005). *Managing customers as investments*. The Strategic Value of Customers in the Long Run, Wharton School Publ.

Gupta, S., Leszkiewicz, A., Kumar, V., Bijmolt, T., & Potapov, D. (2020). Digital analytics: Modeling for insights and new methods. *Journal of Interactive Marketing*, *51*, 26–43.

Haenlein, M. (2013). Social interactions in customer churn decisions: The impact of relationship directionality. *International Journal of Research in Marketing*, *30*(3), 236–248.

Haenlein, M. (2017). How to date your clients in the 21st century: Challenges in managing customer relationships in Today's world. *Business Horizons*, *60*(5), 577–586.

Haenlein, M., & Kaplan, A. (2009). Unprofitable customers and their management. *Business Horizons*, *52*(1), 89–97.

Haenlein, M., & Kaplan, A. (2019). A brief history of artificial intelligence: On the past, present, and future of artificial intelligence. *Californi Management*, *61*(4), 5–14.

Haenlein & Kaplan. (2012). The impact of unprofitable customer abandonment on current customers' exit, voice, and loyalty intentions: An empirical analysis. *Journal of Services Marketing*, *26*(6), 458.

Haenlein & Libai. (2019). Comparing automated text classification methods. *International Journal of Research in Marketing*, *36*(1), 20–38.

Hofacker, C. F. (2019). Notes on the growing importance of software as a driver of value exchange. In A. P. Rindfleisch & A. J. Malter (Eds.), Review of Marketing Research. Academic Press.

KEY TERMS AND DEFINITIONS

Artificial Intelligence: Artificial intelligence (AI) is wide-ranging branch of computer science concerned with building smart machines capable of performing tasks that typically require human intelligence.

Customer Defection: Customer attrition, also known as customer churn, customer turnover, or customer defection, is the loss of clients or customers.

Customer Relationship Management: A customer relationship management (CRM) system allows businesses to monitor and analyze their relationships with customers, suppliers, and employees. It aims to increase sales efficiency and profitability by improving and maintaining these business relationships.

Innovation: An innovation is an idea that has been transformed into practical reality. For a business, this is a product, process, or business concept, or combinations that have been activated in the marketplace and produce new profits and growth for the organization.

Quality: Quality is the totality of features and characteristics of a product or service that bear on its ability to satisfy given needs.

USP: A unique selling point (USP), also called a unique selling proposition, is the essence of what makes your product or service better than competitors.

Value: Value has to do with how much something is worth, either in terms of cash or importance.

Chapter 10
Framework to Understand and Deploy AI-Based Smart CRM in the Airline Industry

Vikram Bawa
HCL Technologies, India

ABSTRACT

This is the age of AI. Soon what customers think will be understood by the smart applications on their mobile devices and the information—most of which will be pre-processed based on the customer personas—will be available at the blink of an eye. In this chapter a critical analysis of how AI bolsters CRM capabilities in the airline industry is conducted. To understand that, AI capabilities are surveyed and its transformational effects on CRM and its impact on customer acquisition, retention, loyalty, and experience are explored in depth. In the end, a customer journey-based deployment framework is presented that supports the finding of the AI-CRM implementation use cases.

INTRODUCTION

In this Chapter a critical analysis of how AI bolsters CRM capabilities in the Airline industry is conducted. To understand that, AI capabilities are surveyed and its transformational effects on CRM and its impact on Customer Acquisition, Retention, Loyalty and Experience is explored in depth. In the end a Customer Journey based deployment framework is presented which supports the finding of the AI-CRM implementation use cases.

DOI: 10.4018/978-1-7998-7959-6.ch010

UNDERSTANDING CUSTOMER NEEDS

This is the age of AI. Soon what customers think will be understood by the smart applications on their mobile devices and the information – most of which will be pre-processed based on the Customer Personas will be available at the blink of an eye.

Has anyone ever fully understood the Customer needs? Customers didn't ask for an IPod but relished the experience, neither did they ask for a Smartphone but today it's like a commodity, similarly customer needs are never well articulated yet they are looking for an experience full of convenience and pleasant surprises. Upgrade an Economy class customer to First Class and he or she will surely have a memorable experience. On the contrary, a customer getting late for a business meeting due to flight delays or losing his baggage will never fly again with the same airline.

Kingfisher Airlines, India was a great example of an airliner surprising its customers with its superior service experience and offering freebies on all festival occasions. No wonder, no one ever said they don't want to fly Kingfisher.

Southwest Airlines, USA is another great example of an airliner creating and maintaining its niche and creating happy customers despite being a no frills airliner. Not only the low cost and on time flight experience it's the liveliness and courteousness of its staff which makes the flying experience with Southwest memorable.

Customers don't want to spend time looking for information. Customer Profiling, Advanced Segmentation, Customer Lifetime Value (CLV) models the holy grail of strategic marketing are being commoditized as customers are seeking services at the touch of a button and sometimes even at the blink of an eye.

NEED FOR AI BASED SMART CRM

Use of advanced analytics and AI has made Omni channel experience feasible and with loads of customer data, firms can offer hyper personalized services to grow customer lifetime value and enhance profitability (Rust and Huang, 2014, Gupta et al., 2020).

AI enabled CRM will ensure hyper personalization of services albeit at a lower cost and thus changing the way the customer service functions (Kaplan and Haenlein, 2019, Hoyer et al., 2020; Grewal, Kroschke, Mende, Roggeveen, & Scott, 2020).

The proliferation of AI in any customer facing industry is inevitable. Delta served more than 80 million people in 2017 (AltexSoft, 2018). As organizations face an uphill task to organize and make sense of the data, AI comes to the rescue. There is no Customer Issue AI cannot help resolve. Delta through its Asset Performance Management was able to prevent more than 1200 flight delays, service interruptions and cancellations in a calendar year (AltexSoft, 2018).

Use of Chatbots/ Voicebots, Voice Recognition and Face Detection Systems, Augmented Reality are on the rise. According to prnewswire.com - AI in the aviation market alone is expected to be valued at $152.4 million in 2018 and to reach $2,222.5 million by 2025 (PRNewswire, 2018). Chatbots for customer service has been found to mitigate risks for service failure and preventing Customer Churn (De Keyser, Arne, Alkire, Verbeeck, & Kandampully, 2019). The next few years will see Chatbots mimicking human behaviour in their service interactions with customers (Luo, Tong, Fang, & Qu, 2019).

UNDERSTANDING THE AIRLINE DIGITAL CUSTOMER JOURNEY

Figure 1. Airline digital customer journey

Customer Lifecycle of Airlines highlights some of the key issues Customers have been facing over the years, possible resolution includes using advanced AI and sophisticated Analytical systems:

1. **Research and Plan Trip:** Researching and planning a trip is still a big area to explore and is a time consuming activity. AI can help track a customer's online behaviour to suggest places to explore based on browsing behaviour, affordable getaways thus ensuring focused targeting of the potential customers and avoiding costly, less productive mass targeting.

2. **Ticket Bookings and Pricing:** Ease of Ticket Bookings across channels using bots and Dynamic Pricing based on advance data analytics. Customers can be in any geography and may like to book tickets and check pricing at 1am, bots can be faster, more precise and can be available at any hour of the day with the same accuracy.
3. **Security and Check Ins:** Voice Recognition and Face Detection Systems play a huge role in Airport and In Flight security. Some of these solutions provide unprecedented sophistication, is convenient and solves a lot of security challenges which humans cannot possibly solve without the help of these AI based systems. For example, face detection system coupled with the CRM system can recognise and provide complete profile of the customer in a few seconds and thus can prevent any security lapses and provides faster check ins and security clearances.
4. **Lounge Access and Entertainment:** Customers nowadays demand Personalized Experience which can be looked as a combination of past interactions with the Airlines and is an important part of the Customer Lifecycle and Customer Loyalty.
5. **Self Service Kiosks** featuring Augmented Reality are helping customers resolve issues faster and more efficiently. Kiosks powered with multilingual capabilities help resolve challenges which humans can't possibly resolve by themselves, such kiosks can function as buddies, help resolve customer queries in multiple languages, guide them on the airport and beyond, thus helping improve customer experience and increase customer loyalty.
6. **Connecting Flights and Bumping:** Connecting flights and bumping is a big pain area for customers across the globe and impacts Customer Experience in a big way, having a command centre powered by AI and Analytics can help resolve a part of it.
7. **Boarding / In-flight Services and Entertainment:** In the era of hyper personalization not having a personalized entertainment program can impact customer satisfaction in a negative manner. Some of the personalized experiences to be looked at are
    a. **Refreshment Preferences** – Can refreshments, both paid and free be personalized? For an airline focusing on high customer loyalty, it will be a yes. As a prerequisite, enough data has to be captured to understand every customer's preferences and then find a close match to surprise the customers. Ideally the types of refreshments or the assortments would not exceed ten as it will be a mix and match of common customer meal preferences. British low cost carrier Easy Jet uses AI to predict the bacon baguette's demand on a single flight by modelling attributes such as

weather, types of passengers on board and the time of the year (AltexSoft, 2018).

b. **Entertainment Preferences** – Similar to meal preferences could be entertainment preferences menu, specially curated for an individual customer. Imagine on a long haul flight, a tired customer is just looking to listen to some good music he or she prefers or watch some engaging content before slipping into slumber.

8. **De boarding Assistance:** De boarding assistance can be a small area but imagine the inconvenience caused to the first time fliers or customers facing language issues, a multilingual, interactive voice bot can help provide a personalized experience without a glitch.
9. **Baggage Handling –** So many customers around the world lose their baggage resulting in poor customer experience and customer churn, many airlines have started face detection systems to ensure only the authorised passengers are picking the baggage and that too the right ones. The video camera based system can verify the identity of the person claiming the bag, match it and let the person pick the bag and all of this in a few seconds. In May 2017, Delta deployed four self-service bag checking machines with a kiosk equipped with face recognition technology to confirm passenger's identity by recognising the photos on their passport (AltexSoft, 2018).
10. **Airport Exit and Customer Complaints Handling**
    a. The case of Jet Blue receiving 15k emails – The glitch happened with Jet Blue flights and a result was more than 15000 emails. They would have lost a good number of customers if they would not have replied to each of these 15000 emails with a personal touch understanding the context and helping to resolve it. It was not humanely possible to understand and reply to such a huge number of emails in a short span of time, a text mining solution came to their rescue, they were able to respond to each of these emails, understanding the context and providing the personal touch in a record time, no wonder they rank in top 3 in customer experience rankings by Forrester every year.
    b. Use of Social Media as a Customer Feedback channel - JDPower 2017 North America Airline Satisfaction study suggests that about 21% of business travellers and 8% of leisure travellers actively share their experiences on Social Media and this figure can be much higher if we take into account close groups. No wonder, to understand and track customer wants and preferences analysing the sentiment on the social media has become an absolute must. Not only that ensuring the customer

DEVELOP AND DEPLOY CONSIDERATIONS

AI Is Not Enough, Structure Has to Be Right Too

Can AI enriched CRM be enough to deliver superior returns, ensure better Customer Lifetime Value (CLV) and make marketers understand their customers better? If it could have been so easy the custom industry solutions would have been enough to ensure every organization enjoys similar customer and brand equity and delivers superior returns year after year.

A big Telecom service provider in Singapore was maintaining two CRM solutions one was maintained by the Sales division and the other by the Marketing division with no easy sync up between the two data sets. While they were enjoying a good market position due to the nature of competition, barriers to entry in the state and stable customer base, they were lacking efficiencies and competitiveness vis a vis the global telecom players. Such structural ambiguities cannot ensure sound financial performance unless it's a monopolistic geography where the firm's interests are protected due to entry barriers, otherwise it's a road to perdition.

Design Considerations

In the era of Cloud, AI and Analytics an airline need not worry about IT infrastructure irrespective of its size – small or big and the number of customers it is serving. All the sophisticated AI tools coupled with the traditional CRM we have talked about in this chapter can be easily supported by a variety of cloud infrastructure will the bulk of AI algorithms running on cloud interface exchanging information with the mobile devices and smart systems (voice recognition, face recognition and intelligent bots). Even best of breed analytics can run on the back end cloud systems with the flexibility of increasing or decreasing infrastructure based on the market or customer load. These design considerations tend to suit both low cost and full service airlines. Within the cloud space airlines can choose to opt for private or public cloud as per their prevalent needs. Similarly, developing proprietary AI algorithms or opting for standard ones can be a design consideration in the AI space and have an impact on the long term customer experience. A lot of these design considerations and how it impacts customer convenience is influenced by the market positioning of the airliner and its IT, Operations and Marketing strategy.

CUSTOMER LOYALTY AND CUSTOMER EXPERIENCE

The popular debate in the late 90's to early 2000's was whether to be Product Centric or Customer Centric with both having its pros and cons. With the steady rise of social media and online channels, Omni channel Customer Experience has become the norm. Organizations do not have a choice but to be in top 3 in delivering Customer Experience in their industry.

Do customer centric organizations enjoy higher customer equity? As they say, the proof lies in the pudding. Southwest Airlines dropped to number 3 spot in the Forrester's Customer Experience Index for 2019 behind Jet Blue due to the cancellation of more than 100 flights per day but regained the top spot in the 2020 rankings because of its long term Customer Centric strategy, design and processes. AI enabled CRM and other digital technologies will help marketers make improved decisions leading to higher customer lifetime value (Agrawal et al., 2019).

So while AI, IOTs can support and augment customer relationship management, Long term Customer Experience Strategy remains the key to a successful AI based CRM implementation delivering its intended benefits year after year. What can augment customer experience and thus loyalty? A comprehensive loyalty management solution.

Loyalty Management is now seen as a necessity rather than an option. Nowadays, Customer Loyalty looks beyond traditional fly, earn and burn model. Loyalty management is definitely a tool for Customer Retention, ensuring Customer needs are met and exceeded. AI can help in personalized loyalty management solution by rolling out personalized offers basis on Customer Persona gathered from social tracking and past transactions with the Airline. Data Science has shown to have a significant impact on Customer acquisition campaigns (Schwartz, Bradlow, & Fader, 2017) to predict churn well in advance (Ascarza, 2018) and suggest offers to enhance customer retention (Overgoor, Chica, Rand, & Weishampel, 2019).

AI powered CRM will facilitate detailed insights about the customers by following their detailed digital journeys (Batra & Keller, 2016). This works as a feedback loop to optimize the customer journeys and improve Customer Lifetime Value (Verhoef & Donkers, 2005).

AI powered online customer journeys can be used for meaningful targeting and retargeting basis the interactions. For example, a customer living in a very cold weather may be interested in a vacation on the beach side, so planning a vacation for this customer and throwing in relevant offers will really be appealing for the customer.

AI AND SMART TECHNOLOGIES INITIATIVES ACROSS THE GLOBE IMPACTING CRM AND CUSTOMER SATISFACTION DURING THE PANDEMIC

"According to a recent survey (Business Wire, 2018) 97.2% of the aviation companies are working towards deploying big data, and artificial intelligence, with 76.5% of the firms are leveraging the value of collected data and empowering AI for cognitive learning initiatives."

The current pandemic has accelerated adoption by aviation industry, many airlines and airports have started using facial recognition systems and robots to help maintain social distancing and avoid the spread of infection. Some of the noteworthy initiatives are discussed below

- Use of humanoid robot (Travel + Leisure, 2018) for helping travellers with the boarding process at Bangalore International Airport, India very similar to the one at Incheon (Future Travel Experience, 2020).
- DigiYatra introduced by Ministry of Civil Aviation, India which will process information through facial recognition at checkpoints, provide digital guidance systems, offer interactive kiosks and augmented reality apps for travellers.
- Airports in Singapore and Hong Kong are relying on thermal screening for monitoring passengers and robots to sanitise the airport.
- Airlines, like Etihad, has been working on developing interactive automated kiosks that are an all-in-one system to check travellers' temperature and heart rate before issuing their tickets and can process the massive volume of biometric data.

DEVELOPING THE CRM DEPLOYMENT FRAMEWORK

In this section we will develop a framework which will help us understand the Customer Lifecycle of Aviation Industry and successfully deploy AI based Smart CRM system.

An Airliner can successfully deploy an AI powered Smart CRM system by following a rigorous four step process.

1. Define – Define the objectives of a Smart CRM system – how it caters to and adjusts to the needs of the customers dynamically? Align these objectives with the Customer Journey to ensure all facets of the Customer Journey are

Figure 2. Customer lifecycle in aviation

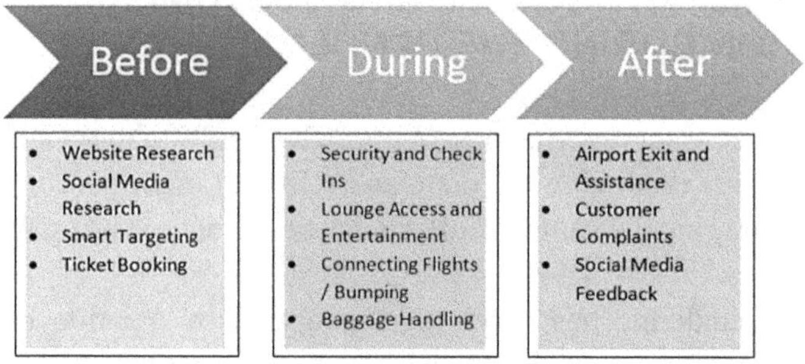

covered. A robust and well-articulated define step ensures 60% less issues in the successive steps.

2. Design – After a successful and smart definition of the objectives and customer strategy a robust design is a key to any Smart CRM implementation. Many of these design considerations including the right organizational structure, IT strategy, Marketing strategy is the key to successful and fructifying implementation.
3. Develop – A robust design makes the development so much easy. An agile based implementation using CI/CD pipeline and having a flexible cloud strategy can be the game changer. With the advent of newer technologies and upgradation of the existing ones a flexible architecture saves cost and ensures long term alignment with the overall customer and marketing strategy of the organization.

Figure 3. Framework for deploying AI based smart CRM using customer lifecycle

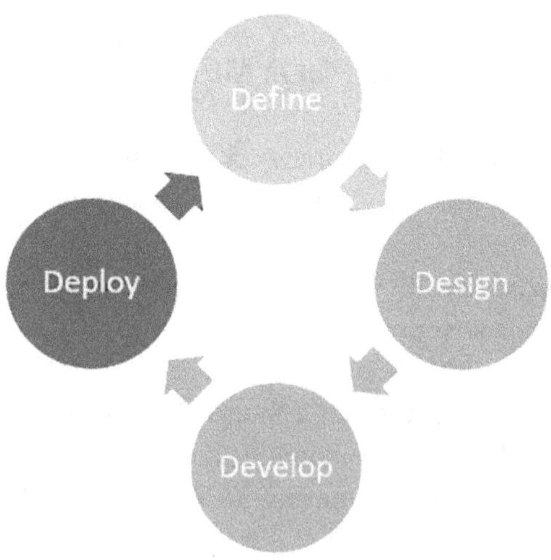

4. Deploy – If an organization has diligently followed the first three steps – define, design and develop as mentioned above, the fourth step is a cake walk with 60-80% less bugs, unpleasant surprises, and cost overruns.

CONCLUSION AND THE ROAD AHEAD

The current pandemic has pushed the adoption of digital systems to an unprecedented level, what the industry may have witnessed after four or five years has been realized in the last two years. In the next five years we may see this adoption getting exacerbated with sophisticated AI powered systems replacing all manual systems in most of the industries. Airlines may be the front runner in contactless customer recognition and surveillance to a point that everything in the airline customer journey may get automated.

It will be a world of hyper personalization, the trip is planned for the customer by the smart bot, ensuring a value for money deal for the customer. On the day of the travel the moment the customer enters the airport lobby he or she is virtually recognized, checked in, standard security procedures are done on the fly and the passenger is directed using Augmented Reality for the boarding lounge. There is no queue and no waiting, everything is well organized, and whatever a customer prefers to drink and eat is served at the airport and in flight when he or she needs it. Inflight entertainment is again hyper personalized based on the content he or she prefers to watch. Each and every minute is well spent, overall turnaround time is reduced. A voice bot on the customer's mobile or a nearby kiosk can be the trusted guide if a customer is looking for additional information in the language preferred by him or her.

Unarguably the use of AI in CRM will enhance customer satisfaction levels in the Airline industry, however the marketers have to be prudent in its selection to ensure they are not crossing the boundaries to become intrusive and hyper targeting should not lead to customer discrimination (World Economic Forum, 2018).

REFERENCES

Agrawal, Gans, & Goldfarb. (2019). Economic policy for artificial intelligence. *Innovation Policy and the Economy, 19*(1), 139–159.

Altexsoft. (2018). *7 Ways Airlines Use Artificial Intelligence and Data Science to Improve Operations.* https://www.altexsoft.com/blog/datascience/7-ways-how-airlines-use-artificial-intelligence-and-data-science-to-improve-their-operations/

Ascarza. (2018). Retention futility: Targeting high-risk customers might be ineffective. *JMR, Journal of Marketing Research*, *55*(1), 80–98.

Batra, R. (2016). Integrating marketing communications: New findings, new lessons, and new ideas. *Journal of Marketing*, *80*(6), 122–145.

Business Wire. (2018). *New Vantage Partners Releases Annual Big Data Executive Survey for 2018, Data and Innovation: How Big Data and AI are Driving Business Innovation*. https://www.businesswire.com/news/home/20180108005172/en/NewVantage-Partners-Releases-Annual-Big-Data-Executive

De Keyser, S. K. (2019). Frontline service technology infusion: Conceptual archetypes and future research directions. *Journal of Service Management*, *30*(1), 156–183.

Future Travel Experience. (2020). *Incheon Airport presses ahead with AI, biometrics and big data plans amid global COVID-19 pandemic*. https://www.futuretravelexperience.com/2020/05/incheon-airport-presses-ahead-ai-biometrics-big-data/

Haenlein & Kaplan. (2019). A brief history of artificial intelligence: On the past, present, and future of artificial intelligence. *California Management*, *61*(4), 5-14.

Hoyer, W. D., Kroschke, M., Schmitt, B., Kraume, K., & Shankar, V. (2020). Transforming the customer experience through new technologies. *Journal of Interactive Marketing*, *51*, 57–71.

Huang, M. H., & Rust, R. T. (2018). Artificial intelligence in service. *Journal of Service Research*, *21*(2), 155–172.

Luo, X., Tong, S., Fang, Z., & Qu Frontiers, Z. (2019). machines vs. humans: The impact of artificial intelligence chatbot disclosure on customer purchases. *Marketing Science*, *38*(6), 937–947.

Overgoor, G., Chica, M., Rand, W., & Weishampel, A. (2019). Letting the computers take over: Using AI to solve marketing problems. *California Management Review*, *61*(4), 156–185.

Power, J. D. (2017). *Despite Inflammatory Incidents, Airline Customer Satisfaction Keeps Improving, J.D. Power Finds Alaska Airlines, Southwest Airlines Rank Highest in Respective Segments*. https://www.jdpower.com/business/press-releases/jd-power-2017-north-america-airline-satisfaction-study

PRNewswire. (2018). *Global $2.2 Bn Artificial Intelligence in Aviation Market 2018-2025: Market to Grow at a CAGR of 46.65%*. https://www.prnewswire.com/news-releases/global-22-bn-artificial-intelligence-in-aviation-market-2018-2025-market-to-grow-at-a-cagr-of-4665-300618741.html

Schwartz, E. M., Bradlow, E. T., & Fader, P. S. (2017). Customer acquisition via display advertising using multi-armed bandit experiments. *Marketing Science*, *36*(4), 500–522.

Travel + Leisure. (2018). *Humanoid Robot, KEMPA, Introduced for Passenger Assistance at Bengaluru Airport*. https://www.travelandleisureindia.in/trending/humanoid-robot/

Verhoef, P. C., & Donkers, B. (2005). The effect of acquisition channels on customer loyalty and cross-buying. *Journal of Interactive Marketing*, *19*(2), 31–43.

World Economic Forum. (2018). *How to prevent discriminatory outcomes in machine learning*. Working Paper.

Chapter 11
The Role of Artificial Intelligence in the Automation of Human Resources

Anjali Rai
Vignana Jyothi Institute of Management (VJIM), Hyderabad, India

Amar Kumar Mishra
Graphic Era University, India

ABSTRACT

Organizational effectiveness is dependent on how resourcefully and effectively people, process, and technology unite and bring value at best cost. Artificial intelligence facilitates to automate most of the back office transactional effort in that way enabling rapid service delivery. AI competencies are scaling new heights and changing the way employee work in this ever-changing corporate world. AI has the power to change various employee skill through quick and accurate processing of a large amount of the data from recruitment to talent management.

INTRODUCTION

Organizational effectiveness is contingent on how resourcefully and effectually individuals, processes, and technical knowhow unite to deliver the cost effective value. AI facilitates mechanization of the majority of back office transactional efforts thus enabling rapid service delivery. AI as a new technology defines the new normal in working trade. This new methodology automates and complete majority of the human resource functions of low value nature thus a better focal point of the strategic

DOI: 10.4018/978-1-7998-7959-6.ch011

length of work may be determined. AI as a technology implemented presents the scope to upgrade various employee skills via accurate processing of a huge amount of the data like recruitment to talent management and that too in short amount of time. Additionally, AI competencies are ever scaling new heights and changing the work ethos in today's dynamic corporate world. Besides, AI can be successfully integrated into the employee lifecycle, right from hiring and onboarding, to various HR functions and career opportunities thus paving way for a personalized worker experience. AI enables HR teams to draw understandings from the data and provide real-time feedback. It also eliminates many human errors and predispositions in a function as important and responsible as human resource management. Therefore, any resolution influenced by AI has the potential to be time-saving, precise, reliable, and unbiased.

A new norm in today's demand is Intelligent Automation. It is achieved when AI blends with automation and facilitates machines to be intelligent self-learning capable of performing on their own or with least human support. Intelligent automation has potential to achieve physical capabilities and cognitive abilities to make decisions as any human might do. AI competency level enables machines to diagnose processes and identify any deviation. Moreover, AI can be deployed across all repeating processes to increase their efficiency and productivity thus bringing about innovation. AI in HR enables ever-increasing prospects and generates ground breaking value for the Human Resources Professional.

EVOLUTION OF ARTIFICIAL INTELLIGENCE IN HUMAN RESOURCES

Artificial Intelligence began as a research area in the 1950s, to understand the nature of intelligence in living organisms, exclusively of the humans (Mesquita, L. Daniel, 2018). The increase of the information quantity in the databases, initiate in many practical troubles of optimization, has encouraged the study and relevance of unconventional techniques in the investigate of techniques that can attain good solutions, such as, to conjugate concepts of Optimization and Artificial Intelligence (Cançado, L. Vera, Vendramine F. M. Corrêa, A. Dalila, Oliveira, J. Elizângela, and Castro. P. S. Dagmar, 2017). Recently, much concentration has been given to the machine learning, most likely due to the countless possibilities of automation brought by recent advances in Artificial Intelligence (Nascimento, M. Alexandre, and Queiroz. M.C Anna, 2017). Further, it is anticipated that the force of Artificial Intelligence development will go away from modifying the nature of work, causing transformation in economic mechanisms and business models, which will probably bring impacts to management (Loebbecke, Claudia, and Picot, Arnold, 2015). In human resources areas, this has been one of the most impacted by new trends and is undergoing a major changing in repositioning terms and their new role within organization. Human Resource Management (HRM) has become a strategic movement in organizations (Barreto, M. Leilianne., Silva, P. Maíra, Fischer, L. André, Albuquerque, G. Lindolfo, and Amorim, A.C. Wilson, 2011). HRM has been growing, driven by economic, political, social and mainly technological revolutions, as well as by the demands of competitiveness and operational excellence Cançado, L. Vera, Vendramine F. M. Corrêa, A. Dalila, Oliveira, J. Elizângela, and Castro. P. S. Dagmar,2017).It is essential to comprehend that Human Resources Management (HRM) strategy is concerned with employment policies and practices, which includes recruitment, selection, evaluation, development and retention of employees, as well as recruitment, consultation and negotiation with people (Boxall, Peter, and Purcell, John,2011). The integration of human resources and organization strategies is comprised by depiction of HRM's at the organization's top level of decision-making (Brewster, Chris, and Hegewisch, Ariane, 1994). Thus, the higher the reliability of information, the more confident the decision-making will be. In this perspective, AI comes as a system of tremendous significance, performing as a supporter and powering the effectiveness of the Human Resources (HR) area.

POSSIBILITIES OF AI CAPABILITIES WITH HR FUNCTIONS

AI presents intellectual engines that enable employees to take the day-to-day workplace decisions. Few of the decisions and responsibilities are as follows:

- **Maintaining Employee Data:** This includes personal information like address, emergency contact number, organizational records, and leaves status, etc. Informal AI may also facilitate KPI-oriented and analytical data.
- **Skill Training:** In the present scenario of skill development, AI is a game changer by removing training gaps. AI is helping in creating a personalized learning path via informal analytics which helps attaining new heights in the learning and development. To plan digital training opportunities manager can identify the skill gap in his current workforce. Apart from these, managers and employees can track digital training with the help of Conversational AI.
- **Recruitment:** To enable the screening of candidates accurately, intellectual solutions provided by AI helps in analyzing multiple sources of data at once. Also AI is helping in removing human preconceptions in the candidate shortlisting. Huge organizations moving towards developing & implementing the Job Descriptions which are AI-oriented, thus helping the organizational requirement in the screening of candidates.

- **Automation for Day to Day Responsibility:** Usually various small responsibility takes a lot of time of HR professional e.g. Induction orientation, employee queries regarding attendance leave and basic benefit questions. In such a situation AI can regulate and automate the HR process and employee expectation from HR by providing support to strategic work performed by HR Professionals.
- **Employee Engagement**: AI provides employee engagement responsibility such as intelligent surveys, real-time feedback for better results, keeping a record for reward and recognitions and many more.AI is a strong catalyst in creating an ecosystem where organization requirements and expectations from the employee is clear.
- **AI Role in Human Resource Management:** AI has an essential role in combining the major HR functions thus revamping the total employee experience. It provides support to the talent processes so as to decrease the attrition thus controlling important areas such as talent acquisition, human resource planning, learning and development, performance management, HR analytics, and self-service online support.

BARRIERS TO IMPLEMENTING AI IN HR

- **Dearth of Skilled Workforce**: Integrating HR function with technology can be a very costly process as there is a huge gap a skilled employee. Keeping dearth of skilled workforce organizations are facing a lot of challenges in adopting AI-based HR functions. Due to the lack of skilled technical people for integrating HR functions, it is very costly.
- **Confidentiality Apprehension**: Due to highly confidential nature of the HR data, its security is paramount. In such a situation Data protection is a big worry while integrating HR function and technology through AI. Most of the organization is facing a big challenge in maintaining the data security concern.
- **Process Maintenance:** As we know every technology-driven process needs regular maintenance. Just like other technologies, AI involved process needs regular feedback, up-gradation, and meticulous maintenance process.
- **Multifaceted Integrating Capacity:** As most of the organization is going through a technological transformation due to this reason data availability is very limited therefore HR function with technology through AI is facing challenges.

KEY CONCERN AREAS IN ADOPTING AI IN HR

As technological advancements are growing at a rapid pace, the organization needs to use the AI systems with utmost care. This chapter will provide insights for the cautions organization should follow while implementing AI systems effectively:

- **Discovering Accurate Data Sets:** Organization vision with AI-enabled process needs Real-time and exact data for better AI results. For better effectiveness, unbiased data need to be processed. Thus organizations need to get the right set of data and then an understandable purpose for result-oriented output.
- **Enabling the Right AI Process:** AI implementation requires a specific set of knowledge skills and attitudes to integrate the HR function with technology. The specific set of o KSA consists of the right set of data sources for AI-enabled organization function. However, AI functioning is unlike the IT environment.
- **Transparency:** It becomes vital to achieve clear understanding; therefore, the process should have a result-oriented objective.
- **Remove Unfairness: As AI is Known for Fast and Accurate Unbiased Results.** Make sure data should be accurate and always keep this in mind, AI will do what organizations want it to do and will not make a decision for the organization.

ROLE OF AI IN RESHAPING THE WORLD OF HR

In today's competitive world to uncover and retain the best talent and to shift the struggle while doing so human resources (HR) and talent acquisition professionals are revolving to the enormous power of AI. As per a survey of HR leaders by Oracle (2019), "AI is becoming more prominent, with 50 percent of workers currently using some form of AI at work compared to only 32 percent last year Vargas, 2018." The struggle for top talented human resources is as difficult as ever. To discover and catch the attention of the talented human resource for a given role has become a competitive advantage, the talent can develop a loyal and impartial atmosphere for those talents with whom organizations do end up hiring.

AI is constantly reshaping the HR function for better and accurate results. Organizations are regularly seeking a new way to do their day-to-day HR function such as recruiting induction training and many more. In recent years, The HR world has changed. A massive motive for this change has been the beginning of technology in many of its functions. AI is ready to change it even further and this can be an encouraging revolution if a suitable concern is taken to make certain exact implementation. To change the HR function with the AI's power to change will be particularly obvious in the startup prospect. The new normal with AI's power to change HR functions are at the next level such as the hiring, administrative to managerial function, and workforce engagement.

The most recent progressions in machine learning and AI are quickly accomplishing the majority, according to Emily He, SVP, Human Capital Management Cloud Business Group at Oracle. This has a huge consequence on the way people across the globe interrelate with technology and their groups. The relationship amongst individuals and machines is redefined at work, and there is no one-size-fits-all tactic to efficaciously manage this change. Most of the organizations need to collaborate with Human Resource organizations to personalize the move toward employing Artificial Intelligence at the workplace to gather the changing prospects of the players across the world.

- AI role in Empowering Startups to Hire the Right Talent:

AI not only reduces the time-consuming HR day-to-day function, apart from this AI helps the organization to transform their hiring process. Earlier in absence of AI, Startups might have faced a lot of difficult scenarios in competing against large companies; However, AI has the power to transform any process of the startup organizations. AI-enabled software provides complete automation to HR functions such as hiring process. AI resolved the problem of the startup, simply such organization needs to share the job opening and explain the expected attribute of the ideal employee, rest of AI-enabled software provide the expected solution. As we all know the technology is too smart therefore HR department need not worry about hiring procedures such as resume screening, candidate inquiries reply, and keeping in contact with the candidate. ATS (Applicant Tracking System) was the beginning of an AI transform HR process. Now startups are transforming their HR functions with the help of Chatbots. These can keep candidates in conversations and resolve routine recruitment problems immediately. As startups have lesser human resources, thus AI-powered HR transformation helps the organization for an automation process to manage and retain talent.HR professionals have a lot of work, time management is the key to competitive advantage.AI in empowering the startups to manage their day-to-day work accurately.

- Developing Talent Management to Improve Productivity and Contentment

Startups have to work hard to retain talented human resource once they get it. AI enabled solution provide enormous opportunities. Managing Employee engagement and recruitment become very easy with chat bots. Not only has this employee felt more comfortable with AI driven solutions. They can easily check their concern about things like payroll, healthcare facility provided by organization and their leaves without bothering any HR professional. Talent retention is purely based on employee engagement and new learning and challenging opportunity. Higher productivity is a key output of this process. Faster startup growth is based on highly productive workforce. Performance management based on employee surveys, these process need to be regular and simple, requiring plethora of manual data analysis. AI driven process powered the organization to conduct employee evaluation on a daily basis. AI driven system facilitates mentoring and monitoring of employee performance at any point of time. Employee training and development is possible because of AI-driven solutions.

- Allocating Employees to be Part of the Process

AI automation and machine learning supported a lot to make the employee engagement activities. AI-driven solutions are not only serving the HR profession but also helping the employee by resolving their concern. AI are playing a very crucial role in the decision making process. AI allowing the system to resolve the problem before they even arise. AI provides a conducive environment where everyone in the team can communicate with each other. The Human Resource division is accountable for psychological resilience and emotional health of an employee separately from their work involvements. AI-enabled systems facilitate observing and analyzing employees' feel related to the business process. The HR professional is then able to decide whether the individual employee needs a break or can continue.

- Providing a Result-Oriented System

As per the World Economic Forum's Future of Jobs Report (2020), "97 million new roles may emerge that are more adapted to the new division of labour between humans, machines, and algorithms." However, keeping that human feel will linger a vital part of keeping a brawny, brilliant, and proficient human resource. As the COVID-19 pandemic demanding many employees to work from home, reports says that HR and Admin opening will be in demand in the upcoming months. As the last decade guided in major shifts in the industry, containing the growing adoption of AI, HR and Admin professionals can expect to see exciting developments with their profession.

AI-driven processes are offering collaborative partnerships between human and machine-oriented work. The presence of AI in HR function means to have experts on board to keep confirm such ongoing systems and processes are operating effectively.

Usually, AI trainers handled manual data translation into AI-ready data where they keep a proper record of ins and out of job openings. Usually they will identify the important information, making sure the right information is shared in proper way during the recruitment process. Most of the HR admin role will be handled by AI in future. This way these departments can focus largely on strategic work and future planning of the organizational development. AI enabled process will pay more crucial role as new employee navigate a virtual workshop for better understanding of the work and organization.

Integration of Artificial Intelligence to the Human resource process makes an organization effective as AI-enabled systems becomes more efficient in analyzing, predicting and diagnosing its support to HR professionals for right and accurate decisions.

- AI-Supported Chatbots Make Engagement Conversation Going

In an organizational structure employee engagement is considered as a science, and as the definition of states, it is a systematic knowledge means gauging, analyzing and observing employees feeling on regular or day-to-day basis. AI-supported chatbots empowers both the individual employee and HR professionals to keep the engagement with a continuous dialogue, over the time. These conversations are then analyzed and utilized to comprehend the precise apprehensions, requirements of the individual employee. But it doesn't over here. The deed following the discussion is just equivalent as taking the feedback for the first time. AI-supported chatbots let's HR professionals to comprehend believing thus they can take care of the potential barriers while taking an action and show to the individual employee their influences, it in turn enhances engagement and negatively effects turnover.

- Improving Learning and Development Programs

In the near future, learning and development departments integrated with Artificial Intelligence will improve enormously. Most of the Learning and development departments will be anticipated to create readily adaptable and agile learning and development programs that are proficient enough in meeting the personal requirements of the employees. To showcase the impact of AI-driven processes most of the professionals will start using the data analytics extensively.

Training and development is not just responsible for training people in skills of Artificial Intelligence and digital agility but also need to prepare employees for new or different roles that will undoubtedly call for more human skillsets: analytical skill, strategic mindset, critical thinking, cultural awareness, emotional intelligence. To familiarize with these alterations, L&D departments are adapting to responsive and receptive learning models that supports individual learning as opposed to just providing organizations with the broad-based solutions. To support the organization process and employee day to day responsibilities, there are the ways by which organizations are improving their employee engagement and experience by adopting AI:

- Special learning program based on the job role and responsibility, current skillfulness, growth and development strategy, expected key result areas or goals, and proactively making a strategy to fill any existing skills gaps based on the current job and responsibilities.
- Allocating broaden assignments and cross-functional team's projects based on employee skill sets and projects listed across the organization through social learning channels.
- The allocated project should be based on the competency of employees and a background check should be conducted on employee interest areas.
- Most of the time employees are facing loads of problems related to their current role and for such concern accessibility of chatbots for frequently asked questions for a real-time response should be given. For real-time problem employees can easily type the questions and immediately get an automated response.
- For all the frequently asked questions via chatbots, a Real-time response is readily accessible to all employees.
- A well-observed chatbots accessible to leaders helps then in their roles.
    - Impact of Transactional Workforce Data

As we are living in the world of data HR professionals can HR utilize AI-enabled systems to influence transactional workforce data to foresee employee latency, tiredness, carelessness leading to risk, and their complete engagement, eventually leads to more productive and effective conversations which eventually helps employee engagement, performance and retention.

Today, it is very easy to utilize Artificial Intelligence and make smart personalized schedules for an individual employee and real-time change requests can be included for the benefits fits of the organization so change can be incorporated on time. AI empowers employee, usually, those who are coordinating with multiple people and multiple departments, their job expectation is very high. In order to improve the work-life balance, AI is playing a very crucial role in managing repetitive administrative requests. It also facilitates free space for the manager and in return they have ample time for handling the customer and designing the job role-oriented training program.

- Empowering Workforce Analytics

Most of the establishments are spinning to workforce analytics and planning. Role of AI and machine learning is day-by-day becoming more evident across these workforce analytics functions. Integration of AI with the HR process supports HR professionals to resolve complications and can direct towards more efficient choices that influence individual employee and complete organizational growth.

CONCLUSION

This chapter provides the benefits of Integrating HR function with technology through AI. AI and HR together can definitely help in increasing employee productivity and a better understanding between the employee and HR resource can also be achieved. HR applications along with AI are capable of examining, predicting and supporting decision-making for the key stakeholders. Adopting AI solutions that organization need, considering the culture of your organization and build up the required Digital platform. Employees will be eventually obligated by the AI functioning and can affirm about having a prompt and perfect user experience. Thus it is essential to focus on needs of the employees and get the expected outcomes that organization is expecting.

HR data security concern is quite a challenge in AI development. All employee data must be secured and proper set of instructions must be setup for managing AI-driven HR involvement. The instructions must not just deal with technical and accurate set of data recording processes; it must also check the diverse legal aspects.

A well-built AI system will encourage a deeper thoughtfulness towards human resource behavior. By combining and broadly analyzing employees, attitudes, and intentions on different digital platforms human behavior can be replicated and validated for useful employee experience.

REFERENCES

Barreto, Silva, Fischer, Albuquerque, & Amorim. (2011). Emerging issues in people management: An analysis of academic output. *Administration Magazine UFSM, 4*(1), 215-232.

Boxall, P., & Purcell, J. (2011). *Strategy and Human Resource Management*. Macmillan International Higher Education.

Brewster, C., & Hegewisch, A. (1994). Human resource management in Europe: Issues and opportunities. *Policy & Practice*.

Cançado. Corrêa, Oliveira, & Dagmar. (2017). Revisiting the Four Faces of Human Resource Management. *ANPAD Meetings – Enanpad*, 1-4.

Loebbecke, C., & Picot, A. (2015). Reflections on societal and business model transformation arising from digitization and big data analytics: A research agenda. The Journal of Strategic Information Systems, 24(3), 149–157.

Mesquita, L. D. (2018). The "Artificial" Consumer: Approaches between Artificial Intelligence and Marketing. *ANPAD Meetings –Enanpad*, 3-6.

Nascimento, Alexandre, & Queiroz. (2017). Overview of research on Artificial Intelligence in Administration in Brazil. *ANPAD Meetings – Enanpad*, 1-4.

Oracle. (2019). *New Study: 64% of People Trust a Robot More Than Their Manager*. Retrieved from: https://www.oracle.com/corporate/pressrelease/robots-at-work-101519.html

World Economic Forum. (2020). *The Future of Jobs Report 2020*. Retrieved from: https://www.weforum.org/reports/the-future-of-jobs-report-2020

Chapter 12
Conceptualizing the Use of Artificial Intelligence in Customer Relationship Management and Quality of Services:
A Digital Disruption in the Indian Banking System

Parag Shukla
https://orcid.org/0000-0002-7014-163X
The Maharaja Sayajirao University of Baroda, Vadodara, India

Sofia Devi Shamurailatpam
Faculty of Commerce, The Maharaja Sayajirao University of Baroda, India

ABSTRACT

In this chapter, the authors have conceptualized a hypothetical comprehensive model of AI, CRM, and quality of services by banks given the underlying pull and push factors that determine the extent of AI adoption by the banks. This chapter shall also serve as a primer to demonstrate the effects of use of artificial intelligence in the Indian banks and is also aimed to encapsulate the restraining and facilitating forces that drive adoption of AI. This chapter examines the blooming development of artificial intelligence and its significance in the operational efficiency in terms of management of issues related to customers while accessing different products and services offered by banks. In other words, the use of artificial intelligence technologies

DOI: 10.4018/978-1-7998-7959-6.ch012

can dramatically improve banks' ability to achieve four key outcomes: higher profits, at-scale personalization, rapid innovation cycles, strategic customer relationship management (CRM), and distinctive omni-channel experiences. The role of artificial intelligence (AI) is significant in the banking industry for operational efficiency.

INTRODUCTION

India has witnessed waves of technological disruptions eased by the advancement of Information and Technology (IT) sector, covering vast ecosystem under the digital platform of over 700 million internet users, making as world's second largest country in digitalization. One such outcome of technological innovation and digitization is the emergence of Artificial Intelligence (AI) and adoption of the same in different sectors of the economy. As we know that there the use of artificial intelligence (AI) by organizations including the government institutions is on the rise for dealing with governance mechanisms in the deployment of qualitative and efficient services. Indeed, most of the industries are aware about the concept of artificial intelligence and potentials of such technology, recognizing that if firms do not deploy such highly skilled technologies within the short span of one to two years; such firms will face difficulty to compete with their counterparts in the years to come who will offer the value added services. Banking industry has been gradually adopting the new technology in the form of digital mode of banking, financial innovations under digitalization reforms and working jointly with the FinTech firms in the delivery of services and products. However, banking industry has a very specific feature given its complex and heterogeneous products & services which covers multiple groups of heterogeneous customer data, which requires high degree of compliance for a smooth regulatory framework. It is thus imperative to understand the regulatory expectations around the use of AI for its implementation and monitoring as a first step if firms are to fully exploit the potential of AI and machine learning (ML) technology, in a sustainable and operationally resilient manner (PWC, 2019).

Over the period, the Reserve Bank of India have geared towards developing efficient and secure payment and settlement systems with focus on their greater penetration through availability of user-friendly platforms at affordable cost (RBI, 2020). The Indian banking industry has been in the forefront of adoption of newer technologies to redefine more sophisticated and qualitative services to the customers. Banks have been significantly improving the use of technology in the form of user interfaces, multiple delivery channels, payment gateways, dashboards, core banking solutions and internal control mechanisms for protection so as to increase the overall operational efficiency. Above these, use of AI-powered platforms reduces costs or production in terms of data storage and processing, which makes easier for banks to connect and access across time and space. The outcome of the use of these services has brought higher automation and improvement in quality of human decision making in terms of speed as well as accuracy to reduce and mitigate the inherent risks involved. In other words, the use of artificial intelligence technologies can dramatically improve banks' ability to achieve four key outcomes viz., higher profits; at-scale personalization; rapid innovation cycles; strategic CRM and distinctive Omni-channel experiences. For example, the deployment of AI is now taking place to help categorize different payments, offer a source of advice and a resource for answering queries via chat bots and provide suggestions to customers based on their spending history. Indian banks have already started on their journey to use of artificial intelligence and most of the banks have experienced improvements in better customer engagement, higher competitiveness, accelerated innovation, higher margins and improved business intelligence, among others and hence aggregate potential cost savings for banks from application of such artificial intelligence in front, middle and back offices estimated at USD 447 billion by the year 2023 (IDRBT, 2020).

Given the digital platform and intense competition, banks earnestly attempt to provide efficient and qualitative services to multiple customers and it remains as the primary objectives in the day to day businesses. Digitalization of banking services and products not only provide the better services to customers but it also increase operational efficiency in terms of the time taken in delivery of services and products. Banks are therefore, converging towards the technology and its digital innovations in order to leverage out for delivering superior banking experience to its customers with a view to adapt customer centric approach from time to time. The successful business of the banking industry relies on how it can manage and adapt different customer relationships in a given integrated solution across all customers' information systems of the bank. This not only provides better experience to customers but also impacted total sales potentials, profitability and net margins for a healthy balance sheet. Customer relationship management (CRM) is an important term that banks need to focus in their banking practices, strategy mechanisms and the relevant suitable technologies adopted to control and manage data for different customers with a view to improve the overall business relationships with customers through meeting the requirements of the customers for better operational efficiency. A superior experience to customers can produce significant impact and long-term benefits to performance of banks and its operational efficiency.

This chapter gives a comprehensive content of how the adoption of AI by banks can influence the working and functioning of Indian banking system from the perspectives of quality of services and products offered to customers. We have developed a conceptualized model that depicts the linkages between adoption of AI by banks, the role of customer relationship management (CRM) and the consequent output that can be operationalized as superior quality of services delivered to different customers under the given digital platform. The entire chapter contains seven sections. Section II gives a brief review of literatures and some aspects of theoretical underpinnings followed by Section III, describing the existing literature gaps in the domain. Section IV highlights the main objectives of the study and research methodology. The next section presents a brief note on the evolution of AI and its underlying factors in the banking industry. Section VI explains about technology and the factors of digitization in banking sector in India. In Section VII, the interplay of facilitating and restraining forces for adoption of AI in Banking. The next Section VIII explains the conceptual model in which the association between AI, CRM and quality of services in banks is conceptualized. Section IX gives the managerial implications of the adoption of AI in banking sector. At the end, Section X concludes with some policy recommendations.

REVIEW OF RELEVANT LITERATURE: THEORETICAL UNDERPINNINGS

Research in the field of artificial intelligence and its integration with customer relationship management of banks is in the nascent stage. Our study shall be a novel contribution in the existing literature of the ongoing landscape in application of diverse aspects of AI in Indian banks highlighting its antecedents and barriers to enhance the service quality to customers.AI technology has enormous potential to shape India's economic and national security future (Vempati, 2016) and recently adopted as one of tools for bank failure prediction (Altman et al., 1994; Martin, 1977 & Wang et al., 2014). One of the significant challenges of the commercial banks is the customer relationship management (CRM) under the oligopolistic nature of market structure, wherein banks are producing more or less similar types of products. Customer relationship management is significant in organizational structural process in the formation, exertion and enhancement of long-term associations with customers and many firms have invested in CRM technology which has brought new technology-based solutions to manage customer relationships designed in such a way to suit IT solutions to support the CRM process (Srivastava, Shervani & Fahey, 1999; Rigby, Reichheld & Schefter, 2002; Day, 2000). In other words, the management of relationship with customers is one of the prime functions of banking operations and has significant impact in the overall performance and value addition towards generating of loyalty to customers. CRM technologies help with the interaction between commercial banks and their customers (Jayachandran et al., 2005). From various reports and studies on the issues of adoption and use of AI in financial services, it is clear that it can be used in different core business of commercial banks. Application of AI in commercial banks suggest that using artificial intelligence, commercial banks can reduce losses in lending, increase security in processing payments, automate compliance related work, and improve customer targeting (Konigstorfer & Thalmann, 2020). Retrospective studies on the applications of artificial intelligence particularly in the field of behavioural finance constitutes major significance undertaken by promising AI experts that describes about how lenders are able to predict the creditworthiness of people which they have never met and also to analyse from the annual reports to predict financial distress (Onay and Ozturk, 2018; Oskarsdottiretet al., 2018; Diakopoulos, 2016; Gomez Martinez et al., 2019; Gandhi et al., 2019). In addition to theses, studies in behavioural finance also investigated how financial information can be made understandable for individual investors and how to mitigate the investors' biases in wealth management (Agnew and Szykman, 2005; Bhatia et al., 2020). Another aspects of behavioural finance is the how effective is the different measures of AI in preventing AI experts from manipulating and harming investors - this requires explaining AI models and keeping track of data the AI are trained on, any human involvement in the development of AI process, how and where the AI is used in business processes; and to exploit the behaviour of investors (Diakopoulos, 2016; Bhatia et al. (2020).

Ironically, the significance of artificial intelligence in digital marketing practices, particularly in financial services is no exception, benefiting both the businesses and customers whilst its complexities in businesses targets. Looking from the perspectives of this digital era, artificial intelligence has numerous roles for financial services industry particularly the banking industry, as such from data collection at a numerous range through chatbots, emails, websites, social media platform in mass, altogether generating big data that can analyze cognitive and unstructured data which are non-verbal in nature, generally in the form of images collected through various biometric information and/or facial recognition systems. The emergence of big data and advances in technology has led to importance of integration of artificial intelligence to enhance their business practices of financial services providers on the one hand (Dwivedi et al., 2019; Haenlein and Kalpan, 2019) and better understanding of the customers effectively target them with personalized digital messages (Mogaji et al., 2020). To sum up, we can say that digital marketing has become as one of the significant digital channels and has been seen as more suitable for the new business environment (Saura et al., 2019) in the process of acquiring and retaining customers, building brands, and managing customer relationships (Kannan and Li, 2017; Mogaji et al., 2016). To say, digital revolution like artificial intelligence in financial services has contributed greatly in the expansion of financial inclusion plans of the government, and strategies to target financially vulnerable customers (Gabor and Brooks, 2017; Costa and Ehrbeck, 2015; Leong et al., 2017) in unbanked customers and underserved areas, specifically in developing countries. In other words, the artificial intelligence has far superior performance relative to human beings in the process of decision making, compilation of data and generation of huge qualitative and quantitative data of such kind in terms of volume and speed, with undue advantage of overcoming judgmental biases associated with the human beings. These all makes easier in handling, fulfilling and resolving the various dimensions of queries and complaints by diverse customers for the goods and services delivered by the banking firms.

However, despite the significant advantages of the use and adoption of artificial intelligence in banks, it is highly associated with financial frauds and constitutes an important challenge for successful operations of the financial institutions. There are other school of thoughts that have significant views of artificial intelligence as controversial as because of its independence from external inputs during and post operations (Van Esch et al., 2019) as well as the mere involvement of human is crucial in the successful adoption and operation of technologies (Agarwal & Venkatesh, 2002). But artificial intelligence is also controversial because of its independence from external inputs during and post operations Some suggest that AI should be viewed as a multifaceted concept through a human-computer interaction lens (Van Esch et al., 2019), asserting that the human factor is crucial to the successful adoption of technologies (Agarwal & Venkatesh, 2002). Study by (Mogaji et. al., 2020) has highlighted the often-ignored implications of the artificial intelligence to developers of artificial intelligence, marketers, policy makers and academicians while adopting artificial intelligence must understand the data challenges and modeling necessary for artificial intelligence deployment and evaluation to effectively reach the customers fairly and reducing information gaps in delivering various services. Therefore, ethically adoption of artificial intelligence while collecting, processing of information should look up from the perspectives of mass and vulnerable customers as well, towards well-being and satisfaction of the customers.

Given this backdrop, the role of artificial intelligence in dealing with the financial behavior and predictions specifically for banks to take precise decision in the lending process and also to redress the complaints of different customers under the intense advancement of information and technology is the need of the hour. No doubt, there are theoretical underpinnings of the use of AI in terms of its optimal size to adapt by banks and also protective mechanisms to safeguard the confidentiality of data of the customers remain deficient, requiring more area to explore about. In all, these discussions and views on different aspects of artificial intelligence framework established make a major foundation for the present study.

GAPS IN EXISTING LITERATURE

Studies in commercial banks with focus on customer relationship management have received little attention so far. Based on this research gap, this study attempts to fill up this gap by incorporating different dimensions of CRM given the adoption of artificial intelligence and digitization in delivery of banking services with the object of meeting satisfaction of the customers. Though the concept of AI and its adoption by banks are much debated recently by academicians and policy authorities to bridge the gaps in the quality products and services offered, there are no such studies wherein the concept of CRM is conceptualized in a hypothesized model of AI and efficient service delivery by banks. This study is specific in the sense that it highlights the various significant roles of the customer relationship management for meeting the expectations of the different customers leading to an increase the sales proceeds and net profits of the banks for a healthy balance sheet. Further, our study is unique and tries to fill such gaps in such a way that formulate the research agenda in a framework of association between AI and possible outcome in quality of services through leveraging the CRM as an intermediating variable to supply superior experience to customers. This conceptualized model can visualize the operational aspects of banks in a broader framework in dealing with all demands and prerequisites of customer under digital platform particularly in view of the recent post-pandemic COVID-19 experience of social and physical distancing norms.

METHODOLOGY AND OBJECTIVES

This section explains the main objectives of the present study and the methodology used to establish the linkages between adoption of artificial intelligence by banks and customer relationship management resulting into quality services to customers. The following are some of the pertinent questions that are theoretically examined in this chapter:

1. Does the use of AI increase the operational efficiency of banks?
2. How efficient are the banks in redressal of complaints of customers under the AI platform?
3. Does the use of AI improve the delivery of qualitative banking services?
4. What is the optimal size of adoption of ÀI by banks for feasible solutions?
5. How safe is the use of AI in protecting the resources of both the customer and banking institution?

These research questions are examined in the context of scheduled commercial banks in India. Data on the use and adoption of artificial intelligence by specific banks are also reported in the following section. The main contribution of this chapter is the conceptualization of hypothetical description of complex entity or process that is established in the Model 2 to portray the linkages between adoption of artificial intelligence by banks and its significant outcomes in performance to meet the requirements of different customers at their end.

EVOLUTIONARY TRENDS OF AI IN BANKING INDUSTRY

Though countries across the globe have realized the concept of 'Artificial Intelligence' in the recent years as a strategy roadmap to development, its evolution can be traced years back to the early part of 1950s. The seminal contribution by McCarthy and its team in 1955 on artificial intelligence, United States is considered as the founding father of modern revolution of Artificial Intelligence and accordingly defined it as "the science and engineering of making intelligent machines" (McCarthy et al., 2006). The basic idea behind the introduction of this innovation is to make enable machines to understand languages, concepts and sophisticated mental tasks such as interpreting conversations and problem solving without human intervention. Gradually, driven by the innovations and novel development of availability of big data, with continuous flow of mobile connectivity, accessibility and affordability to internet, new development of machine learning algorithms, among others to cite, has contributed and enabled adoption of AI within the digital platform to society. Considering the quality of services feasible using AI in terms of volume, speed, space and cognizable performance of human actions, there is a significant rise in the use of AI over the period for operational efficiency and quality services.

At this current pace in technology advancement, it will be difficult for the banking industry to deploy the traditional approach or strategic principles alone to create value in banking through firms' growth, efficiency, amalgamations and scale economies, new products development as the systematic plan of action for long-term potential growth. A new paradigm shift in banking industry performance requires including the roles of other non-bank players particularly FinTech firms, who are entering the market to grab the larger share in the supply chain of banking industry. The much talked issues on financial inclusion of targeting the underprivileged and excluded masses could only be achieved with the involvement of such FinTech firms to connect yet unreached remote areas of the country. In India, the Ministry of Commerce and Industry (2018) under the task force on artificial intelligence has identified ten specific domains of which the financial sector services have faced the challenges of FinTech to accelerate the adoption of AI based technologies. Accordingly, some of the major challenges facing FinTech companies includes balancing the scale and innovation; and anticipation of market demand. Even though the adoption of AI in the financial system may pose challenges in the form of restrictions and secrecy of data, high risk of frauds and cyber security, use of AI will help the FinTech firms in terms of volumes, storage of data with paperless, predictive analysis in project finance and investment decisions in credit and lending processes in particular. AI often requires a new structure of both centralized and decentralized activities, that can be challenging to implement and hence firms need to embrace the adaptive and agile ways of working and setting strategy that are common at startups and AI pioneers, in which AI-enabled processes requires a constant learning and adaption for both man and machine (RBI, 2017). There is significant scope of the use of artificial intelligence, machine learning and data science in core services of banks such as segmentation of customers, particularly in retail banking; prediction of non-performing assets, emotions & sentiment analysis, which are aspects of behavioral finance; credit scoring and project appraisal; market analysis; detection of frauds and malwares; big data analytics; and credit recovery mechanism; etc. To summarize, predictive and machine learning-based analytics models are also helping banks increase revenue, reduce cost and improve risk profile by facilitating informed decisions on credit underwriting, detecting frauds and defaults early, improving collections, increasing employee efficiency and transparency (IDRBT, 2020).

Along with the involvement of the FinTech firms, the penetration of internet facilities which is available at affordable prices, across geographical and demographic dimensions is significant for successful achievements with a view to bring more population under the roof of financial inclusion. This implies that the intensity of adoption of AI and its scope will be determined by the degree of internet users and its affordability to access the services from the safety, security and reliability aspects of the customers' point of view. The technological innovation of artificial intelligence in banking is a major breakthrough that empower the banking industry that are usually burdened with a vast amount of data handling, large volume and values of transactions, heavy documentation and cumbersome processes. Generally, a typical artificial intelligence in a bank uses expert systems, speech recognition, natural language processing, knowledge assimilation, human capabilities such as planning, reasoning, problem solving, perception, motion, and manipulation by using biometric information of the customers. These digital disruptions in the banking industry have impacted the culture at many financial services firms, compelling banks and financial institutions to shift from a largely product-centric perspective to a customer-centric.

The future of banking industry depicts a wider scope in working and functioning in a given complex structure with a greater role of digital technology. Unlike the global financial crisis of 2008-2009, the novel corona virus did not produce devastating impact to banking industry but it experienced the central banks of countries to alert and how to encounter such unprecedented situations, with much role of technology to fight for it upfront, other things remaining the same. This new banking model calls for a digital economy and banks' business model wherein technology is rapidly changing the contours of the financial services. It is impacting diverse ways of providing contact less financial services and products; lowering costs for users; and better information management so as to bring an overall outcome of scale economies and manage externalities and mitigate risks (Carletti et al., 2020).

TECHNOLOGY AND DIGITAL DISRUPTIONS IN INDIAN BANKS

This section gives a brief overview of the use of technology and digital revolution in the context of banking industry in India. Digitalization has transformed the traditional manual process of operational aspects of banking industry, thereby reducing human error and appended efficiency in management of time as well as building of customer loyalty. It has benefited consumers in different ways. For example, customers can access to banking services and products by sitting different corners at home/places based on their convenience and availability of timings. To sum up, it becomes very easy for the customers to do transactions through the digital payment modes or online banking services from one account to another account at any given place and point of time. Incentives in the form of cash-back money, coupons, E-wallets, National Electronic Fund Transfer (NEFT), Real Time Gross Settlement (RTGS), Unified Payment Interface (UPI), and mobile banking are some of the advantages that led to abrupt digital transformation of the banking industry. Further, digitization makes it easy and convenient for the customers as well as the bankers to provide different baskets of products and services at affordable cost with less time. The digitalization in banking industry is also sufficed by the availability of internet facilities at affordable cost that revised from time to time by the government so as to increase its outreach easily across different parts of the country and introduction of e-governance mechanism in the country with a view to bring more accountability, responsibility and transparency for good governance.

The expansion in the use of internet across the country overtime can be explained with the help of Table 1. From the table it is clear that there is a continuous rise in the use of internet facilities in India, from 27 percent in 2015 to 34 percent in 2017 to the level of 50 percent in 2020 as per the latest data from Statista (2020). This is also supported by the increase use of mobile phones with internet users, implying the share of total population that has access to internet with mobile as a medium to access all types of e-commerce services. India is emerging as one the countries in the developing world that has humongous Smartphone user base, and crosses 696.07 million of smartphone users in 2020 and is expected to rise to 875.39 million by the year 2023. The ratio of smartphones to total population indicates the penetration of smartphone users in the country, which has a share of 19.13 percent in 2015 to 50.38 percent in 2020, indicating that almost half of the entire population has access to smartphones over the period and is predicted to reach to 61.49 percent in the year

2023. All these indicators show that in the near future, Indian economy will convert into a highly digitized economy with above 50 percent of the population has access to internet facilities and two-third of the population has access to smartphone, an instrument for digitization platform and well-situated use of artificial intelligence.

Table 1. Trends in the internet use and smartphones penetration in India

Year	Internet Penetration Rate in India *(percent)*	Mobile Phone Internet User Penetration in India		Number of Smartphone Users in India	Smartphones Penetration in India
		(in millions)	*percent (%)*	*(in millions)*	*percent (%)*
2015	27.00	242.92	18.55	250.66	19.13
2016	34.80	281.81	21.28	304.51	22.99
2017	34.40	351.6	26.00	394.82	29.49
2018	38.02	390.9	29.00	479.34	35.44
2019	48.48	420.7	31.00	634.58	46.40
2020	50.00	448.2	32.00	696.07	50.38
2023	--	500.9	35.00	875.38	61.49

Source: The statistic portal, n.d.

Table 2. Mobile banking transactions data for scheduled commercial banks as on March 2010 to March 2020

Periods	Number of Banks Started Providing Mobile Banking	Volume (lakh)	Value (Rs.in crore)
March 2010	32	2.72	23.62
March 2011	36	10.47	84.63
March 2012	48	31.23	232.53
March 2013	55	64.01	991.93
March 2014	63	107.40	3407.06
March 2015	66	197.57	16913.83
March 2016	65	494.77	57280.40
March 2017	74	1136.50	173088.15
March 2018	180	2399.02	141503.46
March 2019	280	8729.27	440152.75
March 2020	363	13830.33	520199.11

Source: Reserve Bank of India Database.

The increase in the number of smartphone users is also reflected in the mobile banking data of scheduled commercial banks in India, in which as on March 2010 only 32 scheduled commercial banks provided mobile banking facilities with an actual volume of 2.72 lakh amounting to a value of Rs.23.62 crore. However, with the digitization and availability of internet facilities at affordable prices, there is gradual increase in the use of mobile banking in terms of both volume and value over the period, which reaches to an actual volume of 13830 lakh with a value of Rs.520199 crore in March 2020. Simultaneously, the number of banks providing the mobile banking facilities has jumped up from 32 banks in 2010 to 74 banks in 2017 to an abrupt figure of 180 banks in 2018, particularly with the entry of small finance banks, payment banks in the list of scheduled commercial banks. Further, the provision of mobile banking transactions to regional rural banks and co-operative banks has also added to the number of banks that offer mobile banking services and reach the number to 363 banks in March 2020.To summarize, mobile apps have become the touchpad of choice of millions of people to access banking products and services at a convenient way. Banks are facing challenges to understand the diverse features and possible outcomes of the use of mobile banking to ensure that they build and identify best practices in finding new ways to improve their mobile services. A snapshot about the mobile banking transactions by scheduled commercial banks is depicted in Table 2.

Moreover, the recent technological development in the banking industry defines scope and structure of adoption of artificial intelligence by leading banks in India. Some of the banks have incorporated artificial intelligence in delivery of products and services which are reported in Table 3.

State Bank of India has AI-based chatbot to assist and addresses queries of customers instantly and help in redressing any tasks just like a bank representative handles. Similar is the Eva chatbot of the HDFC Bank, which can address the problems within a short period of less than 0.4 seconds. Yes Bank, Axis Bank, Kotak Mahindra Bank and IndusInd Bank are private sector banks that adopted the artificial intelligence technology as a part of financial innovation to deal with the different complaints and requirements of the customers. In other words, the Indian scheduled commercial banks were in the initial stage to incorporate the AI technology under the digital platform for providing varied services and products to customers. And it is certain that in the coming years of two to three years, there will be big revolution of Industry 4.0 making futuristic banks of India a highly digitalized AI centric industry. All these indicated that the role of artificial intelligence is very significant in the efficient delivery of products and services and in generating as well as creating loyalty to customers by providing quality services.

Table 3. Artificial intelligence adoption by select banks

Sr. No.	Name of the Banks	Artificial Intelligence	Uses
1.	State Bank of India	SIA Chatbot	AI-powered chat assistant that addresses customer enquiries instantly and helps them with everyday banking tasks just like a bank representative.
2.	HDFC Bank	EvaChatbot	It can assimilate knowledge from thousands of sources and provide simple answers in less than 0.4 seconds.
3.	Bank of Baroda	Baroda Brainy and Digital Lab	An innovative concept of hi-tech digital branch equipped with advanced gadgets like artificial intelligence robot with free Wi-Fi services
4.	ICICI Bank	iPal -Robotic Software	A kind of software generally focused on automating office work, which emulates human actions to automate and perform repetitive, high-volume and time-consuming business tasks.
5.	Yes Bank	YES TAG	Allows customers to perform banking transactions on various social messengers.
6.	Axis Bank	AI & NLP enabled app	Natural Language Processing enabled app, Conversational Banking, to help consumers with financial and non-financial transactions, answer FAQs and get in touch with the bank for loan other products.
7.	Kotak Mahindra Bank	'Keya' Chatbot	With the voicebot, customers can now complete simple transactions such as ordering a cheque book or paying bills through voice instructions. It also responds to a customer's query, provides actionable buttons that enable customers to complete the action associated with the query at that very instant.
8.	Canara Bank	A humanoid robot-Mitra	A humanoid robot which helps customers to navigate the bank.
9.	IndusInd Bank	Alexa Skill -'IndusAssist'	Bank account holders can conduct financial and non-financial banking transactions with Alexa, Amazon's virtual assistant.
10.	City Union Bank	Banking robot - 'Lakshmi'	Can interact with customers on more than 125 subjects. Apart from answering generic questions, the robot is also programmed to connect with the core banking solution.

Source: Compiled by authors from various reports of the respective banks.

AN INTERPLAY OF FACILITATING AND RESTRAINING FORCES FOR ADOPTION OF AI IN BANKING

In the previous section we have given a detailed concept about the factors that led to adoption of artificial intelligence by banks and the significant benefits accrued in overall operational performance, though there are no exceptions to limitations. This section examines how the customer relationship management can be enhanced through the adoption of AI in banking operations. Some of the primary by-products of adoption of AI in banks include chatbots, voice banking, robo-advice, biometric authentication and authorization, customer segmentation, reporting, complaints management, document classification, KYC document processing and credit scoring, compliance monitoring, anti-money laundering detection, fraud prevention and cyber risk prevention measures that are used by the banks for improvement of customer services. The availability of such hi-tech solutions helps banks in wise decision and behavioral analysis of customers in providing core banking services on the one hand and also superior experience towards customers to redress any sorts of issues and queries without much involvement of the bank representative at a shorter time.

The adoption of AI in banks can be expressed from two perspectives viz., (a) the push factors that are the restraining forces and (b) the pull factors that facilitate forces to adapt such technological innovation. The push factors in general are the factors that are the driving force behind the use and adoption of AI in banks, which is the outcome of digitization and entry of FinTech firms in the industry. These factors among others include competition among firms/rivals; process driven services in the form of redressing complaints, meeting customers' needs and winning new customers at the end; skilled employee base that increases the extent of efficiency and productivity of assets; qualitative human capital and strategic decision making capability; and overall operational efficiency; are some of the driving forces towards adoption of AI in banks. On the other hand, there are various pull factors that facilitated forcibly the adoption of AI in banks. These include accounting process wherein huge programming of AI is necessary to deal with all dimensions of accounting and probable risks associated with the accurate data and structuration; to mitigate risk against any sort of cyber security and frauds that is highly existent in the financial institutions like banks. In the context of management of risks there are various forms ranging from credit risk to liquidity risk. It also serves as a platform for compliance mechanism to meet the terms and conditions of the regulation of banking system and in quick decision to finance credits and sanctioning of loans and advances.

The adoption of AI by banks has significant benefits and advantages while delivering its different products and services to multiple customers on the one hand; and on the other hand the customers have superior experience under the AI platform in terms of attending their queries, issues, within a short span. To elaborate, the use of AI in banks has certain advantages such as improvement in the skills of employees, productive and operational efficiency, dealing with multiple customers in shorter time frames, sanctioning of loans and advances in a shorter duration, enhanced capacity to analyze heterogeneous customers, and to cognize, detect frauds and cyber threats. On the other hand, customers do benefitted from AI platform in

Figure 1. A framework of artificial intelligence (ai) adoption in banks: interplay of pull v/s push factors and resultant benefits

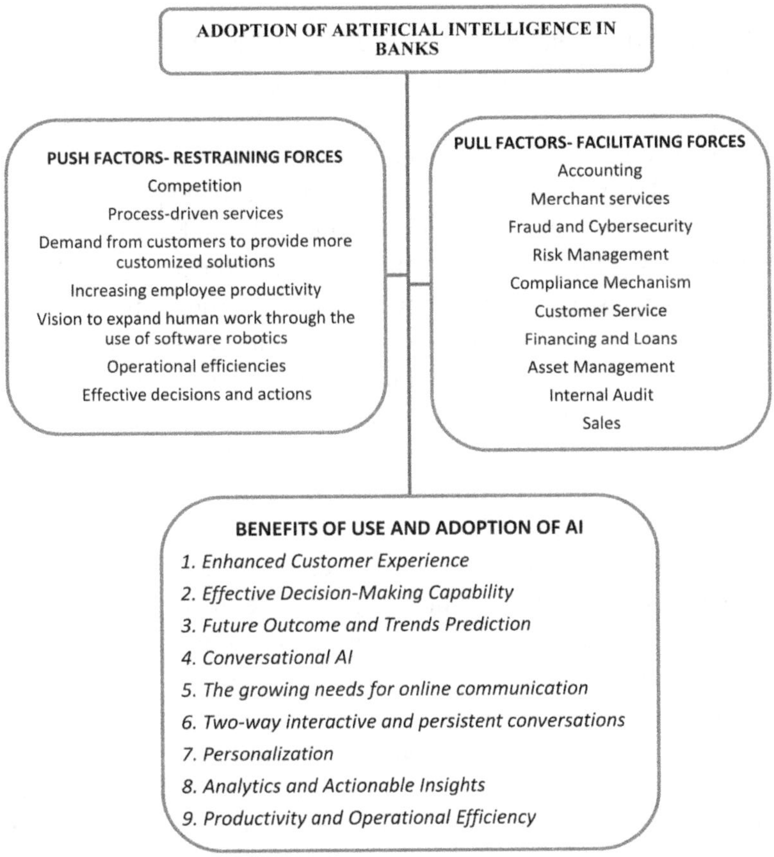

meeting the needs and requirements in recognizing accurate data in a much secure and safe way with the use of biometric information, can deal with services request by connecting through corners of the space, personalization, and efficient delivery of services. The use of AI, particularly in banking industry it requires constant regulatory and monitoring mechanism to adapt with safety and security of data, governance, accountability and responsibility through ethical considerations. A detailed of adoption of Artificial Intelligence in banks, given its underlying factors and the relevant benefits associated with such mechanisms in banking industry is conceptualized in Model 1.

CONCEPTUALIZING THE FRAMEWORK OF AI, CRM AND SERVICE QUALITY

The model proposed by the authors enunciates the relationship between use of Artificial Intelligence (AI) technologies and its application to banking industry in the delivery of products and services. Our conceptualized model portrays the linkages between adoption of AI by banks and its significant performance towards customer relationship management leading to delivery of qualitative services to customers. To start with, as shown in the Model 2, banks used AI in different aspects of working and functioning and these activities ranges widely from specific tools such as Analytics, Chatbots, Robotics Process Automation, and to Report Generation. The use of such technologies can have miraculous results to banks in terms of Risk Modeling, Biometrics, Fraud Detection, and Underwriting to name a few among others. Rather than rebuilding or re-architecting, financial institutions need to turn to innovative technologies like AI and robotic process automation to automate antecedently manual workflows and to test the results through the eyes of the digital customer. These technologies can help financial institutions focus on businesses and consumers that can help in maintaining the type of quality services at the functionality, performance and utility of software and its applications based on the user experience. The entire end result produces an astonishing digital experience.

Indeed, huge changes are taking place in the domain of data that is being churned in the banking industry. The banks are migrating away from legacy on-premise data warehouses to the cloud as a tremendous opportunity for their clients. All these produce benefits in the form of improved performance, availability, cost effectiveness, better manageability and flexibility without compromising on security and safety. However, when we compared banks with other industries, it is observed that banking sector remains less digitally enabled and requires much challenges for meeting the requirements of the customers with more customer-centric, competitive, compliance and profitable in serving and ensuring last mile delivery through cost-effective, user friendly and up-to-date technologies. One possible reason for relatively slower process of adoption of AI in banks is the complex and heterogeneous nature of banking industry, involving mass data for customers, requiring much more safety, security, biased and fairness, accountability and ethical responsibility towards the well-being of the customers. Notwithstanding these specific features, the entry of FinTech firms in the banking industry has gradually led to a paradigm shift in the use and adoption of AI and machine learning technologies by banks in both physical and virtual modes of delivery of services.

Ironically, banks under the traditional and conventional framework processes faced significant operational cost and risk issues due to the probable for human errors associated with the cumbersome and heavy paper work. However, with the advancement of technology in banking sector, such operational inefficiency tends to minimize over the period and significant changes occurred in the functioning of banks. For example by replacing humans with intelligent, automated assistants, banks not only improve their risk management but they can also focus their human resources on higher-value tasks, such as client relationship management and customer services. In addition, many financial services companies are offering robo-advisers that can help their customers with portfolio management which can provide high-quality guidance on investment decisions and be available whenever the customer needs their assistance. Further, by replacing these human processes with AI-based automation, banks can impose audit and regulatory control where they previously have been unable to do so. Robotic Process Automation (RPA), software that mimics rules-based digital tasks performed by humans, is being applied in banking to eliminate much of the time-intensive and error-prone work involved in entering customer data from contracts, forms and other sources. Coupled with improved handwriting recognition, natural language processing and other AI technologies, RPA bots become intelligent process automation tools that can handle an increasingly wide range of banking workflows. Moreover, banks are using smart, AI virtual assistants to monitor transactions, keep an eye on behavior of customers, and audit and log information to various compliance and regulatory systems. Even the introduction of big-data-enhanced fraud prevention has made a significant impact on credit card and loan underwriting processes. Similarly, banks are using AI-based systems to help make more informed, safer and profitable loan and credit decisions. Currently, many banks are still too confined to the use of credit scores, credit history, customer references and banking transactions to determine whether or not an individual or company is creditworthy. AI-based loan decision systems and machine learning algorithms can look at behaviors and patterns to determine if a customer with limited credit history might in fact make a good credit customer or find customers whose patterns might increase the likelihood of default.

To put together, the outcomes of the use and adoption of AI in banking services are manifold, benefiting the overall operational efficiency of banks. Those banks and other companies moving in this direction are rethinking structural and operating models, data access, hiring practices, training, and incentives for employees. At the branch level, employees are learning new skills, as they evolve from being reactive service providers to becoming 'live' customer interface agents and counselors. The use of AI Technologies in the banking sector yields dividends in terms of effective customer relationship management (CRM) strategies viz., customer acquisition, customer response, customer knowledge and customer value. In other words, the CRM practices of the banks should be able to culminate into the digital innovation under the increasingly via mobile applications and online tools in the banking industry to meet the requirements of the customers. Banking is rapidly becoming

Figure 2. An overarching model of embedding artificial intelligence in customer relationship management and improving service quality of banks

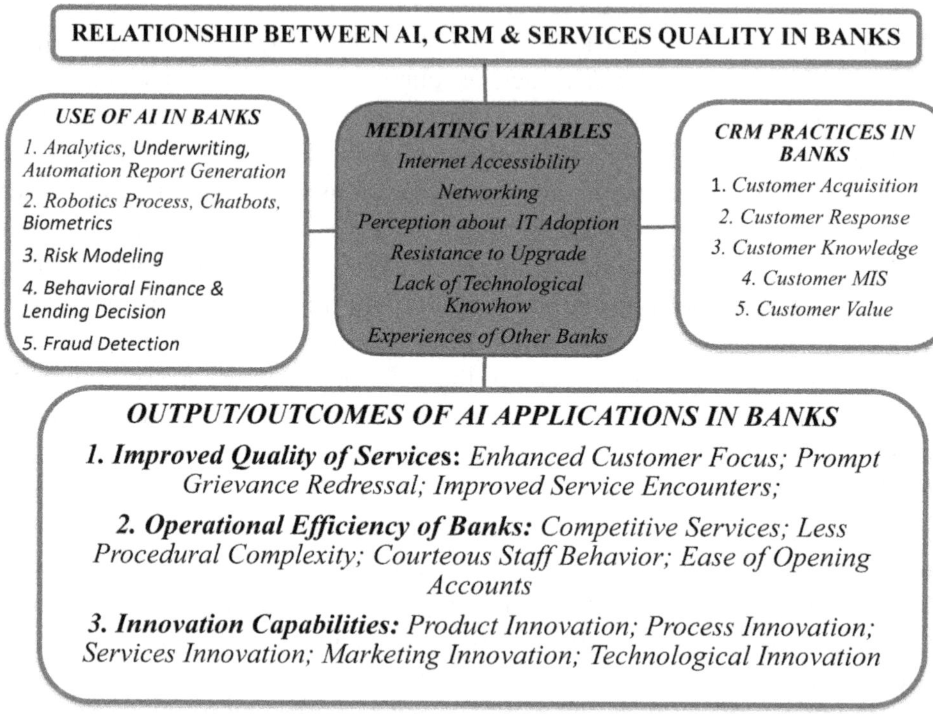

an "anytime, anywhere" omni-channel experience, as tech-enabled and tech-savvy customers drive the need for more and more flexibility, agility, and innovation. Consumers want seamless, convenient banking experiences, regardless of which channels they use or when they use them.

The end result of this entire thoughtful strategy will lead the banks towards Improved Quality of Services and Improved Performance of Banks. The other consequences of adoption of AI that can be realized by Banks are the development of Innovation capabilities that helps the bank to not only to position itself in competitive scenario but also to deliver the services better. No doubt, there are distinct advantages in the use of AI by banks in overall operational efficiency. However, there are constraints in the form of increase in profiteering and fraud events because of increased online transactions compelled by the pandemic. The Model 2 clearly enunciates the relationship between AI, CRM & services quality in banks.

STRATEGIC MANAGERIAL IMPLICATIONS

This section reports brief managerial implications with reference to the application of artificial intelligence for optimal feasible solutions of Indian banking industry. We have grouped four important strategic implications of AI technology in banking sector for better customer relationship management. These are as follows:

1. **Consumer Behavior:** We know that consumers behave rationally and attempts to maximize its satisfaction/utility through the selection of preferences from the given basket of goods and services available under the given budget constraints. In a similar way to banking products and services, customers under the digitized platform with AI driven technology will choose those products and services which has the features of high returns, tax benefits, lower interest rates of loans, easy to redress complaints, better services in all aspects with safety and security in transactions. In this context the customer relationship management is very important in creating or generating assurance and trusts towards customers about the extent of safety and security of all the virtual modes of transactions provided by banks. For example, when it comes to the transactions for huge amount of money the customers still prefer to go for the conventional modes of transactions like using cheques, demand drafts and deposit slips among others rather than opting for internet and mobile applications because of the associated risks of online frauds, transaction failures which makes him juggle between many apps and adapting to varied forms of technologies. Therefore, meeting the expectations of the customer is one of primary objective of any banks and the products and services available should meet such requirements particularly with reference to safety and security to protect the information of consumers.
2. **Incentives and Schemes:** One of the biggest demands for digital services is the mobile banking services. Most of the non-banks come up with wallets, points system, various schemes which forms more incentives and tips to customers to adopt newer applications. The banks through the involvement of FinTech firms can introduce a universal digital platform or mobile apps that can serve a common path to access such benefits for larger coverage of digitized financial services. This is important because there is lack of trust on the part of the customers and hence limitedly used such benefits to such digital wallets system. Hence, much involvement of the FinTech firms is required for filling such gaps in the allocation of services from the core banks, particularly the public sector banks in India.
3. **Economic and Social Implications:** In the light of pandemic COVID-19, the significance of digital transformation is dramatically accelerated and financial

sector is no exception to it. For example, to access the various financial services, the days of visiting your local branch for traditional purposes are waning due to social distancing norms and retail banks are scrambling to add digital services to replicate and enhance the array of sophisticated offerings that branches provide. AI-based mobile applications can make the transaction quicker and safer. Banks can handle the customer-oriented operations with ease while reducing the cost of hiring additional employees. However, when we talk about the rural connectivity, it is the biggest drawback. Much attention be given to encompass the majority illiterate farmers by coming up with simple and easy technologies under multi-lingual apps that is available at affordable price and using the system of miscall alert to farmers, etc.

4. **Adaptability to Technologies:** We had discussed in the previous sections about the technological advancement and its feasible solutions to the access of products and services. The increased accessibility will drive the need for omni-channel support so that both the teams from the customer relationship management and customers on the other side can work seamlessly between them. For example, CRM teams in banks can respond to meet the requirements and queries of different customers to address with and in case there is discrepancy in meeting such demands, the team can pass it on to another respective support team to deal with the complaints received. Operating from a central help desk, it can connect to different teams under the CRM to settle all sorts of customer demands under a connected team interface rather than operating in silos.

In general, these are some of the common and major perspectives for strategic management of the requirement of different customers under the CRM teams of the banks. Hence, expertise in these aspects for providing superior service and building loyalty towards customers is essential for successful businesses.

KEY DISCUSSIONS AND CONCLUSION

This chapter demonstrates the effects of artificial intelligence in the Indian banks and the role of customer relationship management in the delivery of qualitative services and superior experience to the customers. The chapter highlights the changing trend of use in mobile banking as one of the major platforms of digitized financial services provided by banks to use and access various products and services offered from time to time. The increase in the use of mobile apps is also facilitated with the easy access and availability of internet services at affordable charges that updated over the periods. Further, the increase in the penetration of smartphone users given the easy access to internet facilities has also made the increase in outreach of the then excluded remotes of the country. Given the availability of internet and penetration in smartphones it becomes easier for the banks to supply products and services at a faster way. However, a successful business and operations of the banks require much role of the customer relationship management in banks to assure superior experience as well as meeting expectations of customers for generating loyalty towards different customers.

Gone are the days when customers would have to wait for long on calls while the staff in the bank manually looked up the information needed to resolve their queries. With the advent of technology like artificial intelligence and machine learning, customer support is now simplified and automated to suit the needs of the customers and the convenience of enterprises. Customer service automation is nothing but a purpose-built process that aims to minimize or eliminate the need for human interference when assisting with customer requests. The reason for increase in customer service automation becomes so popular and widely used is because it eliminates several unnecessary steps for the customer while searching for a solution. One of the main factors at play when customers use this service is speed or efficacy in redressing all types of complaints. Self-service is the future scope of customer support and hence the adoption of AI in the banking operations will be indispensable. Using self-service portals, customers can find answers to their questions and also perform simple, actionable tasks without depending on a support agent. Is it finding out the time of delivery of a certain package or cancel the delivery self-service portals are the best? Through this tool, we can engage customers with discussion forums whenever they want to find answers. Another aspect of addressing the banking system is the concept of financial inclusion strategy wherein the Reserve Bank of India in its endeavor has taken up several steps so far since its inception as social banking though scheme like PMJDY plays a significant role to increase the credit outreach to the excluded masses of society. In this connection, it is imperative for the banks to focus on financial inclusion and financial literacy programs for delivering financial services at affordable costs to disadvantaged and low-income sections of society. Advanced banking technology will be required for inclusive banks to harness these new opportunities for financial inclusion. Of particular importance is Cloud computing and the Software as a Service (SaaS) delivery model. Cloud and SaaS present an alternative way of running a bank's IT infrastructure. Core banking and/or the digital front office operates on a public or private Cloud rather than on physical infrastructure in the bank's premises. Banks pay a subscription to access the solutions. Both Cloud and SaaS carries lower infrastructure costs, they allow products to be created, delivered and changed faster, and they offer immense resilience, scalability and security. Cloud-based SaaS platforms are also continuously updated, meaning banks benefit from the latest innovations. Cloud and SaaS adoption will be a key to future success in inclusive banking for these three major reasons viz.,

(i) It is a hyper-efficient model, largely in terms of cost (ii) Its elastic scalability makes inclusive banking manageable and efficient and (iii) It helps along financial inclusion in the developed world too.

To sum up, most of the Indian banks have been on various stages of their digital transformation journey, which in most cases was limited to a customer facing digital layer. The new challenges upon financial institutions have accentuated the need for a more holistic approach. Digitization will start with evolving the customer experience creating more cohesive and personal digital journeys by combining and integrating every aspect into a single platform and tooling. Moving beyond the customer interface, digitization includes middle- and back-office operations, and support functions where processes are transformed and automated into intelligent workflows.

REFERENCES

Agarwal, R., & Venkatesh, V. (2002). Assessing a firm's web presence: A heuristic evaluation procedure for the measurement of usability. *Information Systems Research, 13*(2), 168–186. doi:10.1287/isre.13.2.168.84

Agnew, J. R., & Szykman, L. R. (2005). Asset allocation and information overload: The influence of information display, asset choice, and investor experience. *Journal of Behavioral Finance, 6*(2), 57–70. doi:10.120715427579jpfm0602_2

Altman, E. I., Marco, G., & Varetto, F. (1994). Corporate distress diagnosis. Comparisons using linear discriminant analysis and neutral network (the Italian experience). *Journal of Banking & Finance, 18*(3), 505–529. doi:10.1016/0378-4266(94)90007-8

Bhatia, A., Chandani, A., & Chhateja, J. (2020). Robo advisory and its potential in addressing the behavioral biases of investors - A qualitative study in Indian context. *Journal of Behavioral and Experimental Finance, 25*, 100281. doi:10.1016/j.jbef.2020.100281

Carletti, E., Claessens, S., Fatas, A., & Vives, X. (2020). *The Bank Business Model in Post-Covid-19 World, The Future of Banking 2. Report sponsored by IESE*. Bank for International Settlements.

Costa, A., & Ehrbeck, T. (2015). A market-building approach to financial Inclusion. *Innovations: Technology, Governance, Globalization, 10*(1-2), 53–59. doi:10.1162/inov_a_00229

Day, G. S. (2000). *Capabilities for Forging Customer Relationships*. Working Paper, Report No. 00-118. Cambridge, MA: Marketing Science Institute.

Diakopoulos, N. (2016). Accountability in algorithmic decision making. *Communications of the ACM*, *59*(2), 56–62. doi:10.1145/2844110

Hughes, K., Ismagilova, L., Aarts, E., Coombs, G., Crick, C., Duan, T., Dwivedi, Y., Edwards, R., Eirug, J., Galanos, A., Ilavarasan, V., Janssen, P. V., Jones, M., Kar, P., Kizgin, A. K., Kronemann, H., Lal, B., Lucini, B., & Williams, B., M. D. (2021, April). Artificial Intelligence (AI): Multidisciplinary perspectives on emerging challenges, opportunities, and agenda for research, practice and policy. *International Journal of Information Management*, *57*, 101994. doi:10.1016/j.ijinfomgt.2019.08.002

Gabor, D., & Brooks, S. (2017). The digital revolution in financial inclusion: International development in the fintech era. *New Political Economy*, *22*(4), 423–436. doi:10.1080/13563467.2017.1259298

Gandhi, P., Loughran, T., & McDonald, B. (2019). Using annual report sentiment as a proxy for financial distress in US banks. *Journal of Behavioral Finance*, *20*(4), 424–436. doi:10.1080/15427560.2019.1553176

GOI. (2018). *Report of the Artificial Intelligence Task Force*. The Ministry of Commerce & Industry, Government of India (GOI). https://dipp.gov.in/whats-new/report-task-force-artificial-intelligence

Gomez Martinez, R., Prado Román, M., & Plaza Casado, P. (2019). Big data algorithmic trading systems based on investors' mood. *Journal of Behavioral Finance*, *20*(2), 227–238. doi:10.1080/15427560.2018.1506786

Haenlein, M., & Kaplan, A. (2019). A brief history of Artificial Intelligence: On the Past, Present, and Future of Artificial Intelligence. *California Management Review*, *61*(4), 5–14. doi:10.1177/0008125619864925

IDRBT. (2020). *AI in Banking: A Primer*. Institute for Research and Development in Banking Technology. http://www.idrbt.ac.in/assets/publications/Best%20Practices/2020/AI_2020.pdf

Jayachandran, S., Sharma, S., Kaufman, P., & Raman, P. (2005). The role of relational information processes and technology use in customer relationship management. *Journal of Marketing, 69*(4), 177–192. https://journals.sagepub.com/doi/10.1509/jmkg.2005.69.4.177

Kannan, P. K., & Li, H. (2017). Digital marketing: A framework, review and research agenda. *International Journal of Research in Marketing, 34*(1), 22–45. doi:10.1016/j.ijresmar.2016.11.006

Konigstorfer, F., & Thalmann, S. (2020). Applications of Artificial Intelligence in commercial banks – A research agenda for behavioural finance. *Journal of Behavioral and Experimental Finance, 27*(2020), 1-15.

Leong, C., Tan, B., Xiao, X., Tan, F. T. C., & Sun, Y. (2017). Nurturing a FinTech Ecosystem: The case of a Youth Microloan Startup in China. *International Journal of Information Management, 37*(2), 92–97. doi:10.1016/j.ijinfomgt.2016.11.006

Martin, D. (1977). Early warning of bank failure: A Logit regression approach. *Journal of Banking & Finance, 1*(3), 249–276. doi:10.1016/0378-4266(77)90022-X

McCarthy, J., Minsky, M., Rochester, N., & Shannon, C. E. (2006). A Proposal for the Dartmouth Summer Research Project on Artificial Intelligence, August 31, 1955. *AI Magazine, 27*(4), 12–14.

Mogaji, E., Farinloye, T., & Aririguzoh, S. (2016). Factors shaping attitudes towards UK bank brands: An exploratory analysis of social media data. *Cogent Business Management, 3*(1), 1223389. doi:10.1080/23311975.2016.1223389

Mogaji, E., Soetan, T.O., & Kieu, T.A. (2020, May). The implications of artificial intelligence on the digital marketing of financial services to vulnerable customers. *Australasian Marketing Journal*, 1-8.

Onay, C., & Ozturk, E. (2018). A review of credit scoring research in the age of Big Data. *Journal of Financial Regulation and Compliance, 26*(3), 382–405. doi:10.1108/JFRC-06-2017-0054

Oskarsdottir, M., Bravo, C., Sarraute, C., Baesens, B., & Vanthienen, J. (2018). Credit scoring for good: Enhancing financial inclusion with smartphone-based micro lending. *Thirty Ninth International Conference on Information Systems*. https://www.researchgate.net/publication/328826594_Credit_scoring_for_good_enhancing_financial_inclusion_with_smartphone-based_microlending#fullTextFileContent

PWC. (2019). *AI in financial services - Are you meeting the regulators' expectations?* https://www.pwc.co.uk/financial-services/assets/pdf/ai-in-financial-services.pdf

RBI. (2017). *Report of the Working Group on FinTech and Digital Banking*. Reserve Bank of India. rbi.org.in

RBI. (2020). *Annual Report 2019-20*. Reserve Bank of India. https://rbi.org.in

Rigby, D. K., Reichheld, F., & Schefter, P. (2002). Avoid the Four Perils of CRM. *Harvard Business Review*, *80*(2), 101–109. PMID:11894676

Saura, J. R., Palos-Sanchez, P. R., & Correia, M. B. (2019). Digital Marketing Strategies Based on the E-Business Model: Literature Review and Future Directions. In A. G. Guerra (Ed.), *Organizational Transformation and Managing Innovation in the Fourth Industrial Revolution* (pp. 86–103). IGI Global. doi:10.4018/978-1-5225-7074-5.ch005

Srivastava, R. K., Shervani, T. A., & Fahey, L. (1999). Business Processes and Shareholder Value: An Organizationally Embedded View of Marketing Activities and the Discipline of Marketing. *Journal of Marketing*, *63*(4), 168–179. doi:10.1177/00222429990634s116

Statista. (n.d.). *The statistics portal.* https://www.statista.com/

Van Esch, P., Black, J. S., & Ferolie, J. (2019). Marketing AI recruitment: The next phase in job application and selection. *Computers in Human Behavior*, *90*(January), 215–222. doi:10.1016/j.chb.2018.09.009

Vempati, S. S. (2016). *India and the Artificial Intelligence Revolution. Carnegie Endowment for International Peace*. Carnegie India. https://carnegieindia.org/2016/08/11/india-and-artificial-intelligence-revolution-pub-64299

Wang, G., Ma, J., & Yang, S. (2014). An improved boosting based on feature selection for corporate bankruptcy prediction. *Expert Systems with Applications*, *41*(5), 2353–2361. doi:10.1016/j.eswa.2013.09.033

Chapter 13
Artificial Intelligence in Retail:
Enhancing Customer Experience and Profitability

Renu Sharma
Amity University, Noida, India

Mamta Mohan
Amity University, Noida, India

Prabha Mariappan
National Institute of Technology, Tiruchirappalli, India

ABSTRACT

This chapter gives an overview of how artificial intelligence is used by the retail sector to enhance customer experience and to improve profitability. It provides information about the role of the pandemic in stimulating AI adoption by retailers. It deliberates on how AI tools help retailers to engage customers online and in stores. Firms gain better understanding of customers, design immersive experiences, and enhance customer lifetime value using cost-effective technology solutions. It discusses popular AI algorithms like recommendation algorithm, association algorithm, classification algorithm, and predictive algorithm. Popular applications in retail include chatbots, visual search, voice search engine optimisation, in-store assistance, and virtual fitting rooms.

INTRODUCTION

Artificial Intelligence is gradually replacing traditional data analysis in data driven

DOI: 10.4018/978-1-7998-7959-6.ch013

retail sector. This fact is envisaged in number of deals signed by AI start-ups. Between 2013-2018, 374 deals amounting to 1.8 Billion Dollars were finalised (*Artificial Intelligence for Retail in 2020: 12 Real-World Use Cases*, n.d.). The number of retailers deploying AI has gone up from 4% in 2016 to 28% in 2020 marking a sevenfold increase (*Artificial Intelligence for Retail in 2020: 12 Real-World Use Cases*, n.d.).

Artificial intelligence makes understanding of customers possible and these insights, combined with human intelligence can lead to significant changes in customer experience. For example AI can help a retailer analyse feed from the in-store cameras, locate customers in frames, trach each customer's position, match it to location of product, and also signal sales staff whether a customer is standing for too long and may require assistance. The insights provided by such system can be integrated with CRM to predict demand for a particular product, create personalised promotional offers and customise pricing strategies to align with different customer groups.

Retail organisation who aggressively adopted AI showed revenue increase through applications of AI in multiple operational areas. Revenue increases from sales and marketing are reported when AI is used in pricing, predicting buying preferences and customer service analytics(Cam et al., 2019).

This chapter will attempt to provide answers to following questions:

1. How pandemic acted as a helped in adoption of AI tools?
2. How Artificial Intelligence can help in improving customer experience?
3. How can Artificial intelligence enhance retail profitability?
4. Which technology tools and algorithms are commonly used in a retail organisation?
5. What are the popular AI tools used by retail sector?

PANDEMIC AS A CATALYST FOR AI

During pandemic customers were forced to shop online resulting in unprecedented growth rate of e-commerce revenue. In 2020, e-commerce sales grew by 20% and brick & mortar sales dropped by 14% (*Shopping in 2020: 6 Intriguing Experiments in Digital Retail*, n.d.).The amount of sales revenue lost can not be compensated with growth of e-commerce. Therefore, retail brands are under tremendous pressure to entice customers and provide them seamless and memorable experience. Customer interfacing technologies and back end technologies became harbinger of sweeping changes in retail. Covid 19 proved a catalyst for Artificial Intelligence in customer interface, sales, marketing, and logistics as retailers were forced to find different ways to engage and entice customers. Mobile apps, online shopping, digital payments, contactless delivery, chatbots are the norms in retail now(Roggeveen & Sethuraman, 2020). As a result all stages of a shopper's journey has some influencing technology component be it search for information, pre-purchase stage, purchase process and post purchase stage. AI is also a game changer in supply-chain management as tools like sales and demand forecasting and spend analytics helped retailers increase their revenues(Cam et al., 2019).Reduced cost and availability of CRM and CDP (Customer Data Platform) became important factors for usage of AI by small and big retailers. According to Mckinsey's Global Survey, usage of AI witnessed a 25% year on year increase in business processes(Cam et al., 2019). AI revenue is projected to reach $97.9 billion in the year of 2023 as per International Data Corporation (IDC).

However, the intention of using AI and related tools should be on increasing the human experience through technology. The success of organisations will be measured by how they enrich human experience rather than just numbers of tools employed or money invested in AI(Accenture, 2020).

Consumer behaviour changed significantly during Covid 19 and following trends can be noticed(Ready, 2020):

Multiple Devices, More Internet Browsing

Web browsing went up by 70%; social media engagement by 61% and consumers spent 20% more time using app data.

Information Search for Essential Needs

As retailers moved to online space during pandemic, people searched for specific information about nearby retailers, their timings, options of home delivery etc. Retailers had to create online store fronts and link them to important data like stock availability, and delivery information.

Around 30,000-40,000 kirana stores listed on Paynearby every day during pandemic in an effort to reach customers during lockdown period(*Tech Industry Leading India's Recovery Post Covid - The Financial Express*, n.d.)(*Tech Industry Leading India's Recovery Post Covid - The Financial Express*, n.d.).

Consumers Opted for Internet First

Pandemic changed routines and schedules which resulted in emergence of new online habits. In India and China, over 1 in 4 consumers did majority of their shopping online. Moreover, 1 in 3 consumers opted for store/ curb side pick-up in India, China and Australia.

Retailers were expected to update information about their opening hours, status of each location- whether it's open or close and also information about inventory. Consumers preferred contact less deliveries and stores are required to provide information about same.

ARTIFICIAL INTELLIGENCE AND CUSTOMER EXPERIENCE

In the context of customer experience, a popular theory is UTAUT2((Unified theory of acceptance and use of technology2)(Venkatesh et al., 2012). Originally UTAUT was developed after combining eight theories/ models to explain technology acceptance by employees(Venkatesh et al., 2003). Further UTAUT2 explained technology usage and acceptance by customers. According to UTAUT, four major factors determine intention for technology usage. These factors are: Performance Expectancy, Effort Expectancy, Social Influence and Facilitating Conditions. Performance expectancy is the extent to which technology will benefit the consumers. Effort Expectancy is extent of ease of using a particular technology .Social influence is the impact of other important people(family, friends) as to how they believe that technology should be used. Facilitating conditions refer to the resources and support available for using technology.

In addition to these factors, three more factors were added to original model to explain how consumer intention for using any technology(Venkatesh et al., 2012). These factors are hedonic motivation, price and habit. Therefore, while designing technology solutions novelty/enjoyment, its cost to the customer and also consumer habits should be taken into consideration. As these factors are influenced by age, gender and experience, clarity about target customers will make usage of AI more effective.

Therefore, marketers and retail professionals are increasingly making use of AI and real time data to provide hyper-personalized customer experience. Simply creating personalised experiences are not enough; brands need to make them memorable for customers. Besides the product and services can be improved and developed using new AI-based products and new AI-based enhancements leading to increased sales, better customer experience and increased revenue for the organisation(Cam et al., 2019). Amazon is an example of creating and adopting multiple technological innovations for increasing efficiencies, reducing cost, and growing revenues(Grewal et al., 2020). It makes use of robotic technologies to assist workers in its fulfilment centres besides using predictive analytics to provide sophisticated personal recommendations. Its patented, innovative one click ordering sets it apart from its competitors.

Tools like conversational AI is make a shopper's journey more convenient and personalized. Rather than conventional ways of interacting with retailer, calling up, holding on a phone call, making multiple clicks to reach the information that one requires, conversational AI changed it all and is now a part of majority of ecommerce portals.

Retailers are striving to build holistic IOT solutions. For instance, autonomous shelf-monitoring technology is used by Auchan Retail Portugal, a grocery retailer, in its supermarkets and hypermarkets. The technology makes use of moving robots which capture photos of every shelf and aisle, digitize and convert them into metrics and provides information about out-of-stock merchandise and pricing to decision makers.

Figure 1. The Fogg behaviour model

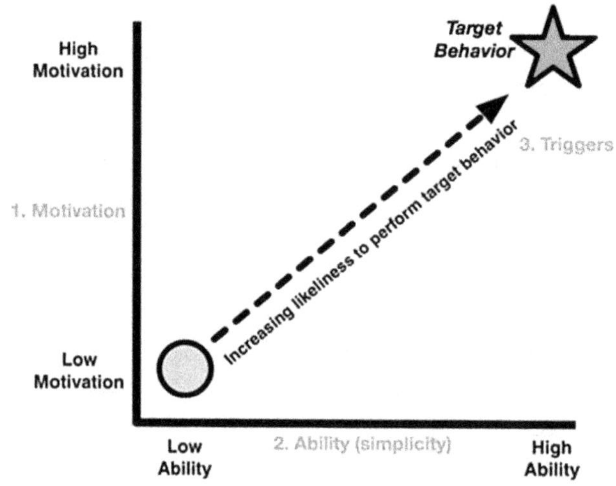

Retailers can make use of The Fogg Behaviour Model (FBM) which postulates that persuasive technology automates behaviour. According to FBM model (Fig. 1) for creating persuasive technologies, behaviour is a product of motivation, ability and trigger(B. Fogg, 2009). To get desired behaviour, motivation, ability and trigger should be present simultaneously(B. Fogg, 2009).Motivation includes pleasure/pain, hope/fear and social acceptance/rejection. Triggers are effective when people notice it, associate with target behaviour and they will require both motivation and ability.

Retailers need to ensure that technology ensures a smooth journey of customer by improving ability and by providing triggers at right time. Providing information about merchandise through QR code is an example of improving 'ability' and sending automated messages during weekend can be a 'trigger' to bring motivated customer to the store.

AI helps in improving customer experience in the following ways(Fig. 2):

Figure 2. AI and customer experience

Better Understanding of the Customer

Retailers use AI tools which are based on retail specific data. Within a few months these tools can learn behaviour and preferences of actual customer base. Retailers Experience- and intuition-based selling to data-driven selling, Online customer interactions can be easily tracked with the help of browsing history, click through rates, email open history. Robots inside stores can also provide aisle browsing data. Retailers can thus have smarter conversations, provide personalised recommendations and can make entire customer journey more pleasant.

AI can make companies reach top 1% of the customers, which can add 18 times the value of other customers(Ameen et al., 2021)

Uniqlo Reads Human Mind Through UMood Kiosks

Uniqlo has set up UMood which show customers a variety of products and colours. The reactions of customers are observed through neurotransmitters. They don't even have to press any button, the machine reads brain signals. Based on the each person's response, kiosk recommends merchandise.

Hyper Personalisation

AI along with real time data can enable hyper personalisation of customer experience. With the aid of clustering algorithms, companies can provide better recommendations and improve footfalls and conversion. Most of the online retailers show merchandise suggestion as "recommended products" and also "people who viewed this product also viewed.....".

Customers frequently are disappointed with call centres due to long waiting time, time sapping queues, confirmation / re-confirmation of personal data, and call drop rates. With conversational AI, now servers can store earlier chat history and purchase history of customer making the complaint resolution faster and more convenient.

Immersive Customer Experience

Retail brands need to interact with customers and ensure quality information exchange in real time during shopping experience. The extent to which a customer feels that he is "being there" is known as immersion. This concept gained importance during pandemic as most of the customers could not visit store but wanted to have an experience of being present there. Two major concepts that define immersion are number of touchpoints (breadth) and quality of information exchange across these touchpoints(depth)(Parise et al., 2016). As more retailers are building omni channel presence, number of customer touchpoints has gone up. The challenge is to ensure smoother flow of information across various channels.

American Eagle Creates Augmented Reality Store on Snapchat

American Eagle created an immersive experience for its customers using a mix of entertainment, social media and shopping. They opened an augmented reality store on Snapchat for launching their holiday collection, which featured collaboration with Disney. Customers could see the products stocked in the digital store when they visited the brand page on Snapchat. They could click and buy the products from Snapchat itself. Disney characters like Mickey Mouse and Goofy added to the entertainment by doing some mischief like climbing a fixture or dancing on a table. The visuals were refreshed three times giving users a different experience on repeat visit. American Eagle registered 26, 000 purchases amounting to $1.9 Million and garnered 41 million impressions.(*Shopping in 2020: 6 Intriguing Experiments in Digital Retail*, n.d.)

Customer Satisfaction Tracking

Business leaders now use terms like BX (Business of experience) where they obsess with customer needs and build entire processes, structures and technology around customer satisfaction. Leaders now strive to build listening organization to understand what shoppers are talking and how are they behaving by picking up signals through data and research.

Macy's Enriches Consumer Experience Through in Store Apps

Macy's is using On Call App to help customers navigate inside each of their stores. Customers can open the app in store and they can converse with AI chatbot and find if an item is available and where is it displayed. The bot is capable of sensing customer's mood and can alert an employee if a customer is getting frustrated.

Customer Behaviour Prediction

Retailers cannot gain a strategic advantage merely by tracking customer's purchases. What can give them an edge is what customers wanted but could not purchase. Aisle robots can help in making such predictions possible. Retailers need to collect and analyse data from multiple touchpoints including website, physical stores, mobile applications and social media platforms. This data combined with knowledge about target customer segment can provide more accurate predictions about likely needs and demands of shoppers.

Customers Help Marks and Spencer Choose Product Names

Marks and Spencer wanted to launch swimwear made up of recycled polyester and needed inputs for naming the product. They also wanted to find out if customers will be attracted by sustainability aspect. The same product was tested with four different names. With the help of data scoring, M&S found that eco aspect performed better in terms of sale than the fashion oriented brand. (*Actionable Data From Customer Experience Analytics Helping Retailers To Get Better*, n.d.).

ENHANCING RETAIL PROFITABILITY THROUGH AI

AI leads to increase in business revenues and reduction in costs(Cam et al., 2019). There is a sizable difference between companies who are aggressive in adoption AI compared to adoption laggards(Cam et al., 2019). Profitability can be enhanced by applying technology to corresponding applications such as cost analysis, efficiency promoting, customer vulnerability analysis, customer relationship management Tudor et al.,(2016) .According to Mckinsey's Global Survey, companies which make use of AI platforms or apps in their sales and marketing department achieve higher revenue growth. Marketing and sales department increased their revenue by 40% and supply chain management decreased their costs by 31% due to AI adoption (Fig 3)

Figure 3. Cost decrease and revenue increase from AI adoption (function wise), % age of respondents

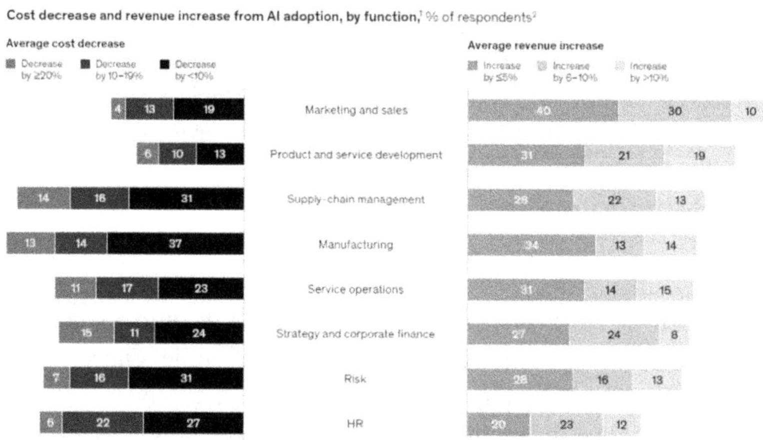

Figure 3 Cost decrease and revenue increase from AI adoption (function wise), % age of respondents Source: Mckinsey's Global AI Survey (Cam et al., 2019)

Improved Product Categorization

Product categorization is the classifying and placing the products in different categories. Although it sounds simple, it becomes a challenging task considering the sheer volume and number of categories handled by e-commerce portals. For example, products can be classified into multiple categories.

Men's Fashion- Men's accessories- Men's ties
Gifts - For Men- Accessories- Men's ties

Product categorization makes it easier for customers to reach their desired products and thereby improves conversion rate and also search engine rankings. Automated product categorization tools can help customer choose the right category by adding just a few keywords. As millions of products are listed on e-commerce portals, accuracy pf product categorization makes a significant difference to sales and revenues.

Better Price Predictions and Price Optimization

Footwear retailer Dan Post wanted to study the impact of country of origin on value of its products. They tested boots at same price but mentioned country of origin as China on one and Mexico on another. Studies revealed that consumers placed less value on boots made in China even though they were similar (*Actionable Data From Customer Experience Analytics Helping Retailers To Get Better*, n.d.)

Retail stores can use AI to predict likely impact of multiple pricing policies. Based on demand of products, inventory level, promotional activities, sales data and customer profiles marketers can offer dynamic pricing to attract new customers. eBay and Kroger use artificial Intelligence for their price optimization and stay flexible with their ability to adjust prices and promotions according to the information obtained.

Lower Cost to Reach Customers

With the help of AI, terabytes of data generated in daily transactions by retailers like Ikea, Costco etc. can be integrated with historical data of millions of customers and billions of shopping journeys. This capability ensures that right message reach the customer at the right time which has a direct impact on sales volume. The cost involved in reaching customer is much lower due to AI.

Another popular tool to get customer traffic is through affiliate marketing where firms use affiliates to attract customers to their site and improve conversion (Singh, 2017a)

Reduction in Cost of Human Resources

Smart shelves, robots, spillage sensor etc. have automated the process of getting information about product quantities on shelves i.e., whether the shelves need restocking. In context of supermarkets and grocery stores, AI based management can alert staff about products nearing their expiry date and also to apply pricing updates. This automation excludes the need for manual collection of this data which is time consuming and keeps the staff busy. HR costs can be optimized as staff can be deployed for other quality functions like conversing and relating with customers.

Improved Conversion Rates - Marketing Qualified Lead (MQL) to Sales Qualified Lead (SQL)

Leads are qualified prospective customers who are contacted by sales people. The customer data is generally collected and filtered by marketing systems. However, sales representatives need more specific information about prospects to close sales. AI algorithms can empower sales representative with dashboards that can provide qualified leads, customers' data, IP addresses, pricing variables for different groups of customers. Using lead generation algorithms for three months a Harley Davison store generated 40 qualified leads per day, increasing its total qualified leads by 2930% (Syam & Sharma, 2018). Combined with a Gainsight system it helped sales people to decide when to upsell or cross sell a product to a particular customer.

Promotional campaigns can be analysed for their acceptance or rejection rates, how the content influences the lead growth, and how the amount of time spent at various stages of qualification impacts sales closures.

Enhanced Customer Lifetime Value (CLV)

Customer Lifetime Value refers to the estimated total amount money that a consumer will spend on buying products or services during their entire lifetime.AI systems can help in better prediction of CLV based on collected data. Machine learning can help in better customer acquisition (targeted promotions, superior recommendations), enhancing customer retention, and better handling of complaints, exceptional requests (chatbots, conversational AI).

Ai backed CRM can help in customer acquisition, development and retention at a lower cost. Tools like text mining can analyse user generated content (UGC) to provide quick and valuable insights. Marketers wish to focus their resources on customers with strategic advantage i.e., the ones who will have higher CLV. Retailers can design message contents to target specific needs of prospects which can lead to customer acquisition at lower cost. Moreover, customer lifetime value can be increased by cross selling, upselling; improving purchase frequency with the aid of AI backed CRM. Technology design can automate customer behaviour leading to smoother decision making. Customers don't have to think too much as they get recommendations and a number of decisions are made by AI tools for ensuring quick product choices and fast check outs. Retailers design their technology interface in such a manner that they become habit forming for shoppers which makes their visits regular and frequent.

Nir Eyal proposed The Hook Model (Fig. 4)to explain the process of creating habit forming products/ experiences. One of the ways brains can learn complex behaviours is through habits. If a new behaviour occurs more frequently, it will take

Figure 4. The Hook cycle model
Source: Hooked: How to build habit-forming products by Nir Eyal(Eyal, 2014)

less thinking and will form a habit. For example Google created a habit of internet search. One no longer need to consciously think about searching on Google, rather it has become a habit. Creating consumer habits can provide retailers a base of active and engaged shoppers.

Companies can create hooks to trigger habit formation so that customers will keep coming back without heavy spending on promotion. Hook process has four main components(ref Fig 4)(Eyal, 2014): Triggers, Action, Variable awards and Investment.

Triggers are the internal and external prompts to tell the prospect what to do. External triggers can be emails, app icons, alert messages, notifications, one click purchase button etc. Internal triggers reside in user's mind and can be in the form of emotions, memory, association etc. Negative emotions can be a trigger for seeking escape to social media. For example people start browsing Facebook/ Instagram when they feel lonely.

Next step is when users take an action prompted by trigger. For example user will click on the link in a notification or promotional message or a social media post and they anticipate a reward from this action.

Next, rewards should be designed in such a manner that they vary every time when product is used depending on time and efforts of user. Some of these rewards can be satisfaction for doing a great product hunt, getting recognition from others, and solving a problem.

Last phase of the Hook Model is Investment which refers to data, time, effort or money put in the product or services. This part ensures that customer will keep coming to the hook cycle again and may invite friends or others users also in the next visit.

Repetition of hook cycles creates a habit and the user keeps visiting certain sites/ stores without doing much thinking. This automated behaviour is lucrative for business as it does not require heavy promotions; it only requires a good product or technology design.

Efficient Supply Chain Management and Logistics

Inventory optimization is a critical area for success of a retailer as there are direct and indirect costs associated with it. Direct costs include storage and maintenance cost. Indirect cost can be due to non-availability of stocks and loss of business as a result. ANN (Artificial Neural Networks) and machine learning is widely used to predict ABC classification of inventory where A is the category which will register highest sale and C is the category of product which will have least sale. Ai makes this predictions more accurate helping retailers improve their GMROII (gross margin return on investment).

Automated picking programmes are being used at many warehouses. E-commerce players are frequently using robots to pick up ordered items from shelves, pack them in a box, and even deliver to the customer. Robots are also used for patrolling job reducing the number of security guards.

In addition AI is helping truckers by reducing the paper documentation by inventing more touchless experiences. OCR (optical character recognition) and e-signature technology ensures delivery of products without physical handling of documents(*How AI Can Support The Supply Chain And Overcome Hurdles*, n.d.).

Zara Using Robots to Handle Deliveries

When customers orders online at Zara, they get PIN codes, which can be read by an optical barcode reader. Once the shopper scan the code, a dynamic robot will go to the warehouse, pick up merchandise and delivers the merchandise to a mailbox where the customer can collect it. Each robot can handle 2400 packages simultaneously. Thousands of Zara stores are transformed into a pickup point for online orders.

COMMON AI TECHNOLOGIES AND ALGORITHMS IN RETAIL

AI universally signifies tools such as machine learning, predictive analytics, IoT, language processing, deep learning, and big data. Retail sector makes use of following AI technologies:

Figure 5. Recommendation system

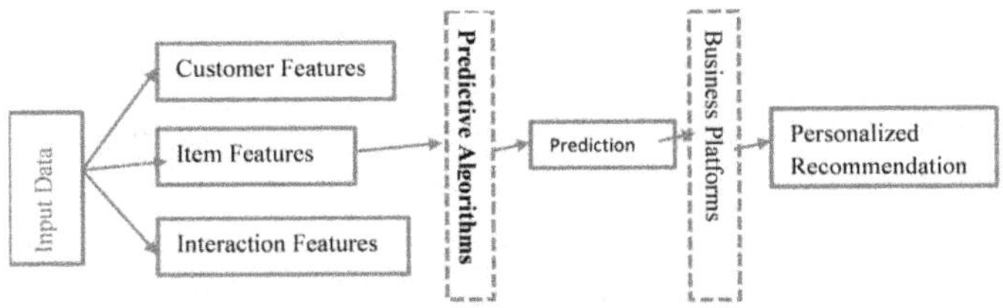

1. **Machine Learning** which help in identifying hidden patterns, segmenting the data and in predicting future outcomes through data analysis.
2. **Deep Learning** where machine learning is used to conceptualise model based on multiple layers of neural networks of the human brain.
3. **Natural Language Processing** makes it possible to understand meaning and extract intent from text in a readable, grammatically correct form.
4. **Computer Vision** is used to derive meaning and intent from graphics and visual elements including classifying content in images like faces, activities, objects, identifying characters in documents.

Common Algorithm in Retail CRM

Recommendation algorithm, Association Algorithm, Classification Algorithm, and Predictive algorithm are commonly used by retail organisations.

Recommendation System Algorithm

This algorithm enhances personalised in and out of store recommendations for the customers based on their earlier choices. When the customer open a store app, the in store sensor sense the customer choices and track the customer activities and envelope the customer behaviour. Also, it finds data about customer's last visit, products bought and frequency of the visits. Based on the criteria the AI can compile personalized recommendation of the product, offers, rewards and loyalty points, etc., for the present purchase (Fig. 5).

Amazon was the first one to introduce recommendation system in the year of 2000 and it increased product sales by 35%. Next JD sports used AI recommendation system for outdoor products which increased its revenue by 332%. Almost 50% of online sales happen through recommended systems. Therefore, the retailer should use this system to channelize the customer and increase the sale.

The out-store recommendation system have AI enabled stores which can collect the customer purchase details and preferences of product details. This data can helps to design the marketing campaigns, promotions, media plan for particular customers to hike store footfalls and increase the cart value too.

In this case the system use predictive analytics to recommend the products. The recommended system can identify the customer behavioural pattern from the leverage of past and present retail data, statistical model, and mathematical model. Thus, the retailer can spot the customer's purchase behaviour and can detect the sales opportunities. In addition, information about the sales traffic can generate valuable insights for designing the store layouts, and guiding customer's journey in the store.

There are three major sources of recommended systems: a) Collaborative Filtering, b) Content Based Filtering c) Hybrid Filtering.

Collaborative Filtering

It involves collecting and analysing data from user's behaviour, activities, and preferences and comparing these data with data from other users. The recommendation depends on item-to-item collaboration and user-to-user collaboration. The first recommendation is based on item and its similarity with other items. So products which are visually or categorically similar, to the products viewed or added to wish list by the customer, are recommended for purchase. The user-user filtering is more intensive with customer preferences and behaviours. That is the customer A prefers x, y, z products and customer B prefers m, x, y products means the recommended system assume that A also prefers m product and B prefers z product.

Content Based Filtering

It recommends the products based on the user's history of purchase choices or state of the product preferences. It also interprets the keywords, which describe the product and are enlisted from the user's browsing history. For example if the user purchased mobile phone last week, they may want to add mobile case, head set to complete the ensemble. Thus, the recommendation system assumes that the user will express his interest on purchasing the related items.

Hybrid Filtering

It is a combination of collaborative and content based filtering for precise product recommendation. Netflix is the best example for this recommendation system as it boosts the customer satisfaction through layers of data filtered by hybrid filtering. The searching pattern is spotted using rating of the film, favourite actor/actress, geographical location, age and genre of the film. Some other companies which use recommendation algorithms are Social Media Channels like LinkedIn; Video platforms like Netflix, YouTube, and Amazon Prime; Music streaming services like

Apple Music and Spotify; Online food delivery platforms like Grab, Uber Eats, and Foodpanda; Online Retail Stores like Amazon, Flipkart, Snapdeal.

Association Algorithm

Association algorithm is the technique used to analyse huge amount of unrelated variables. Association rule mining is a very popular technique in market basket analysis and it consists of the common algorithms include Apriori, K-Apriori and FP growth. Association rule based approach has a two-step approach, frequent item generation i.e. find all the frequency of items and rule generation i.e. calculate support and confidence for all association rules. The association between the items improves cross selling and provides information about frequently purchased items to the retailer (Dalal Al Attal et al., 2018). This association discovery can help in formulating the retail strategies including customer behaviour pattern analysis, designing a product catalogue, add-on sales, rearranging the store layout according to trends, frequency of trending items purchase etc.

Apriori algorithm is the very famous association algorithm implemented in market basket analysis. This is useful to find the frequency set of items for each transaction. The assumption of this case is the subset of frequent item set must be frequent. The association rule quantified by the support, confidence and lift measure can be formulated as shown in Fig 6. The Support (X, Y) incur the frequency of X and Y items and N is the total items. The confidence infers the frequency of transaction involving both X and Y divided by the transaction frequency of X. The lift infers when increase the sale of X by selling Y. In this algorithm, the frequency of subset items access from database makes some computational complexity.

Classification Algorithm

This algorithm is used to classify the occurrence of independent dataset based on the pattern, identified from the training dataset. The main classification algorithms are: Decision Tree, Bayesian Network, Support Vector Machine, and Multilayer Perceptron

Decision Trees

Decision trees perform supervised classification by recursively partitioning the training dataset. Initially all the instances are in the same class and it is trying to identify exact class with respect to target attribute. The algorithm used for constructing a decision tree is a recursive partitioning algorithm and it can be represented by tree like structure. The compact visual representation of data and rules makes decision

Figure 6. Quantified rule for association

$$Rule:\ X \Rightarrow Y$$

$$Support = \frac{frq(X,Y)}{N}$$

$$Confidence = \frac{frq(X,Y)}{frq(X)}$$

$$Lift = \frac{Support}{Supp(X) \times Supp(Y)}$$

tree to interpret and use it with ease. This also gives enough attention to description of data and picks the most important predictor variable for particular outcome. These added descriptions can help in better understanding of shopper behavior leading to improved customer retention in retail sector.

Specifically in retail, the customer behavioral patterns (purchase, transaction history and retention) are analyzed with data mining tools to improve customer loyalty, sales and increase the market share. Decision tree can construct nonlinear interactive relationship model(Agarwal & Ranjan, 2013; Tinabo, 2011). Some common algorithms used to construct decision tree are CHAID (Chi-square Automatic Interaction Detection), C5.O (a proprietary algorithm) and CART (Classification and Regression Trees).

CHAID

In the CHAID process the lowest p-value in the Chi-square test considered as a predictor variable to segment a data set into two more nodes. This method of splitting ends when there is no significant relationship between the dependent variable and set of predictors (Magidson, 1993). CHAID tree can significantly differentiate the dependent variables into segments which can be ranked by its segmentation process (Gallarza et al., 2017).

Some unique advantages by CHAID, in the retail sector, based on the customer satisfaction and group of the customer application, the predominant customer is identified directly. Additionally, the direct marketing campaign is used to identify the potential customer with reference to the customer profile (CHAID Analysis I Decision Tree Analysis I B2B International, n.d.)

CART

This is the concept of binary child node tree based classification and prediction method for splitting the records based on the similar output field values in large datasets (Fig. 7). The retail decision tree is used to predict the pattern of product purchased, best prospects and customers, target in marketing.

Figure 7. Tree based classification

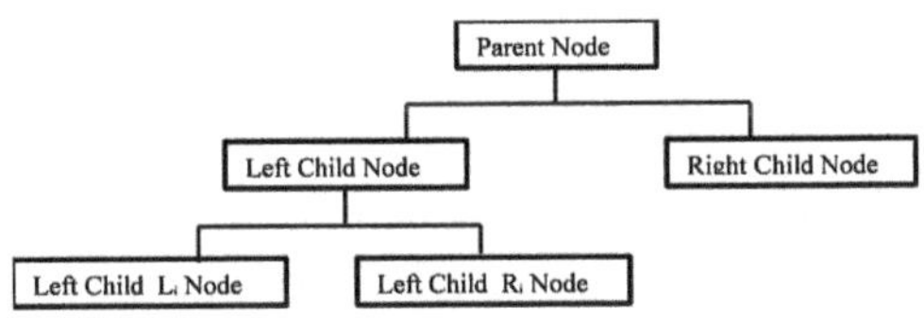

The tree based classification is a partitioning technique which is used to classify the database recursively. That is the training data partitioned with similar output values in a single segment. For example, database (Parent node) classified into two child nodes (left and right child). Also, the classification of the left child improved into the left child ith node and right child ith node. Moreover, it has hierarchical structure represented internal nodes that consists of values of features and leaf node represents as a class label.

C5.0

Ross Quinlan developed C5.0 is the improved version and combination of C4.5 and ID3 (Iterative Dichotomiser 3) algorithms. This is the common splitting algorithm which includes entropy based for maximum information gaining method. The process of splitting still continuous until otherwise for further splitting of large data set. Each subsamples splits again and again based on the different attributes combinations. This will improve the information gain before splitting. Finally the low level sample removed from the tree i.e. the model is pruned. Error Based Pruning (EBP) is the powerful boosting method of classification and thus will increase the classification accuracy(Chi et al., 2019; Elsayad & Elsalamony, 2013).

C5.0 gives best optimum while handling missing data and more number of variables. It can trim the tree by excluding the unwanted features. Interpretation of the model is very easy. Sometime it may over fit or under fit. The effect of a training data implies more on decision making (Chi et al., 2019).

Nilima Patil et al., (2012) discussed customer membership card classification method using C5.0 algorithm(Patil et al., 2012). Based on the customer income and their family size the customer card type will be classified as gold, silver and bronze.

Bayesian Networks

Naïve Bayes classifier (NBC) are probabilistic models and this will visually represent the dependency among the attributes. NBC have the combination of both prior knowledge as well as current knowledge. It is faster, efficient, and easy to use, doesn't require much training data and can handle both continuous and discrete data. Sentiment analysis, recommendation engines, and spam filtering are the common applications by NBC.

SVM Models

SVM is the classification tool using statistical learning theory proposed by Vapnik(Bottou & Vapnik, 1992). This theory enhances the closest optimum between training data to reality(Cao et al., 2020; Zendehboudi et al., 2018). Also, it follows minimizing the structural risk principal and therefore, it necessitates less amount of data for classification compared to other machine learning techniques (Güven & Şimşir, 2020). SVM models are used in the both linear and nonlinear mappings of classification. For linear classification the regression line is used as a classifier between two classes(Fig. 8). For non-linear mapping the higher dimensional feature space can be split using different kernel methods(Cao et al., 2020). The non-linear functions can be mapped by SVM without any prior assumptions of features of data to avoid overfitting of the model (Xie et al., 2008).

Figure 8. Linear SVM

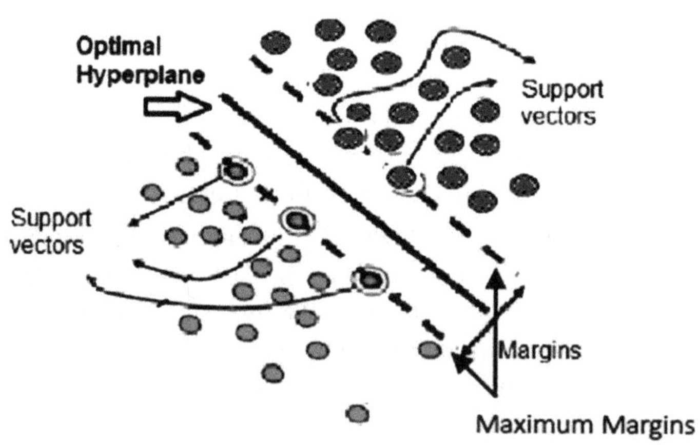

Using SVM, the data integrity can be checked for different timeline. For example, the product sale can be compared between 49th week of 2014 and 52nd week of 2018. The input data set consists of color of the product, gender, sales week, etc., For all the features it is possible to build individual models like SVM with and without color details and this will predict the customer preference details (Güven & Şimşir, 2020). The SVM can do wonders with retail data like sales prediction, detect fraudulent transactions, customer behavior, pattern analysis, market trend analysis and etc., The ORACLE corporation ensure that the SVM possibility analysis like employee sales analysis, customer loyalty prediction, store analysis, product price elasticity, customer life time value analysis, churn customer analysis, sentiment analysis etc. (Retail et al., n.d.).

The challenge for deciding on a single machine learning algorithm is how to imitate the human decision making process of selecting, transferring and extracting information from multiple sources(Torrey & Shavlik, 2010).

POPULAR AI APPLICATIONS IN RETAIL

Customer interactions are facilitated by features like co-browsing, content sharing and screen sharing. An intelligent mix of tools can lead to better customer satisfaction(Singh, 2017b).Technology applications can be broadly classified in following two divisions in the context of retail(Parise et al., 2016).:

Remote Experts

In this case physical location of expert is different than that of consumer and technology acts like a connection to provide live interaction between the two.

Chatbots/ Conversational AI/Video Chat

Conversational AI includes chatbots/business messages to support customers and sales departments. These tools help in making better connection with customers and prospects on higher scale. Majority of brands worldwide are already using chatbots or about to use them in near future. These chatbots provide a personalised support to shoppers by sending notifications, conversing with them to resolve any queries, and suggesting products. Brands like Burberry Tommy Hilfiger use chatbots to provide product navigation and promote cross selling by suggesting related products. If a customer buys a jacket, chatbot can suggest him to buy a matching bag to complete the look.

Besides video chats are increasingly employed to engage the customer and to give him virtual store experience. These chats make it possible for shoppers to see various product options and also avail recommendations from store employees. Product queries related to size, colour, and design in case of apparel retail can be resolved instantly over video chat. Retail banking makes extensive use of video chats so that customers can get information about complex financial products and take decisions about their purchase with the help of live discussion with experts. Burberry opened its first "social retail store" in China. Through WeChat shoppers can access product and store information, book appointments for store visits, make table reservations in store café.

Visual Search

Rather than using keywords, customers can make use of images/visuals to carry out search using Google Images or any other image search engine. As picture has more details, it can remove inaccuracies of keywords search. Visual search is popular in apparel, home décor and electronics category.

In-store Assistance

Retail brands have come out with robots in various shapes, sizes and capabilities. Retail robots can perform routine tasks so that sales people can devote attention to customers. Retail robots can also be used as data collectors

Robots like Lowebot at Lowe's Home Improvement Chain can answer simple customer questions in number of languages. It can also monitor inventory and thus, frees up sales staff from such routine jobs.

Beauty Counter integrated its brick and mortar store with online customers through live streaming. Inside store, the front portion is traditional retail and rear portion is a studio where products, events, beauty consultations are live streamed throughout the day using Bambuser platform Customers can ask their questions in real time, get consultations from the staff and can buy products by clicking online(*Why Beautycounter Is Live-Streaming Everything inside Its New Store*, n.d.)

Digital Assistants

In this case technology itself provides expert information to employee or shopper, and they are present in same physical location like physical store. Technology may be in the form of app or platform or in store assistance like virtual mirrors etc. The number of virtual digital assistants and of enterprise voice assistants is anticipated to grow to one billion users by 2025(Accenture, 2020). Prevalent examples of digital assistants include:

Cashier-Free Stores

Checkout free stores like Amazon Go can make shopping more efficient as customers need not wait for billing. Technology like Amazon Go and Just Walk Out shopping responds if people pick products from the shelf or keep them back. The billed amount is deducted from your Amazon account when shopper moves out of the store. The result is faster shopping, lower operational costs and lower number of employees required per store.

Voice Search Engine Optimization (VSEO)

Voice search is gaining ground as people use smartphones and devices like Amazon's Alexa to do product searches. Retailers need to create their content for voice searches, use long tail keywords and create voice enabled catalogues so that customers can search products and complete buying process using voice. This technology allows retailers to tap customers speaking diverse languages. During Covid 19, elderly population frequently used voice searches for making purchases on internet.

Indian Railway Catering and Tourism Corporation's (IRCTC) developed a chatbot, AskDISHA to answer passenger queries and it improved the satisfaction of customer interactions by 70%. This chatbot can handle queries on ticket reservation, refund status, PNR search, and cancellations through voice and text capabilities in multiple languages.

Virtual Fitting Rooms/Virtual Mirrors

Retailers have been experimenting with virtual mirrors for number of years but pandemic pushed the efforts further as customer became apprehensive of trying products touched by others. Product trial is critical for closing the sales especially in sector like apparel, footwear, jewellery etc. Digital/virtual mirrors can help resolve the trial issues for retailers. The mirror clicks pictures of shopper from different angles and records the relevant measurements. With the help of mapping recognition software, an image of customer is shown in mirror along with different product options. Shopper can choose different merchandise by using hand gestures/ touch screens and try them on without entering physical trial room.

Luxury retailers and beauty brands like Estee Lauder, Sephora, and L'Oréal etc. are investing in beauty tech so that customers can try their products virtually. Virtual artist app of Sephora enables customers to try make up using digital overlays aided by face tracking and image recognition technology. L'Oréal provides personalized touch through Perso, which can do face analysis and then activates a device to generate suitable foundation shade.

Cashless Payments

Contactless payments increased by 69% as consumers were wary of touching surfaces, cash and cards. Number of alternative options like digital wallets, tap to pay wearables, smartphone applications are available for shoppers. Food delivery players like UberEats, Swiggy, Zomato and grocery retailers adopted and promoted digital payments during lockdown. Many retailers gave customers an option to pay online and then pick up the merchandise from store or curb side avoiding the need to enter a PIN or touch card machine(*NRF | Coronavirus Leads to More Use of Contactless Credit Cards and Mobile Payments despite Cost and Security Concerns*, n.d.).

POINTS TO PONDER FOR CHOICE AND IMPLEMENTATION OF AI

Clarity About Mission

Multitude of technology solutions is available and many a times decision makers become obsessed with AI losing the focus on customers. The starting point for any decision should be how to serve and delight the customer rather than which technology to employ.AI should be a means to an end and not the end in itself. Another point to remember is that business systems should align with technology solutions and vice versa.

Careful Selection of Vendors

Firms should carefully choose vendors for AI technology. Vendor Selection Check List should consider following factors:

1. Capability to provide required technologies, AI tools
2. Sustainability of vendor in future: A number of start-ups are mushrooming in AI business. Pick a vendor which has a sound business plan and can provide services in the long run
3. Flexibility and Adaptability of Vendors to innovate
4. Clear communication: Pick a vendor who can understand and articulate solutions. This is a critical area as organisations and vendors need to regularly & clearly communicate and work together for devising and revising technology solutions
5. Trustworthy
6. Support to Internal staff for testing & training

Action Analytics

Most of the retailers are flooded with data and there are number of tools available for data analysis. However, action taken on basis of predictive analytics should materialize in terms of customer values. To ensure that data offerings are activated by and for customers, following principles should be used(*Actioned Analytics Pave the Way to New Customer Value*, n.d.):

1. Give Priority to customers who are ready to take action and are open to adapt insight

PepsiCo wanted to provide information solution Pep Worx to company's retail partners. It included a suite of capabilities to support innovative marketing programs, space optimization in retail stores, and also product assortment strategies. They chose to initiate the programme with retailers who were willing to take action and eager to learn new skills. Activities that inspire action based on insights.

2. Deliver insights in consumable ways

AI companies can set up customer-centred efforts like onsite support, automated services, and advisory units for retailers. Tripbam offers hotel rate shopping to a major chunk of Fortune 500 companies. As the rates fluctuated, it suggested rebooking opportunities to travel managers. Afterwards, Tripbam designed an automated rebooking feature so that a busy traveller can avail a lower cost opportunity.

3. Monitor action and handle inaction

Customers may not act on all the recommendations given by apps. Cochlear, which deals with hearing implants, was astonished to find that hearing patients did not change their hearing settings despite getting recommendation alerts. Therefore, developers devised a new technology which could analyse the sound environment and do automatic settings for customers to provide best hearing for the conditions. Retail organisations should pay attention to cognitive fit so that shoppers get the information they need and get expertise when they need it (Parise et al., 2016). Besides technology should provide aesthetically pleasing experiences like augmented reality, video content, which makes customers happy and excited.

Adoption of New Systems vs. Reliance on Obsolete Models

Companies find it difficult to implement human centric experiences even though they are capable of creating such solution. Interestingly the problem is due to earlier technology solution which served companies well in the past. Employees and management resist adoption of new systems as they don't wish to let go of their familiarity with the present systems(Accenture, 2020).

Digital technology is now a basic expectation rather than a competitive advantage. The best practices may appear like a shortcoming in the current scenario. Retailers need to rethink their entire business model so that technology can be inbuilt into the system providing smoother access across various levels and aligning better with people.

Human Factor in AI Implementation

Successful choice and implementation require cooperation from employees. Creativity and critical thinking skills of humans can be combined with scalability of technology.

As per Accenture PLC's global study about AI and machine learning usage. new human jobs are emerging in AI which are unique and require entirely novel skills and training. Three job categories can be identified as trainers, explainers and sustainers (Wilson et al., 2017).These roles will support the machines and cognitive technology to ensure an effective and responsible outcome.

Enterprises should rethink core assumptions about intersection of human and technology to survive and thrive in future(Accenture, 2020).

REFERENCES

Accenture. (2020). *We, the post-digital people.* https://www.accenture.com/us-en/insights/technology/_acnmedia/Thought-Leadership-Assets/PDF-2/Accenture-Technology-Vision-2020-Full-Report.pdf

Actionable Data From Customer Experience Analytics Helping Retailers To Get Better. (n.d.). Retrieved February 6, 2021, from https://www.forbes.com/sites/warrenshoulberg/2021/01/13/actionable-data-from-customer-experience-analytics-helping-retailers-to-get-better/?sh=ec4c541e328c

Actioned Analytics Pave the Way to New Customer Value. (n.d.). Retrieved February 3, 2021, from https://sloanreview.mit.edu/article/actioned-analytics-pave-the-way-to-new-customer-value/

Agarwal, R., & Ranjan, J. (2013). An empirical investigation on association rule mining in Indian retail industry. *International Journal of Intercultural Information Management, 3*(3), 226–241. doi:10.1504/IJIIM.2013.057741

Ameen, N., Tarhini, A., Reppel, A., & Anand, A. (2021). Customer experiences in the age of artificial intelligence. *Computers in Human Behavior, 114*. doi:10.1016/j.chb.2020.106548

Ammanath, B., Hupfer, S., & Jarvis, D. (2020). *The state of artifical intelligence in business | Deloitte Insights*. https://www2.deloitte.com/us/en/insights/focus/cognitive-technologies/state-of-ai-and-intelligent-automation-in-business-survey.html?id=us:2ps:3gl:aisurvey:awa:con:071420:ad2:kwd-932327896302:%2Baiinthe%2Benterprise&gclid=EAIaIQobChMIpsyytr2V6wIVBeiGCh

Artificial Intelligence for Retail in 2020: 12 Real-World Use Cases. (n.d.). Retrieved December 12, 2020, from https://spd.group/artificial-intelligence/ai-for-retail

Bottou, L., & Vapnik, V. (1992). Local learning algorithms. *Neural Computation, 4*(6), 888–900. doi:10.1162/neco.1992.4.6.888

Cam, A., Chui, M., & Hall, B. (2019). Global AI Survey: AI proves its worth, but few scale impact. *McKinsey*, (November), 1–16.

Cao, W., Fang, Z., Hou, G., Han, M., Xu, X., Dong, J., & Zheng, J. (2020). The psychological impact of the COVID-19 epidemic on college students in China. *Psychiatry Research, 287*, 112934. doi:10.1016/j.psychres.2020.112934 PMID:32229390

CHAID Analysis | Decision Tree Analysis | B2B International. (n.d.). Retrieved February 24, 2021, from https://www.b2binternational.com/research/methods/statistical-techniques/chaid-analysis/

Chi, D.-J., Chu, C.-C., & Chen, D. (2019). Applying Support Vector Machine, C5. 0, and CHAID to the Detection of Financial Statements Frauds. *International Conference on Intelligent Computing*, 327–336.

Elsayad, A. M., & Elsalamony, H. A. (2013). Diagnosis of breast cancer using decision tree models and SVM. *International Journal of Computers and Applications, 83*(5).

Eyal, N. (2014). *Hooked: How to build habit-forming products*. Penguin.

Fogg, B. (2009). A behavior model for persuasive design. *ACM International Conference Proceeding Series*, 350. 10.1145/1541948.1541999

Fogg, B. J. (2003). Persuasive Technology: Using Computers to Change What We Think and Do. *Persuasive Technology: Using Computers to Change What We Think and Do*. doi:10.1016/B978-1-55860-643-2.X5000-8

Fogg, B. J. (2009). Creating persuasive technologies: An eight-step design process. *ACM International Conference Proceeding Series*, 350. 10.1145/1541948.1542005

Gallarza, M. G., Arteaga, F., Del Chiappa, G., Gil-Saura, I., & Holbrook, M. B. (2017). A multidimensional service-value scale based on Holbrook's typology of customer value: Bridging the gap between the concept and its measurement. *Journal of Service Management*, *28*(4), 724–762. doi:10.1108/JOSM-06-2016-0166

Grewal, D., Hulland, J., Kopalle, P. K., & Karahanna, E. (2020). The future of technology and marketing: a multidisciplinary perspective. Journal of the Academy of Marketing Science (Vol. 48, Issue 1). doi:10.100711747-019-00711-4

Güven, İ., & Şimşir, F. (2020). Demand forecasting with color parameter in retail apparel industry using artificial neural networks (ANN) and support vector machines (SVM) methods. *Computers & Industrial Engineering*, *147*, 106678. doi:10.1016/j.cie.2020.106678

How AI Can Be The Key To Loyalty And Retention For Retail In 2021. (n.d.). Retrieved February 25, 2021, from https://www.forbes.com/sites/jonathantreiber/2021/02/02/how-artificial-intelligence-can-be-the-key-to-loyalty-and-retention-in-2021/

How AI Can Support The Supply Chain And Overcome Hurdles. (n.d.). Retrieved February 20, 2021, from https://www.forbes.com/sites/forbestechcouncil/2020/06/12/how-ai-can-support-the-supply-chain-and-overcome-hurdles/?sh=50420cee330d

How technology is helping to reshape fitness and outdoor recreation. (n.d.). Retrieved December 12, 2020, from https://www.fastcompany.com/90566919/how-technology-is-helping-to-reshape-fitness-and-outdoor-recreation

Magidson, J. (1993). The use of the new ordinal algorithm in CHAID to target profitable segments. *The Journal of Database Marketing*, *1*(1), 29–48.

NRF | Coronavirus leads to more use of contactless credit cards and mobile payments despite cost and security concerns. (n.d.). Retrieved February 20, 2021, from https://nrf.com/media-center/press-releases/coronavirus-leads-more-use-contactless-credit-cards-and-mobile-payments

Parise, S., Guinan, P. J., & Kafka, R. (2016). Solving the crisis of immediacy: How digital technology can transform the customer experience. *Business Horizons*, *59*(4), 411–420. doi:10.1016/j.bushor.2016.03.004

Patil, N., Lathi, R., & Chitre, V. (2012). Customer card classification based on C5. 0 & CART algorithms. *International Journal of Engineering Research and Applications*, *2*(4), 164–167.

Ready, B. (2020). *Navigating your retail business through COVID-19*. https://services.google.com/fh/files/misc/2020_covidretailguide_en-us.pdf

Retail, O., Decision, C., & Science, D. T. (n.d.). Oracle Retail Consumer Decision Tree and Demand Transference Science Cloud Service - Data sheet. Oracle.

Roggeveen, A. L., & Sethuraman, R. (2020). Customer-Interfacing Retail Technologies in 2020 & Beyond: An Integrative Framework and Research Directions. *Journal of Retailing*, *96*(3), 299–309. doi:10.1016/j.jretai.2020.08.001

Shopping in 2020: 6 intriguing experiments in digital retail. (n.d.). Retrieved January 3, 2021, from https://www.fastcompany.com/90585138/the-six-wildest-ways-we-shopped-in-2020

Singh, S. (2017a). *Driving traffic and customer activity through affiliate marketing*. IGI Global.

Singh, S. (2017b). Technological Innovations of Marketing in Digital India. *International Journal of Transformation in Operational & Marketing Management*, *1*(1). www.eurekajournals.com

Syam, N., & Sharma, A. (2018). Waiting for a sales renaissance in the fourth industrial revolution: Machine learning and artificial intelligence in sales research and practice. *Industrial Marketing Management*, *69*, 135–146. doi:10.1016/j.indmarman.2017.12.019

Tech industry leading India's recovery post Covid - The Financial Express. (n.d.). Retrieved February 20, 2021, from https://www.financialexpress.com/industry/technology/tech-industry-leading-indias-recovery-post-covid/2196681/

Tinabo, R. (2011). Decision tree technique for customer retention in retail sector. *International Conference on Integrated Computing Technology*, 123–131. 10.1007/978-3-642-22247-4_11

Torrey, L., & Shavlik, J. (2010). Transfer learning. In *Handbook of research on machine learning applications and trends: Algorithms, methods, and techniques* (pp. 242–264). IGI Global. doi:10.4018/978-1-60566-766-9.ch011

Venkatesh, V., Morris, M. G., Davis, G. B., & Davis, F. D. (2003). User acceptance of information technology: Toward a unified view. *Management Information Systems Quarterly*, *27*(3), 425–478. doi:10.2307/30036540

Venkatesh, V., Thong, J. Y. L., & Xu, X. (2012). Consumer acceptance and use of information technology: Extending the unified theory of acceptance and use of technology. *MIS Quarterly: Management Information Systems*, *36*(1), 157–178. doi:10.2307/41410412

What Robots Can Do for Retail. (n.d.). Retrieved January 3, 2021, from https://hbr.org/2020/10/what-robots-can-do-for-retail

Why Beautycounter is live-streaming everything inside its new store. (n.d.). Retrieved January 3, 2021, from https://www.fastcompany.com/90580782/why-this-beauty-startup-is-live-streaming-everything-inside-its-new-store

Wilson, H. J., Daugherty, P. R., & Morini-Bianzino, N. (2017). The jobs that artificial intelligence will create. *MIT Sloan Management Review*, *58*(4), 14–16. doi:10.7551/mitpress/11645.003.0020

Xie, X., Ding, J., & Hu, G. (2008). Forecasting the retail sales of China's catering industry using support vector machines. *2008 7th World Congress on Intelligent Control and Automation*, 4458–4462.

Zendehboudi, A., Baseer, M. A., & Saidur, R. (2018). Application of support vector machine models for forecasting solar and wind energy resources: A review. *Journal of Cleaner Production*, *199*, 272–285. doi:10.1016/j.jclepro.2018.07.164

KEY TERMS AND DEFINITIONS

Conversational AI: Technology tools to interact or converse with customers.

Digital Assistants: Technology which provides expert information and assistance to employee or shopper, and they are present in the same physical location like a physical store.

Remote Experts: Experts located at a distance, who use technology as a bridge to reach customers.

Triggers: Internal and external prompts to tell the prospect what to do.

Virtual Mirrors: Technology aided replica which can be used for virtually trying on products or assessing the merchandise fit.

Virtual Search: Ability to conduct search on search engine using pictures or images.

Compilation of References

$16.1B of Global EdTech Venture Capital in 2020 – HolonIQ. (n.d.). Retrieved July 26, 2021, from https://www.holoniq.com/notes/16.1b-of-global-edtech-venture-capital-in-2020/

(2006). CRM implementation: Effectiveness issues and insights. *Journal of Service Research, 9*(2), 184–194.

"Virtual patient" helps train medics remotely during pandemic - BBC News. (n.d.). Retrieved July 12, 2021, from https://www.bbc.com/news/uk-england-bristol-55202237

standout start-ups taking an AI leap in India. (n.d.). Retrieved July 12, 2021, from https://www.livemint.com/Leisure/u7M3e5ymwmGf6QRLaXBoAJ/10-standout-startups-taking-an-AI-leap-in-India.html

Abbott, J., & Minasian, P. (2020). The Modern Retailer Imperative: Creating Hyper-personalized. *Connected Customer Experiences*, 1–12.

Abdollahpouri, H., Adomavičius, G., Burke, R., Guy, I., Jannach, D., Kamishima, T., Krasnodebski, J., & Pizzato, L. (2019). *Beyond Personalization: Research Directions in Multi Stakeholder Recommendation*. doi:10.1007/s11257-019-09256

Accenture. (2020). *We, the post-digital people*. https://www.accenture.com/us-en/insights/technology/_acnmedia/Thought-Leadership-Assets/PDF-2/Accenture-Technology-Vision-2020-Full-Report.pdf

Actionable Data From Customer Experience Analytics Helping Retailers To Get Better. (n.d.). Retrieved February 6, 2021, from https://www.forbes.com/sites/warrenshoulberg/2021/01/13/actionable-data-from-customer-experience-analytics-helping-retailers-to-get-better/?sh=ec4c541e328c

Actioned Analytics Pave the Way to New Customer Value. (n.d.). Retrieved February 3, 2021, from https://sloanreview.mit.edu/article/actioned-analytics-pave-the-way-to-new-customer-value/

Agarwal, R., Dugas, M., Gao, G., & Kannan, P. K. (2020). Emerging technologies and analytics for a new era of value-centered marketing in healthcare. *Journal of the Academy of Marketing Science, 48*(2), 9–23.

Agarwal, R., & Ranjan, J. (2013). An empirical investigation on association rule mining in Indian retail industry. *International Journal of Intercultural Information Management*, *3*(3), 226–241. doi:10.1504/IJIIM.2013.057741

Agarwal, R., & Venkatesh, V. (2002). Assessing a firm's web presence: A heuristic evaluation procedure for the measurement of usability. *Information Systems Research*, *13*(2), 168–186. doi:10.1287/isre.13.2.168.84

Aggarwal, A., & Yadav, V. K. (2015). Impact of Technology in E- Retailing Operations: A Consumer Perspective. *Procedia: Social and Behavioral Sciences*, *189*, 252–258. doi:10.1016/j.sbspro.2015.03.220

Agnew, J. R., & Szykman, L. R. (2005). Asset allocation and information overload: The influence of information display, asset choice, and investor experience. *Journal of Behavioral Finance*, *6*(2), 57–70. doi:10.120715427579jpfm0602_2

Agrawal, Gans, & Goldfarb. (2019). Economic policy for artificial intelligence. Innovation Policy and the Economy, 19(1), 139–159.

Agrawal, A., Gans, J., & Goldfarb, A. (2019). Economic policy for artificial intelligence. *Innovation Policy and the Economy*, *19*(1), 139–159. doi:10.1086/699935

Aguiar, M., & Bils, M. (2015). Has consumption inequality mirrored income inequality? *The American Economic Review*, *105*(9), 2725–2756. doi:10.1257/aer.20120599

Aguirre, S., & Rodriguez, A. (2017, September). Automation of a business process using robotic process automation (RPA): A case study. In *Workshop on engineering applications* (pp. 65-71). Springer. 10.1007/978-3-319-66963-2_7

Akroush, M. N., Dahiyat, S. E., Gharaibeh, H. S., & Abu-Lail, B. N. (2011). Customer relationship management implementation. *International Journal of Commerce and Management*, *21*(2), 158–190. doi:10.1108/10569211111144355

Al-Ajlan, M., & Zairi, M. (2006). Critical Success Factors in CRM Implementation: Some Research Issues. Metamorphosis. *Journal of Management Research*, *5*(1), 19–30. doi:10.1177/0972622520060103

Alexander, A., Nell, D., Bailey, A. R., & Shaw, G. (2009). Theco-creation of a retail innovation: Shoppers and the earlysupermarket in Britain. *Enterprise and Society*, *10*(3), 529–558. doi:10.1093/es/khp016

Alibaba Group. (2019). https://www.alibabagroup.com/en/about/overview

Ali, M., & Lee, Y. (2018, April). Crm sales prediction using continuous time-evolving classification. *Proceedings of the AAAI Conference on Artificial Intelligence*, *32*(1), 7727–7734.

Ali, O., Shrestha, A., Osmanaj, V., & Muhammed, S. (2020). Cloud computing technology adoption: An evaluation of key factors in local governments. *Information Technology & People*, *34*(2), 666–703. doi:10.1108/ITP-03-2019-0119

Altexsoft. (2018). *7 Ways Airlines Use Artificial Intelligence and Data Science to Improve Operations.* https://www.altexsoft.com/blog/datascience/7-ways-how-airlines-use-artificial-intelligence-and-data-science-to-improve-their-operations/

Altman, E. I., Marco, G., & Varetto, F. (1994). Corporate distress diagnosis. Comparisons using linear discriminant analysis and neutral network (the Italian experience). *Journal of Banking & Finance, 18*(3), 505–529. doi:10.1016/0378-4266(94)90007-8

Alzahrani, S., & Daim, T. U. (2021). *Technology Adoption. Recent Developments in Individual and Organizational Adoption of ICTs*. doi:10.4018/978-1-7998-3045-0.ch006

Amazon AI Awards 2017: Recognising the future of AI. (n.d.). Retrieved July 8, 2021, from https://yourstory.com/2017/12/amazon-ai-awards-2017/amp

Ameen, N., Tarhini, A., Reppel, A., & Anand, A. (2021). Customer experiences in the age of artificial intelligence. *Computers in Human Behavior, 114*. doi:10.1016/j.chb.2020.106548

Ammanath, B., Hupfer, S., & Jarvis, D. (2020). *The state of artifical intelligence in business | Deloitte Insights*. https://www2.deloitte.com/us/en/insights/focus/cognitive-technologies/state-of-ai-and-intelligent-automation-in-business-survey.html?id=us:2ps:3gl:aisurvey:awa:con:071420:ad2:kwd-932327896302:%2Baiinthe%2Benterprise&gclid=EAIaIQobChMIpsyytr2V6wIVBeiGCh

Amoako, G. K., Arthur, E., Bandoh, C., & Katah, R. K. (2012, January). The impact of effective customer relationship management (CRM) on repurchase: A case study of (GOLDEN TULIP) hotel (ACCRA-GHANA). *African Journal of Marketing Management, 4*(1), 17–29.

André, Q., Carmon, Z., Wertenbroch, K., Crum, A., Frank, D., Goldstein, W., Huber, J., van Boven, L., Weber, B., & Yang, H. (2017). Consumer Choice and Autonomy in the Age of Artificial Intelligence and Big Data. *Customer Needs and Solutions, 5*(1-2), 28–37. doi:10.100740547-017-0085-8

Andrews, M., Goehring, J., Hui, S., Pancras, J., & Thornswood, L. (2016). Mobile promotions: A framework and research priorities. *Journal of Interactive Marketing, 34*, 15–24. doi:10.1016/j.intmar.2016.03.004

Anshari, Almunawar, Lim, & Al-Mudimigh. (2018). Customer relationship management and big data-enabled: Personalization & customization of services. *Applied Computing and Informatics, 15*(2), 94-101.

Antons, D., & Breidbach, C. F. (2018). Big data, big insights? Advancing service innovation and design with machine learning. *Journal of Service Research, 21*(1), 17–39. doi:10.1177/1094670517738373

Arbel, Y. A., & Shapira, R. (2020). Theory of the nudnik: The future of consumer activism and what we can do to stop it. *Vanderbilt Law Review*.

Artificial Intelligence for Retail in 2020: 12 Real-World Use Cases. (n.d.). Retrieved December 12, 2020, from https://spd.group/artificial-intelligence/ai-for-retail

Artificial intelligence trains doctors to be more empathetic to people - The Washington Post. (n.d.). Retrieved July 12, 2021, from https://www.washingtonpost.com/technology/2021/02/16/virtual-ai-hospital-patients/

Arts, J. W. C., Frambach, R. T., & Bijmolt, T. H. A. (2011). Generalizations on consumer innovation adoption: A meta-analysis on drivers of intention and behavior. *International Journal of Research in Marketing*, *28*(2), 134–144. doi:10.1016/j.ijresmar.2010.11.002

Arumawadu, H. I., Rathnayaka, R. M. K. T., & Illangarathne, S. K. (2015, August). Mining Profitability of Telecommunication Customers Using K-Means Clustering. *Journal of Data Analysis and Information Processing*, *3*(03), 63–71. doi:10.4236/jdaip.2015.33008

Ascarza. (2018). Retention futility: Targeting high-risk customers might be ineffective. *JMR, Journal of Marketing Research*, *55*(1), 80–98.

Ascarza, E. (2018). Retention futility: Targeting high-risk customers might be ineffective. *JMR, Journal of Marketing Research*, *55*(1), 80–98. doi:10.1509/jmr.16.0163

Audretsch, D. B., & Feldma, M. P. (1996). R&D spillovers and the geography of innovation and production. *The American Economic Review*, *86*(3), 630–640.

Auto Proctoring - Examity. (n.d.). Retrieved June 19, 2021, from https://www.examity.com/solutions/auto-proctoring/

Avasthi. (n.d.). *ETPWLA 2019: Embibe founder Aditi Avasthi gets "Accenture Vaahini Innovator of the Year" - The Economic Times Video | ET Now*. Retrieved July 12, 2021, from https://economictimes.indiatimes.com/news/company/corporate-trends/etpwla-2019-embibe-founder-aditi-avasthi-gets-accenture-vaahini-innovator-of-the-year/videoshow/68636240.cms?from=mdr

Avolio, B. J., Sosik, J. J., Kahai, S. S., & Baker, B. (2014). E-leadership: Re-examining transformations in leadership source and transmission. *The Leadership Quarterly*, *25*(1), 105–131. doi:10.1016/j.leaqua.2013.11.003

Azam, M. S. (2015). *Diffusion of ICT and SME Performance. E-Services Adoption: Processes by Firms in Developing Nations*. doi:10.1108/S1069-096420150000023005

Bakardjieva, M., Felt, M., & Dumitrica, D. (2018). The mediatization of leadership: Grassroots digital facilitators as organic intellectuals, sociometric stars and caretakers. *Information Communication and Society*, *21*(6), 899–914. doi:10.1080/1369118X.2018.1434556

Balaji, M. S., & Roy, S. (2017). Value co-creation with Internet of things technology in the retail industry. *Journal of Marketing Management*, *33*(1-2), 7–31. doi:10.1080/0267257X.2016.1217914

Balducci, B., & Marinova, D. (2018). Unstructured data in marketing. *Journal of the Academy of Marketing Science, 46*(4), 557–590.

Barney, J. (1991). Firm resources and sustained competitive advantage. *Journal of Management*, *17*(1), 99–120. doi:10.1177/014920639101700108

Barreto, Silva, Fischer, Albuquerque, & Amorim. (2011). Emerging issues in people management: An analysis of academic output. *Administration Magazine UFSM, 4*(1), 215-232.

Bart, Y., Shankar, V., Sultan, F., & Urban, G. L. (2005). Are the drivers and role of online trust the same for all web sites and consumers? A large-scale exploratory empirical study. *Journal of Marketing, 69*(4), 133–152. doi:10.1509/jmkg.2005.69.4.133

Batra, R., & Keller, K. L. (2016). Integrating marketing communications: New findings, new lessons, and new ideas. *Journal of Marketing, 80*(6), 122–145. doi:10.1509/jm.15.0419

Bauer, J., & Jannach, D. (2018). Optimal pricing in e-commerce based on sparse and noisy data. *Decision Support Systems, 106*, 53–63. doi:10.1016/j.dss.2017.12.002

Bawack, R. E., Fosso Wamba, S., & Carillo, K. D. A. (2021). A framework for understanding artificial intelligence research: Insights from practice. *Journal of Enterprise Information Management, 34*(2), 645–678. doi:10.1108/JEIM-07-2020-0284

Berger, J., Humphreys, A., Ludwig, S., Moe, W. W., Netzer, O., & Schweidel, D. A. (2019). Uniting the tribes: Using text for marketing insight. *Journal of Marketing, 84*(1), 1–25.

Berman, B., & Evans, J. R. (2010). *Retail Management: A Strategic Approach* (11th ed.). Pearson Education, Inc.

Berry, L. L., Bolton, R. N., Bridges, C. H., Meyer, J., Parasuraman, A., & Seiders, K. (2010). Opportunities for innovation inthe delivery of interactive retail services. *Journal of Interactive Marketing, 24*(2), 155–167. doi:10.1016/j.intmar.2010.02.001

Bhatia, A., Chandani, A., & Chhateja, J. (2020). Robo advisory and its potential in addressing the behavioral biases of investors - A qualitative study in Indian context. *Journal of Behavioral and Experimental Finance, 25*, 100281. doi:10.1016/j.jbef.2020.100281

Bloom, B. S. (1984). The 2 sigma problem: The search for methods of group instruction as effective as one-to-one tutoring. *Educational Researcher, 13*(6), 4–16.

Blut, M., Frennea, C. M., Mittal, V., & Mothersbaugh, D. L. (2015). How procedural, financial and relational switching costs affect customer satisfaction, repurchase intentions, and repurchase behavior: A meta-analysis. *International Journal of Research in Marketing, 32*(2), 226–229. doi:10.1016/j.ijresmar.2015.01.001

Blut, M., Wang, C., & Schoefer, K. (2016). Factors influencing the acceptance of self-service technologies: A meta-analysis. *Journal of Service Research, 19*(4), 396–416. doi:10.1177/1094670516662352

Boe, O., & Torgersen, G.-E. (2018). Norwegian "Digital Border Defense" and Competence for the Unforeseen: A Grounded Theory Approach. *Frontiers in Psychology, 9*, 555. Advance online publication. doi:10.3389/fpsyg.2018.00555 PMID:29725314

Bohling, T., Bowman, D., LaValle, S., Mittal, V., Narayandas, D., Ramani, G., & Varadarajan, R. (2006). CRM Implementation. *Journal of Service Research*, *9*(2), 184–194. doi:10.1177/1094670506293573

Bolton, R. N., McColl-Kennedy, J. R., Cheung, L., Gallan, A., Orsingher, C., Witell, L., & Zaki, M. (2018). Customer experience challenges: Bringing together digital, physical, and social realms. *Journal of Service Management*, *29*(5), 776–808. doi:10.1108/JOSM-04-2018-0113

Bottou, L., & Vapnik, V. (1992). Local learning algorithms. *Neural Computation*, *4*(6), 888–900. doi:10.1162/neco.1992.4.6.888

Boxall, P., & Purcell, J. (2011). *Strategy and Human Resource Management*. Macmillan International Higher Education.

Boxine GmbH Company Profile | Düsseldorf, Nordrhein-Westfalen, Germany | Competitors, Financials & Contacts - Dun & Bradstreet. (n.d.). Retrieved July 6, 2021, from https://www.dnb.com/business-directory/company-profiles.boxine_gmbh.3a47fbdf271e382eea4c303c27900ccb.html

Bradlow, E. T., Gangwar, M., Kopalle, P., & Voleti, S. (2017). The Role of Big Data and Predictive Analytics in Retailing. *Journal of Retailing*, *93*(1), 79–95. doi:10.1016/j.jretai.2016.12.004

Brewster, C., & Hegewisch, A. (1994). Human resource management in Europe: Issues and opportunities. *Policy & Practice.*

Brynjolfsson, E., & Mcafee, A. (2017). The Business of Artificial Intelligence: what it can and cannot do for your organization. *Harvard Business Review Digital Articles*, 1–20.

Business Wire. (2018). *New Vantage Partners Releases Annual Big Data Executive Survey for 2018, Data and Innovation: How Big Data and AI are Driving Business Innovation.* https://www.businesswire.com/news/home/20180108005172/en/NewVantage-Partners-Releases-Annual-Big-Data-Executive

Cam, A., Chui, M., & Hall, B. (2019). Global AI Survey: AI proves its worth, but few scale impact. *McKinsey*, (November), 1–16.

Cambria, E. (2016). Affective computing and sentiment analysis. *IEEE Intelligent Systems*, *31*(2), 102–107. doi:10.1109/MIS.2016.31

Can Artificial Intelligence Actually Make Classroom Discussion Better? | League for Innovation. (n.d.). Retrieved July 16, 2021, from https://leagueforinnovation.wordpress.com/2020/09/17/can-artificial-intelligence-actually-make-classroom-discussion-better/

Cançado. Corrêa, Oliveira, & Dagmar. (2017). Revisiting the Four Faces of Human Resource Management. *ANPAD Meetings – Enanpad*, 1-4.

Cao, W., Fang, Z., Hou, G., Han, M., Xu, X., Dong, J., & Zheng, J. (2020). The psychological impact of the COVID-19 epidemic on college students in China. *Psychiatry Research*, *287*, 112934. doi:10.1016/j.psychres.2020.112934 PMID:32229390

Cao, Y., & Gruca, T. S. (2005). Reducing adverse selection through customer relationship management. *Journal of Marketing*, *69*(4), 219–229.

Carletti, E., Claessens, S., Fatas, A., & Vives, X. (2020). *The Bank Business Model in Post-Covid-19 World, The Future of Banking 2. Report sponsored by IESE*. Bank for International Settlements.

Carmilovic, D. (2008). Data Mining and CRM in Telecommunications. *Serbian Journal of Management*, *3*(1), 61–72.

Cecilia, F. (2020). E-Leadership: The Implication of Digital Transformation for Leadership in Organizations in Africa. doi:10.31219/osf.io/sj6zf

CHAID Analysis | Decision Tree Analysis | B2B International. (n.d.). Retrieved February 24, 2021, from https://www.b2binternational.com/research/methods/statistical-techniques/chaid-analysis/

Chatterjee, S., Chaudhuri, R., Vrontis, D., Thrassou, A., & Ghosh, S. K. (2020). ICT-enabled CRM system adoption: a dual Indian qualitative case study and conceptual framework development. *Journal of Asia Business Studies*. doi:10.1108/JABS-05-2020-0198

Chatterjee, S., Ghosh, S. K., Chaudhuri, R., & Chaudhuri, S. (2020). Adoption of AI-integrated CRM system by Indian industry: from security and privacy perspective. *Information & Computer Security*. doi:10.1108/ICS-02-2019-0029

Chatterjee, S., Ghosh, S. K., & Chaudhuri, R. (2020). Knowledge management in improving business process: An interpretative framework for successful implementation of AI–CRM–KM system in organizations. *Business Process Management Journal*, *26*(6), 1261–1281. doi:10.1108/BPMJ-05-2019-0183

Chatterjee, S., Ghosh, S. K., Chaudhuri, R., & Nguyen, B. (2019). Are CRM systems ready for AI integration? *The Bottom Line (New York, N.Y.)*, *32*(2), 144–157. doi:10.1108/BL-02-2019-0069

Chatterjee, S., Nguyen, B., Ghosh, S. K., Bhattacharjee, K. K., & Chaudhuri, S. (2020). Adoption of artificial intelligence integrated CRM system: An empirical study of Indian organizations. *The Bottom Line (New York, N.Y.)*, *33*(4), 359–375. doi:10.1108/BL-08-2020-0057

Chen, Y., Lee, J. Y., Sridhar, S., Mittal, V., McCallister, K., & Singal, A. G. (2020). Improving cancer outreach effectiveness through targeting and economic assessments: Insights from a randomized field experiment. *Journal of Marketing, 84*(3), 1–27.

Chen, C., Ibekwe-SanJuan, F., & How, J. (2010). The Structure and Dynamics of Cocitation Clusters: A Multiple-Perspective Cocitation analysis. *Journal of the American Society for Information Science and Technology*, *61*(7), 1386–1409. doi:10.1002/asi.21309

Chen, Y., Lee, J. Y., Sridhar, S., Mittal, V., McCallister, K., & Singal, A. G. (2020). Improving cancer outreach effectiveness through targeting and economic assessments: Insights from a randomized field experiment. *Journal of Marketing*, *84*(3), 1–27. doi:10.1177/0022242920913025

Chi, D.-J., Chu, C.-C., & Chen, D. (2019). Applying Support Vector Machine, C5. 0, and CHAID to the Detection of Financial Statements Frauds. *International Conference on Intelligent Computing*, 327–336.

China and India now 70%+ of Global EdTech VC – HolonIQ. (n.d.). Retrieved July 26, 2021, from https://www.holoniq.com/notes/china-india-now-70-global-edtech-vc/

Chiu, Y. B., Lin, C. P., & Tang, L. L. (2005). Gender differs: Assessing a model of online purchase intentions in e-tail service. *International Journal of Service Industry Management, 16*(5), 416–435. doi:10.1108/09564230510625741

Chris, B. (2018, April 27). *How Fashion Should (and Shouldn't) Embrace Artificial Intelligence | Opinion, Op Ed | BoF*. https://www.businessoffashion.com/opinions/news-analysis/how-fashion-should-and-shouldnt-embrace-artificial-intelligence

Chu, K.-M. (2021). Measuring Customer Service Experience in Offline and Online Retail Environments. doi:10.20944/preprints202102.0250.v1

Chung, T. S., Wedel, M., & Rust, R. T. (2016). Adaptive personalization using social networks. *Journal of the Academy of Marketing Science*, *44*(1), 66–87.

Ciuffo, J. (2019). Artificial Intelligence in Marketing. *Artificial Intelligence and Machine Learning for Business for Non-Engineers,* 71–76. doi:10.1201/9780367821654-6

Colgate, J. E., Wannasuphoprasit, W., & Peshkin, M. A. (1996). Cobots: robots for collaboration with human operators. In American Society of Mechanical Engineers, Dynamic Systems and Control Division (Publication) DSC (Vol. 58, pp. 433–439). Academic Press.

Cooke, A. D. J., & Zubcsek, P. P. (2017). The connected consumer: Connected devices and the evolution of customer intelligence. *Journal of the Association for Consumer Research, 2*(2), 164–178.

Costa, A., & Ehrbeck, T. (2015). A market-building approach to financial Inclusion. *Innovations: Technology, Governance, Globalization, 10*(1-2), 53–59. doi:10.1162/inov_a_00229

Costa, P. B., Neto, G. M., & Bertolde, A. I. (2017). Urban mobility indexes: A brief review of the literature. *Transportation Research Procedia*, *25*, 3645–3655. doi:10.1016/j.trpro.2017.05.330

Cowan, K., & Ketron, S. (2019). A dual model of product involvement for effective virtual reality: The roles of imagination, co-creation, telepresence, and interactivity. *Journal of Business Research, 100*, 483–492. doi:10.1016/j.jbusres.2018.10.063

Creating the HBS Hybrid Classrooms: Collaboration, Experimentation, Equity, and Innovation - News - Harvard Business School. (n.d.). Retrieved June 19, 2021, from https://www.hbs.edu/news/articles/Pages/creating-hybrid-classrooms.aspx

Creative ways students try to cheat on online exams. (n.d.). Retrieved June 24, 2021, from https://www.insidehighered.com/digital-learning/views/2017/09/20/creative-ways-students-try-cheat-online-exams

Daabes, A. S. A., & Kharbat, F. F. (2017). Customer-based perceptual map as a marketing intelligence source. *International Journal of Economics and Business Research, 13*(4), 360–379. doi:10.1504/IJEBR.2017.084381

Dabholkar, P. A., & Bagozzi, R. (2002). An attitudinal model of technology-based self-service: Moderating effects of consumer traits and situational factors. *Journal of the Academy of Marketing Science, 30*(3), 184–201. doi:10.1177/0092070302303001

Dahiya, K., & Bhatia, S. (2015). *Customer Churn Analysis in Telecom Industry*. IEEE. doi:10.1109/ICRITO.2015.7359318

Dash, R., McMurtrey, M., Rebman, C., & Kar, U. K. (2019). Application of artificial intelligence in automation of supply chain management. *Journal of Strategic Innovation and Sustainability, 14*(3), 43–53. doi:10.33423/jsis.v14i3.2105

Daunt, K. L., & Harris, L. C. (2012). Exploring the forms of dysfunctional customer behaviour: A study of differences in servicescape and customer disaffection with service. *Journal of Marketing Management, 28*(1–2), 129–153. doi:10.1080/0267257X.2011.619149

Davenport, T. H., & Ronanki, R. (2018, Feb.). Artificial intelligence for the real world. *Harvard Business Review,* 108–117.

Davenport, T., Guha, A., Grewal, D., & Bressgott, T. (2020). How artificial intelligence will change the future of marketing. *Journal of the Academy of Marketing Science, 48*(1), 24–42. doi:10.100711747-019-00696-0

Davenport, T., & Kalakota, R. (2019). The potential for artificial intelligence in healthcare. *Future Healthcare Journal, 6*(2), 94–98. doi:10.7861/futurehosp.6-2-94 PMID:31363513

Davis, F. D., Bagozzi, R. P., & Warshaw, P. R. (1989). User acceptance of computer technology: A comparison of two theoretical models. *Management Science, 35*(8), 982–1003. doi:10.1287/mnsc.35.8.982

Dawar, N. (2018, May). Marketing in the age of Alexa. *Harvard Business Review,* 80–87.

Dawn, S. K., & Guha, A. (2010). E-CRM: A Critical Analysis by Developing an Effective Model. *Asia Pacific Business Review, 6*(3), 106–114. doi:10.1177/097324701000600309

Day, G. S. (2000). *Capabilities for Forging Customer Relationships*. Working Paper, Report No. 00-118. Cambridge, MA: Marketing Science Institute.

Day, G. S. (2011). Closing the marketing capabilities gap. *Journal of Marketing, 75*(4), 183–195. doi:10.1509/jmkg.75.4.183

de Graaf, M. M., Ben Allouch, S., & van Dijk, J. A. (2019). Why would I use this in My home? A model of domestic social robot acceptance. *Human-Computer Interaction, 34*(2), 115–173. doi:10.1080/07370024.2017.1312406

De Keyser, S. K. (2019). Frontline service technology infusion: Conceptual archetypes and future research directions. *Journal of Service Management*, *30*(1), 156–183.

De Sutter, R., Matton, M., Laukens, N., Van Rijsselbergen, D., & Van de Walle, R. (2011). MediaCRM: Enabling Customer Relationship Management in the Broadcast. *Lecture Notes in Computer Science*, *6987*, 19–26. doi:10.1007/978-3-642-23971-7_3

Deb, S. K., Jain, R., & Deb, V. (2018, January). Artificial Intelligence—Creating Automated Insights for Customer Relationship Management. In *2018 8th International Conference on Cloud Computing, Data Science & Engineering (Confluence)* (pp. 758-764). IEEE.

Decker, R., & Trusov, M. (2010). Estimating aggregate consumer preferences from online product reviews. *International Journal of Research in Marketing*, *27*(4), 293–307.

Dehghanpouri, H., Soltani, Z., & Rostamzadeh, R. (2020). The impact of trust, privacy and quality of service on the success of E-CRM: The mediating role of customer satisfaction. *Journal of Business and Industrial Marketing*, *35*(11), 1831–1847. doi:10.1108/JBIM-07-2019-0325

Deighton, J. (2019). Big Data. *Consumption Markets & Culture*, *22*(1), 68–73.

Dekimpe, M. (2020). Retailing and retailing research in the age of big data analytics. *International Journal of Research in Marketing, 37*, 3–14.

Dekimpe, M. (2020). Retailing and retailing research in the age of big data analytics. *International Journal of Research in Marketing*, *37*(1), 3–14. doi:10.1016/j.ijresmar.2019.09.001

Desai, D. (2019). An Empirical Study of Website Personalization Effect on Users Intention to Revisit E-commerce Website through Cognitive and Hedonic Experience. In V. Balas, N. Sharma, & A. Chakrabarti (Eds.), *Data Management, Analytics, and Innovation. Advances in Intelligent Systems and Computing* (Vol. 839). Springer. doi:10.1007/978-981-13-1274-8_1

Desai, D. (2021). Role of Privacy Concern and Control to Build Trust in Personalized Social Networking Sites. In A. Sheth, A. Sinhal, A. Shrivastava, & A. K. Pandey (Eds.), *Intelligent Systems. Algorithms for Intelligent Systems*. Springer. doi:10.1007/978-981-16-2248-9_10

Devara & Usman. (n.d.). Retrieved June 22, 2021, from https://www.forbes.com/pictures/fmhd45gdgi/adamas-belva-syah-devara/?sh=727b61393cc9

Devara. (n.d.). *2016 has spurred educational technology in Southeast Asia | Harvard Kennedy School*. Retrieved June 22, 2021, from https://www.hks.harvard.edu/alumni/connect/community-stories/adamas-belva-syah-devara-mpa-has-spurred-educational-technology

Diakopoulos, N. (2016). Accountability in algorithmic decision making. *Communications of the ACM*, *59*(2), 56–62. doi:10.1145/2844110

Duan, Y., Edwards, J. S., & Dwivedi, Y. K. (2019). Artificial intelligence for decision making in the era of Big Data–evolution, challenges, and research agenda. *International Journal of Information Management*, *48*, 63–71. doi:10.1016/j.ijinfomgt.2019.01.021

Du, R. Y., Hu, Y., & Damangir, S. (2015). Leveraging trends in online searches for product features in market response modeling. *Journal of Marketing*, *79*(1), 29–43.

Dwivedi, Y. K., Hughes, L., Ismagilova, E., Aarts, G., Coombs, C., Crick, T., ... Galanos, V. (2021). Artificial Intelligence (AI): Multidisciplinary perspectives on emerging challenges, opportunities, and agenda for research, practice and policy. *International Journal of Information Management*, *57*, 101994. Advance online publication. doi:10.1016/j.ijinfomgt.2019.08.002

Dzyabura, D., & Hauser, J. R. (2019). Recommending products when consumers learn their preferences weights. *Marketing Science*, *38*(3), 365–541. doi:10.1287/mksc.2018.1144

Eagle, N., Pentland, A. S., & Lazer, D. (2009). Inferring friendship network structure by using mobile phone data. *Proceedings of the National Academy of Sciences of the United States of America*, *106*(36), 15274–15278.

Eastlick, M. A., Ratto, C., Lotz, S. L., & Mishra, A. (2012). Exploring antecedents of attitude toward co-producing a retailcheckout service utilizing a self-service technology. *International Review of Retail, Distribution and Consumer Research*, *22*(4), 337–364. doi:10.1080/09593969.2012.690775

Elkington, R. (2021). E-Leadership as Enabling Function for Technology-enriched Learning. *Effective Leadership for Overcoming ICT Challenges in Higher Education: What Faculty, Staff and Administrators Can Do to Thrive Amidst the Chaos*, 59–71. doi:10.1108/978-1-83982-306-020211007

Elsayad, A. M., & Elsalamony, H. A. (2013). Diagnosis of breast cancer using decision tree models and SVM. *International Journal of Computers and Applications*, *83*(5).

Embibe - AI - Using AI In Education To Maximize Learning Outcomes. (n.d.). Retrieved July 8, 2021, from https://www.embibe.com/ai

Embibe: A Teacher's Pet Tool | Forbes India. (n.d.). Retrieved July 8, 2021, from https://www.forbesindia.com/article/checkin/embibe-a-teachers-pet-tool/41195/1

Eyal, N. (2014). *Hooked: How to build habit-forming products*. Penguin.

Eyal, N. (2014). *Hooked: How to Build Habit-Forming Products*. Penguin.

Fader, P. (2012). *Customer Centricity: Focus on the Right Customers for Strategic Advantage*. Wharton Digital Press.

Fader, P., & Toms, S. E. (2018). *The Customer Centricity Playbook: Implement a Winning Strategy Driven by Customer Lifetime Value*. Wharton Digital Press.

Filimonova, V. (2020). CRM Systems as a Tool for Improving Business Efficiency. *Bulletin of Science and Practice*, *6*(2), 235–240. doi:10.33619/2414-2948/51/25

Fiore, A., Kim, J., & Lee, H. (2005). Effect of image interactivity technology on consumer responses toward the online retailer. *Journal of Interactive Marketing*, *19*(3), 38–53. doi:10.1002/dir.20042

Florenthal, B. (2019). Young consumers' motivational drivers of brand engagement behavior on social media sites. *Journal of Research in Interactive Marketing, 13*(3), 351–391. doi:10.1108/JRIM-05-2018-0064

Fogg, B. J. (2003). Persuasive Technology: Using Computers to Change What We Think and Do. *Persuasive Technology: Using Computers to Change What We Think and Do*. doi:10.1016/B978-1-55860-643-2.X5000-8

Fogg, B. (2009). A behavior model for persuasive design. *ACM International Conference Proceeding Series*, 350. 10.1145/1541948.1541999

Fogg, B. J. (2009). Creating persuasive technologies: An eight-step design process. *ACM International Conference Proceeding Series*, 350. 10.1145/1541948.1542005

Foltean, F. S., Trif, S. M., & Tuleu, D. L. (2019). Customer relationship management capabilities and social media technology use: Consequences on firm performance. *Journal of Business Research, 104*, 563–575. doi:10.1016/j.jbusres.2018.10.047

Forbes. (2019). Retrieved from: https://www.forbes.com/sites/falonfatemi/2019/08/10/5-ways-artificial-intelligence-is-transforming-crms/?sh=6a8dd2ba5354

Fotiadis, A. K., & Vassiliadis, C. (2017). Being customer-centric through CRM metrics in the B2B market: The case of maritime shipping. *Journal of Business and Industrial Marketing, 32*(3), 347–356. doi:10.1108/JBIM-11-2014-0226

Frow, P. E., & Payne, A. F. (2009). Customer Relationship Management: A Strategic Perspective. *Journal of Business Market Management, 3*(1), 7–27. doi:10.100712087-008-0035-8

Frow, P., Payne, A., Wilkinson, I. F., & Young, L. (2011). Customer management and CRM: Addressing the dark side. *Journal of Services Marketing, 25*(2), 79–89. doi:10.1108/08876041111119804

FT ranking: The Americas' fastest-growing companies 2021 | Financial Times. (n.d.). Retrieved July 20, 2021, from https://www.ft.com/americas-fastest-growing-companies-2021

Future Travel Experience. (2020). *Incheon Airport presses ahead with AI, biometrics and big data plans amid global COVID-19 pandemic*. https://www.futuretravelexperience.com/2020/05/incheon-airport-presses-ahead-ai-biometrics-big-data/

Gabor, D., & Brooks, S. (2017). The digital revolution in financial inclusion: International development in the fintech era. *New Political Economy, 22*(4), 423–436. doi:10.1080/13563467.2017.1259298

Gale, M., & Aarons, C. (2018). Digital Transformation. *Leader to Leader, 2018*(90), 30–36. doi:10.1002/ltl.20390

Galitsky, B. (2020). *Artificial Intelligence for Customer Relationship Management*. Retrieved from https://www.springer.com/series/6033

Gallarza, M. G., Arteaga, F., Del Chiappa, G., Gil-Saura, I., & Holbrook, M. B. (2017). A multidimensional service-value scale based on Holbrook's typology of customer value: Bridging the gap between the concept and its measurement. *Journal of Service Management, 28*(4), 724–762. doi:10.1108/JOSM-06-2016-0166

Gandhi, B. M., & Chinnadorai, K. M. (2017). Retail in India. *International Journal of Engineering Development and Research, 5*(1), 433–435.

Gandhi, P., Loughran, T., & McDonald, B. (2019). Using annual report sentiment as a proxy for financial distress in US banks. *Journal of Behavioral Finance, 20*(4), 424–436. doi:10.1080/15427560.2019.1553176

Gangwar, H., Date, H., & Raoot, A. D. (2014). Review on IT adoption: Insights from recent technologies. *Journal of Enterprise Information Management, 27*(4), 488–502. doi:10.1108/JEIM-08-2012-0047

Garg, R., & Stiller, B. (2015). Factors Affecting Cloud Adoption and Their Interrelations. *Proceedings of the 5th International Conference on Cloud Computing and Services Science.* 10.5220/0005412300870094

Gartner. (2018). *Gartner Says 25 Percent of Customer Service Operations Will Use Virtual Customer Assistants by 2020.* https://www.gartner.com/en/newsroom/press-releases/2018-02-19-gartner-says-25-percent-of-customer-service-operations-will-use-virtual-customer-assistants-by-2020

Gartner. (2019). *Gartner Survey Shows Brands Risk Losing 38 Percent of Customers Because of Poor Marketing Personalization Efforts.* https://www.gartner.com/en/newsroom/press-releases/2019-03-11-gartner-survey-shows-brands-risk-losing-38-percent-of

Gensler, S., Völckner, F., Egger, M., Fischbach, K., & Schoder, D. (2015). Listen to your customers: Insights into brand image using online consumer-generated product reviews. *International Journal of Electronic Commerce, 20*(1), 112–141.

Gerbaudo, P. (2016). Social media teams as digital vanguards: The question of leadership in the management of key Facebook and Twitter accounts of Occupy Wall Street, Indignados and UK Uncut. *Information Communication and Society, 20*(2), 185–202. doi:10.1080/1369118X.2016.1161817

Gerth, A. B., & Peppard, J. (2016). The dynamics of CIO derailment: How CIOs come undone and how to avoid it. *Business Horizons, 59*(1), 61–70. doi:10.1016/j.bushor.2015.09.001

Giatsoglou, M., Vozalis, M. G., Diamantaras, K., Vakali, A., Sarigiannidis, G., & Chatzisavvas, K. C. (2017). Sentiment analysis leveraging emotions and word embeddings. *Expert Systems with Applications, 69*, 214–224. doi:10.1016/j.eswa.2016.10.043

Girdher, S. (2019). Role of Artificial Intelligence in Transforming E-commerce Sector. *Research Review International Journal of Multidisciplinary, 4*(6), 282–284.

Global E-learning Market - Outlook and Forecast 2021-2026. (n.d.). Retrieved June 17, 2021, from https://www.researchandmarkets.com/reports/5327504/global-e-learning-market-outlook-and-forecast?utm_source=BW&utm_medium=PressRelease&utm_code=n8vslb&utm_campaign=1550491+-+Global+E-learning+Market+Outlook+and+Forecast+2021-2026%3A+Market+is+Likely+to+Witness+an+Absolute+Growth+of+About+110%25&utm_exec=chdo54prd

GOI. (2018). *Report of the Artificial Intelligence Task Force*. The Ministry of Commerce & Industry, Government of India (GOI). https://dipp.gov.in/whats-new/report-task-force-artificial-intelligence

Goldsmith, R. E. (2002). Explaining and predicting consumer intention to purchase over the internet: An exploratory study. *Journal of Marketing Theory and Practice*, *10*(1), 22–28. doi:10.1080/10696679.2002.11501913

Gomez Martinez, R., Prado Román, M., & Plaza Casado, P. (2019). Big data algorithmic trading systems based on investors' mood. *Journal of Behavioral Finance*, *20*(2), 227–238. doi:10.1080/15427560.2018.1506786

Gordini, N., & Veglio, V. (2017). Customers churn prediction and marketing retention strategies. An application of support vector machines based on the AUC parameter-selection technique in B2B e-commerce industry. *Industrial Marketing Management*, *62*, 100–107. doi:10.1016/j.indmarman.2016.08.003

Graham, C., Daniel, H., & Doore, B. (2021). Virtual Leadership. *Research Anthology on Digital Transformation, Organizational Change, and the Impact of Remote Work*, 1678–1691. doi:10.4018/978-1-7998-7297-9.ch082

Grewal, D., Hulland, J., Kopalle, P. K., & Karahanna, E. (2020). The future of technology and marketing: A multidisciplinary perspective. *Journal of the Academy of Marketing Science*, *48*(1), 1–8. doi:10.100711747-019-00711-4

Grewal, D., Kroschke, M., Mende, M., Roggeveen, A. L., & Scott, M. L. (2020). Customer experiences in retail, sales, and service settings. *Journal of Interactive Marketing*, *51*, 9–25.

Grewal, D., Kroschke, M., Mende, M., Roggeveen, A. L., & Scott, M. L. (2020). Frontline Cyborgs at Your Service: How Human Enhancement Technologies Affect Customer Experiences in Retail, Sales, and Service Settings. *Journal of Interactive Marketing*, *51*, 9–25. doi:10.1016/j.intmar.2020.03.001

Guerrero, M., Montoya, F. G., Baños, R., Alcayde, A., & Gil, C. (2017). Adaptive community detection in complex networks using genetic algorithms. *Neurocomputing*, *266*, 101–113.

Guo, J., Zhang, W., Fan, W., & Li, W. (2018). Combining geographical and social influences with deep learning for personalized point-of- interest recommendation. *Journal of Management Information Systems*, *35*(4), 1121–1153.

Guo, J., Zhang, W., Fan, W., & Li, W. (2018). Combining geographical and social influences with deep learning for personalized point-of interest recommendation. *Journal of Management Information Systems*, *35*(4), 1121–1153. doi:10.1080/07421222.2018.1523564

Gupta, S., & Lehmann, D. R. (2003). Customers as assets. *Journal of Interactive Marketing*, *17*(1), 9–24.

Gupta, S., & Lehmann, D. R. (2005). *Managing customers as investments*. The Strategic Value of Customers in the Long Run, Wharton School Publ.

Gupta, S., Leszkiewicz, A., Kumar, V., Bijmolt, T., & Potapov, D. (2020). Digital analytics: Modeling for insights and new methods. *Journal of Interactive Marketing*, *51*, 26–43.

Gurău, C. (2012). A life-stage analysis of consumer loyalty profile: Comparing Generation X and Millennial consumers. *Journal of Consumer Marketing*, *29*(2), 103–113. doi:10.1108/07363761211206357

Güven, İ., & Şimşir, F. (2020). Demand forecasting with color parameter in retail apparel industry using artificial neural networks (ANN) and support vector machines (SVM) methods. *Computers & Industrial Engineering*, *147*, 106678. doi:10.1016/j.cie.2020.106678

Haenlein & Kaplan. (2012). The impact of unprofitable customer abandonment on current customers' exit, voice, and loyalty intentions: An empirical analysis. *Journal of Services Marketing*, *26*(6), 458.

Haenlein & Kaplan. (2019). A brief history of artificial intelligence: On the past, present, and future of artificial intelligence. *California Management, 61*(4), 5-14.

Haenlein & Libai. (2019). Comparing automated text classification methods. *International Journal of Research in Marketing*, *36*(1), 20–38.

Haenlein, M. (2013). Social interactions in customer churn decisions: The impact of relationship directionality. *International Journal of Research in Marketing*, *30*(3), 236–248.

Haenlein, M. (2017). How to date your clients in the 21st century: Challenges in managing customer relationships in Today's world. *Business Horizons*, *60*(5), 577–586.

Haenlein, M. (2017). How to date your clients in the 21st century: Challenges in managing customer relationships in today's world. *Business Horizons*, *60*(5), 577–586. Advance online publication. doi:10.1016/j.bushor.2017.06.002

Haenlein, M., & Kaplan, A. (2009). Unprofitable customers and their management. *Business Horizons*, *52*(1), 89–97.

Haenlein, M., & Kaplan, A. (2019). A brief history of artificial intelligence: On the past, present, and future of artificial intelligence. *Californi Management*, *61*(4), 5–14.

Haenlein, M., & Kaplan, A. (2019). A Brief History of Artificial Intelligence: On the Past, Present, and Future of Artificial Intelligence. *California Management Review*, *61*(4), 5–14. doi:10.1177/0008125619864925

Han, J., Kamber, M., & Pei, J. (2014). *Data Mining Concepts and echniques* (3rd ed.). Morgan Kaufmann.

Hanson, J., Wei, M., Veys, S., Kugler, M., Strahilevitz, L., & Ur, B. (2020). *Taking Data Out of Context to Hyper-Personalize Ads*. doi:10.1145/3313831.3376415

Haridasan, V., & Venkatesh, S. (2011). CRM Implementation in Indian Telecom Industry-Evaluating the Effectiveness of Mobile Service Providers Using Data Envelopment Analysis. *IJBRM*, *2*(3), 110–127.

Harrigan, P., Ramsey, E., & Ibbotson, P. (2009). Investigating the e-CRM activities of Irish SMEs. *Journal of Small Business and Enterprise Development*, *16*(3), 443–465. doi:10.1108/14626000910977161

Hennig-Thurau, T., Malthouse, E. C., Friege, C., Gensler, S., Lobschat, L., Rangaswamy, A., & Skiera, B. (2010). The impact of new media on customer relationships. *Journal of Service Research*, *13*(3), 311–330. doi:10.1177/1094670510375460

Henning, T. T., & Klee, A. (1997). The Impact of customer satisfaction and relationship quality on customer retention: A critical reassessment and model development. *Psychology and Marketing*, *14*(8), 737–764. doi:10.1002/(SICI)1520-6793(199712)14:8<737::AID-MAR2>3.0.CO;2-F

Herhausen, D., Binder, J., Schoegel, M., & Herrman, A. (2015). Integrating Bricks with Clicks: Retailer-Level and Channel-Level Outcomes of Online-Offline Channel Integration. *Journal of Retailing*, *91*(2), 309–325. doi:10.1016/j.jretai.2014.12.009

Hew, K. F., & Brush, T. (2007). Integrating technology into K-12 teaching: Current knowledge gaps and recommendations for future research. *Educational Technology Research and Development*, *55*(3), 223–252. doi:10.100711423-006-9022-5

Hilas, C. S., Mastorocostas, P. A., & Rekanos, I. T. (2015). Clustering of Telecommunications User Profiles for Fraud Detection and Security Enhancement in Large Corporate Networks: A case Study. *Applied Mathematics & Information Sciences*, *9*(4), 1709–1718.

Hofacker, C. F. (2019). Notes on the growing importance of software as a driver of value exchange. In A. P. Rindfleisch & A. J. Malter (Eds.), Review of Marketing Research. Academic Press.

Hofacker, C. F. (2019). The Growing Importance of Software as a Driver of Value Exchange. *Marketing in a Digital World*, 85–95. doi:10.1108/S1548-643520190000016007

Home - Packback. (n.d.). Retrieved July 20, 2021, from https://www.packback.co/

How AI Can Be The Key To Loyalty And Retention For Retail In 2021. (n.d.). Retrieved February 25, 2021, from https://www.forbes.com/sites/jonathantreiber/2021/02/02/how-artificial-intelligence-can-be-the-key-to-loyalty-and-retention-in-2021/

How AI Can Support The Supply Chain And Overcome Hurdles. (n.d.). Retrieved February 20, 2021, from https://www.forbes.com/sites/forbestechcouncil/2020/06/12/how-ai-can-support-the-supply-chain-and-overcome-hurdles/?sh=50420cee330d

How technology is helping to reshape fitness and outdoor recreation. (n.d.). Retrieved December 12, 2020, from https://www.fastcompany.com/90566919/how-technology-is-helping-to-reshape-fitness-and-outdoor-recreation

Hoyer, W. D., Kroschke, M., Schmitt, B., Kraume, K., & Shankar, V. (2020). Transforming the customer experience through new technologies. *Journal of Interactive Marketing*, *51*, 57–71.

Hoyer, W. D., Kroschke, M., Schmitt, B., Kraume, K., & Shankar, V. (2020). Transforming the Customer Experience Through New Technologies. *Journal of Interactive Marketing*, *51*, 57–71. doi:10.1016/j.intmar.2020.04.001

Huang, M.-H., & Rust, R. T. (2021). *A strategic framework for artificial intelligence in marketing*. doi:10.1007/s11747-020-00749-9

Huang, M. H., & Rust, R. T. (2017). Technology-driven service strategy. *Journal of the Academy of Marketing Science*, *45*(6), 906–924. doi:10.100711747-017-0545-6

Huang, M. H., & Rust, R. T. (2018). Artificial intelligence in service. *Journal of Service Research*, *21*(2), 155–172.

Huang, M.-H., & Rust, R. T. (2018). Artificial Intelligence in Service. *Journal of Service Research*, *21*(2), 155–172. doi:10.1177/1094670517752459

Hummer, W., Muthusamy, V., Rausch, T., Dube, P., El Maghraoui, K., Murthi, A., & Oum, P. (2019). ModelOps: Cloud-Based Lifecycle Management for Reliable and Trusted AI. *2019 IEEE International Conference on Cloud Engineering (IC2E)*. 10.1109/IC2E.2019.00025

Humphreys, A., & Wang, R. (2018). Automated text analysis for consumer research. *The Journal of Consumer Research*, *44*(6), 1274–1306. doi:10.1093/jcr/ucx104

Hyper-Personalization: A new way of customer-centric marketing. (2019). *Academe, 97*(5).

Iansiti, M., & Lakhani, K. R. (2020). Competing in the age of AI: How machine intelligence changes the rules of business. *Harvard Business Review*, *2020*(January-February), 1–9.

IDRBT. (2020). *AI in Banking: A Primer*. Institute for Research and Development in Banking Technology. http://www.idrbt.ac.in/assets/publications/Best%20Practices/2020/AI_2020.pdf

Im, S., Bayus, B. L., & Mason, C. H. (2003). An empirical study of innate consumer innovativeness, personal characteristics, and new-product adoption behavior. *Journal of the Academy of Marketing Science*, *31*(1), 61–72. doi:10.1177/0092070302238602

Instapage. (2019). *Hyper-Personalized Marketing: How to Do It Right with 3 Examples to Prove It.* https://instapage.com/blog/hyper-personalization

Introducing tonies, The Revolutionary Children's Audio Player And European Toy Sensation Making Its U.S. Debut September 2020. (n.d.). Retrieved June 19, 2021, from https://www.prnewswire.com/news-releases/introducing-tonies-the-revolutionary-childrens-audio-player-and-european-toy-sensation-making-its-us-debut-september-2020-301136398.html

Ivanov, S., & Webster, C. (2017). Adoption of robots, artificial intelligence and service automation by travel, tourism and hospitality companies – a cost-benefit analysis. *Proceedings of the International Scientific Conference "Contemporary tourism – traditions and innovations"*.

Jabbar, A., Akhtar, P., & Dani, S. (2019). Real-time big data processing for instantaneous marketing decisions: A problematization approach. *Industrial Marketing Management, 90*, 558-569. doi:10.1016/j.indmarman.2019.09.001

Jain, G., Rakesh, S., Kamalun Nabi, M., & Chaturvedi, K. R. (2018). Hyper-personalization – fashion sustainability through digital clienteling. *Research Journal of Textile and Apparel*, *22*(4), 320–334. doi:10.1108/RJTA-02-2018-0017

Jayachandran, S., Sharma, S., Kaufman, P., & Raman, P. (2005). The role of relational information processes and technology use in customer relationship management. *Journal of Marketing, 69*(4), 177–192. https://journals.sagepub.com/doi/10.1509/jmkg.2005.69.4.177

Jenner, M. (2021). *The future of learning report.* https://www.futurelearn.com/info/insights/self-education-online-learning-the-future-of-education

Kahai, S., Avolio, B. J., & Sosik, J. J. (2017). E-Leadership. The Wiley Blackwell Handbook of the Psychology of the Internet at Work, 285–314. doi:10.1002/9781119256151.ch14

Kalaignanam, K., Kushwaha, T., & Rajavi, K. (2018). How Does Web Personalization Create Value for Online Retailers? Lower Cash Flow Volatility or Enhanced Cash Flows. *Journal of Retailing*, *94*(3), 265–279. doi:10.1016/j.jretai.2018.05.001

Kamalraj & Malathi. (2013). Apply Data Mining Techniques in Telecom Churn Prediction. *International Journal of Advanced Research in Computer Science and Software Engineering, 3*(10), 363-370.

Kampani, N., & Jhamb, D. (2020). Analyzing the role of e-crm in managing customer relations: A critical review of the literature. *Journal of Critical Review*, *7*(4), 221–226.

Kannan, P. K., & Li, H. (2017). Digital marketing: A framework, review and research agenda. *International Journal of Research in Marketing*, *34*(1), 22–45. doi:10.1016/j.ijresmar.2016.11.006

Kaplan, A. M., & Haenlein, M. (2010). Users of the world, unite! the challenges and opportunities of social media. *Business Horizons*, *53*(1), 59–68. doi:10.1016/j.bushor.2009.09.003

Kaplan, A., & Haenlein, M. (2019). Siri, Siri, in my hand: Who's the fairest in the land? On the interpretations, illustrations, and implications of artificial intelligence. *Business Horizons*, *62*(1), 15–25. doi:10.1016/j.bushor.2018.08.004

Kasthuri, Shanthi, & Manigandan. (2016). Customizing Clustering algorithm for Data mining in CRM. *International Journal of Computer Science and Information Technology & Security, 6*(2).

Kaur, J., Arora, V., & Bali, S. (2020). Influence of technological advances and change in marketing strategies using analytics in retail industry. *International Journal of System Assurance Engineering and Management, 11*(5), 953–961. doi:10.100713198-020-01023-5

Khan, B. H. (2021). A Global Framework for E-Learning. In *Challenges and Opportunities for the Global Implementation of E-Learning Frameworks* (pp. 1–14). IGI Global.

Kımıloğlu, H., & Zaralı, H. (2009). What signifies success in e-CRM? *Marketing Intelligence & Planning, 27*(2), 246–267. doi:10.1108/02634500910945011

Kim, Y. M., & Shim, K. Y. (2002). The influence of internet shopping mall characteristics and user traits on purchase intent. *Irish Marketing Review, 15*(2), 25–34.

Kirkpatrick, K. (2020). Tracking shoppers. *Communications of the ACM, 63*(2), 19–21.

Konigstorfer, F., & Thalmann, S. (2020). Applications of Artificial Intelligence in commercial banks – A research agenda for behavioural finance. *Journal of Behavioral and Experimental Finance, 27*(2020), 1-15.

Koufaris, M. (2002). Applying the technology acceptance model and flow theory to online consumer behavior. *Information Systems Research, 13*(2), 205–223. doi:10.1287/isre.13.2.205.83

Kumar, V., Rajan, B., Venkatesan, R., & Lecinski, J. (2019). Understanding the role of artificial intelligence in personalized en- gagement marketing. *California Management Review, 61*(4), 135–155. doi:10.1177/0008125619859317

Lamantia, J. (2009, August 17). Inside out: interaction design for Augmented Reality. *UXMatters*. https://www.uxmatters.com/mt/archives/2009/08/inside-out-interaction-design-for-augmented-reality.php

Lechman, E. (2015). What Matters for ICT Diffusion? *ICT Diffusion in Developing Countries*, 167–222. doi:10.1007/978-3-319-18254-4_5

Lee, M. J. W., & McLoughlin, C. (2010). Web 2.0-based e-learning: Applying social informatics for tertiary teaching. In *Web 2.0-Based E-Learning: Applying Social Informatics for Tertiary Teaching*. doi:10.4018/978-1-60566-294-7

Lee, M., Cheung, C., & Chen, Z. (2005). Acceptance of Internet-based learning medium: The role of extrinsic and intrinsic motivation. *Information & Management, 42*(8), 1095–1104. doi:10.1016/j.im.2003.10.007

Leong, C., Tan, B., Xiao, X., Tan, F. T. C., & Sun, Y. (2017). Nurturing a FinTech Ecosystem: The case of a Youth Microloan Startup in China. *International Journal of Information Management, 37*(2), 92–97. doi:10.1016/j.ijinfomgt.2016.11.006

Libai, B., Bart, Y., Gensler, S., Hofacker, C. F., Kaplan, A., Kötterheinrich, K., & Kroll, E. B. (2020). Brave New World? On AI and the Management of Customer Relationships. *Journal of Interactive Marketing*, *51*, 44–56. doi:10.1016/j.intmar.2020.04.002

Lichtenstein, S., Bednall, D. H., & Adam, S. (2008). Marketing research and customer analytics: Interfunctional knowledge integration. *International Journal of Technology Marketing*, *3*(1), 81–96. doi:10.1504/IJTMKT.2008.017341

Liebman, E., Saar-Tsechansky, M., & Stone, P. (2019). The right music at the right time: Adaptive personalized playlists based on sequence modeling. *Management Information Systems Quarterly*, *43*(3), 765–786. doi:10.25300/MISQ/2019/14750

Lilien, G. L. (2016). The B2B knowledge gap. *International Journal of Research in Marketing*, *33*(3), 543–556. doi:10.1016/j.ijresmar.2016.01.003

Liu, X. (2019). Analyzing the impact of user-generated content on B2B firms' stock performance: Big data analysis with machine learning methods. *Industrial Marketing Management, 86*, 30-39. doi:10.1016/j.indmarman.2019.02.021

Liu, C., Ready, D., Roman, A., Van Wart, M., Wang, X., McCarthy, A., & Kim, S. (2018). E-leadership: An empirical study of organizational leaders' virtual communication adoption. *Leadership and Organization Development Journal*, *39*(7), 826–843. doi:10.1108/LODJ-10-2017-0297

Liu, X., Singh, P. V., & Srinivasan, K. (2016). A structured analysis of unstructured big data by leveraging cloud computing. *Marketing Science*, *35*(3), 363–388. doi:10.1287/mksc.2015.0972

Loebbecke, C., & Picot, A. (2015). Reflections on societal and business model transformation arising from digitization and big data analytics: A research agenda. The Journal of Strategic Information Systems, 24(3), 149–157.

Lok, C. K. (2015). Adoption of Smart Card-Based E-Payment System for Retailing in Hong Kong Using an Extended Technology Acceptance Model. *Advances in Business Marketing and Purchasing*, 255–466. doi:10.1108/S1069-09642015000023B003

Luce, L. (2019). *Artificial Intelligence for Fashion*. Apress - Springer Nature. doi:10.1007/978-1-4842-3931-5

Luo, X., Tong, S., Fang, Z., & Qu Frontiers, Z. (2019). machines vs. humans: The impact of artificial intelligence chatbot disclosure on customer purchases. *Marketing Science*, *38*(6), 937–947.

Luo, X., Tong, S., Fang, Z., & Qu, Z. (2019). Frontiers: Machines versus humans: The impact of AI chatbot disclosure on customer pur- chases. *Marketing Science*, *38*(6), 937–947.

Luo, X., Tong, S., Fang, Z., & Qu, Z. (2019). Frontiers: Machines vs. Humans: The Impact of Artificial Intelligence Chatbot Disclosure on Customer Purchases. *Marketing Science*, mksc.2019.1192. Advance online publication. doi:10.1287/mksc.2019.1192

Lynn Pulley, M., & Sessa, V. I. (2001). E-leadership: Tackling complex challenges. *Industrial and Commercial Training*, *33*(6), 225–230. doi:10.1108/00197850110405379

Maddodi, S., & Nandha Kumar, K. G. (2020). *Artificial intelligence and hyper-personalization for improving customer experience.* Retrieved from www.drsrjournal.com

Magidson, J. (1993). The use of the new ordinal algorithm in CHAID to target profitable segments. *The Journal of Database Marketing*, *1*(1), 29–48.

Maheshwari, R. U., & Mahesan, S. S. (2014, February). Tamilarasan, and A. K.Subramani, "Role of Data Mining in CRM. *International Journal of Engine Research*, *3*(2), 75–78. doi:10.17950/ijer/v3s2/208

Mangold, W. G., & Faulds, D. J. (2009). Social media: The new hybrid element of the promotion mix. *Business Horizons*, *52*(4), 357–365. doi:10.1016/j.bushor.2009.03.002

Marczewski, A. (2013). *The Intrinsic Motivation RAMP*. Academic Press.

Marinchak, C. M., Forrest, E., & Hoanca, B. (2018). Artificial Intelligence. *International Journal of E-Entrepreneurship and Innovation*, *8*(2), 14–24. doi:10.4018/IJEEI.2018070102 PMID:30145103

Martin, D. (1977). Early warning of bank failure: A Logit regression approach. *Journal of Banking & Finance*, *1*(3), 249–276. doi:10.1016/0378-4266(77)90022-X

McCarthy, J., Minsky, M., Rochester, N., & Shannon, C. E. (2006). A Proposal for the Dartmouth Summer Research Project on Artificial Intelligence, August 31, 1955. *AI Magazine*, *27*(4), 12–14.

McGovern, G., & Moon, Y. (2007). Companies and the customers who hate them. *Harvard Business Review*, *85*(6). PMID:17580650

Medicine & Mindfulness. (n.d.). *How VR Training Is Helping Healthcare Through The Pandemic*. Retrieved July 13, 2021, from https://www.forbes.com/sites/charlestowersclark/2021/02/19/medicine--mindfulness-how-vr-training-is-helping-healthcare-through-the-pandemic/?sh=30fb425a58b9

Meffert, J., & Swaminathan, A. (2018). Leadership and the urgency for digital transformation. *Leader to Leader*, *2018*(88), 44–49. doi:10.1002/ltl.20357

Mesquita, L. D. (2018). The "Artificial" Consumer: Approaches between Artificial Intelligence and Marketing. *ANPAD Meetings –Enanpad*, 3-6.

Milovic, B. (2012). Application of Customer Relationship Management Strategy (CRM) in Different Business Areas. Economics and Organization, 9(3), 341-354.

MIT Solve | Ruangguru - Solver Spotlight | Youth, Skills & Future Workforce Solver | Ruangguru. (n.d.). Retrieved June 23, 2021, from https://solve.mit.edu/challenges/youth-skills-the-workforce-of-the-future/solutions/2359#solution-subnav-offset

Mogaji, E., Soetan, T.O., & Kieu, T.A. (2020, May). The implications of artificial intelligence on the digital marketing of financial services to vulnerable customers. *Australasian Marketing Journal*, 1-8.

Mogaji, E., Farinloye, T., & Aririguzoh, S. (2016). Factors shaping attitudes towards UK bank brands: An exploratory analysis of social media data. *Cogent Business Management*, *3*(1), 1223389. doi:10.1080/23311975.2016.1223389

Mollen, A., & Wilson, H. (2010). Engagement, telepresence and interactivity in online consumer experience: Reconciling scholastic and managerial perspectives. *Journal of Business Research*, *63*(9-10), 919–925. doi:10.1016/j.jbusres.2009.05.014

Morris, M. G., & Venkatesh, V. (2000). Age differences in technology adoption decisions: Implications for a changing work force. *Personnel Psychology*, *53*(2), 375–403. doi:10.1111/j.1744-6570.2000.tb00206.x

Mujawar, S., & Joshi, A. (2015, February). Data Analytics Types, Tools and their Comparison. *IJARCCE*, *4*(2), 488–491.

Nadaf & Kadam. (2013). Data Mining in Telecommunication. *International Journal on Advanced Computer Theory and Engineering*, *2*(3).

Nagarajan, Minu, Vedanarayanan, Sundersingh Jebaseelan, & Vasanth. (2015). CIMTELMining Algorithm for Big Data in Telecommunication. *International Journal of Engineering and Technology*, 7(5), 1709-1715.

Nascimento, Alexandre, & Queiroz. (2017). Overview of research on Artificial Intelligence in Administration in Brazil. *ANPAD Meetings – Enanpad*, 1-4.

Netzer, O., Lemaire, A., & Herzenstein, M. (2019). When words sweat: Identifying signals for loan default in the text of loan applications. *Journal of Marketing Research*, *56*(6), 960–980.

Neumann, N., Tucker, C. E., & Whitfield, T. (2019). Frontiers: How effective is third-party consumer profiling? Evidence from field studies. *Marketing Science*, *38*(6), 918–926.

Ng, I. C. L., & Wakenshaw, S. Y. L. (2017). The internet-of-things: Review and research directions. *International Journal of Research in Marketing*, *34*(1), 3–21.

Ngai, E. W. T., Xiu, L., & Chau, D. C. K. (2009). Application of data mining techniques in customer relationship management: A literature review and classification. *Expert Systems with Applications*, *36*(2), 2592–2602. doi:10.1016/j.eswa.2008.02.021

Nguyen, B., Jaber, F., & Simkin, L. (2020). A systematic review of the dark side of CRM: The need for a new research agenda. *Journal of Strategic Marketing*, *00*(00), 1–19. doi:10.1080/0965254X.2019.1642939

Nguyen, B., & Mutum, D. S. (2012). Customer relationship management: Advances, dark sides, exploitation, and unfairness. *International Journal of Electronic Customer Relationship Management*, *6*(1), 1–19. doi:10.1504/IJECRM.2012.046467

Nicholson, M., Clarke, J., & Blakemore, M. (2002). One brand, three ways to shop: Situational variables and multichannel consumer behaviour. Review of Retail. *Distribution and Consumer Research*, *12*(2), 131–148. doi:10.1080/09593960210127691

NRF | Coronavirus leads to more use of contactless credit cards and mobile payments despite cost and security concerns. (n.d.). Retrieved February 20, 2021, from https://nrf.com/media-center/press-releases/coronavirus-leads-more-use-contactless-credit-cards-and-mobile-payments

Nwaizugbo, I. C., & Ifeanyichukwu, C. D. (2016). Understanding Consumers' Behaviour Towards Online Shopping: A Study of Online Shoppers in Anambra State. *International Journal of Sales. Retailing & Marketing*, *5*(2), 28–37. doi:10.6007/ijarafms.v1i2.8

Okazaki, S., Eisend, M., Plangger, K., de Ruyter, K., & Grewal, D. (2020). Understanding the Strategic Consequences of Customer Privacy Concerns: A Meta-Analytic Review. *Journal of Retailing*, *96*(4), 458–473. doi:10.1016/j.jretai.2020.05.007

Onay, C., & Ozturk, E. (2018). A review of credit scoring research in the age of Big Data. *Journal of Financial Regulation and Compliance*, *26*(3), 382–405. doi:10.1108/JFRC-06-2017-0054

Online Remote Proctoring (Remote Invigilation) Market 2021 Size, Business Growth, Recent Trends and Future Scenario Till 2026| Examity, ProctorU – The Courier. (n.d.). Retrieved June 24, 2021, from https://www.mccourier.com/online-remote-proctoring-remote-invigilation-market-2021-size-business-growth-recent-trends-and-future-scenario-till-2026-examity-proctoru/

Oracle. (2019). *New Study: 64% of People Trust a Robot More Than Their Manager*. Retrieved from: https://www.oracle.com/corporate/pressrelease/robots-at-work-101519.html

Oskarsdottir, M., Bravo, C., Sarraute, C., Baesens, B., & Vanthienen, J. (2018). Credit scoring for good: Enhancing financial inclusion with smartphone-based micro lending. *Thirty Ninth International Conference on Information Systems*. https://www.researchgate.net/publication/328826594_Credit_scoring_for_good_enhancing_financial_inclusion_with_smartphone-based_microlending#fullTextFileContent

Overgoor, G., Chica, M., Rand, W., & Weishampel, A. (2019). Letting the computers take over: Using AI to solve marketing problems. *California Management Review*, *61*(4), 156–185.

Overgoor, G., Chica, M., Rand, W., & Weishampel, A. (2019). Letting the Computers Take Over: Using AI to Solve Marketing Problems. *California Management Review*, *61*(4), 156–185. doi:10.1177/0008125619859318

Pactera Technologies & Nimdizi. (2017). Retrieved from:https://www.nimdzi.com/wp-content/uploads/2019/06/Nimdzi-AI-whitepaper.pdf

Pantano, E., & Pietro, L. (2012). Understanding Consumer's Acceptance of Technology-BasedInnovations in Retailing. *Journal of Technology Management & Innovation*, *7*(4), 483–492. doi:10.4067/S0718-27242012000400001

Parise, S., Guinan, P., & Kafka, R. (2016). Solving the crisis of immediacy: How digital technology can transform the customer experience. *Business Horizons*, *59*(4), 411–420. doi:10.1016/j.bushor.2016.03.004

Parvatiyar, A., & Sheth, J. N. (2000). The Domain and Conceptual Foundations of Relationship Marketing. In J. N. Sheth & A. Parvatiyar (Eds.), *Handbook of Relationship Marketing* (pp. 3–38). Sage Publications. doi:10.4135/9781452231310.n1

Paschen, J., Kietzmann, J., & Kietzmann, T. C. (2019). Artificial intelligence (AI) and its implications for market knowledge in B2B marketing. *Journal of Business and Industrial Marketing*, *34*(7), 1410–1419. doi:10.1108/JBIM-10-2018-0295

Paschen, J., Wilson, M., & Ferreira, J. J. (2020). Collaborative Intelligence: How human and artificial intelligence create value along the B2B sales funnel. *Business Horizons*, *63*(3), 403–414. doi:10.1016/j.bushor.2020.01.003

Patil, N., Lathi, R., & Chitre, V. (2012). Customer card classification based on C5. 0 & CART algorithms. *International Journal of Engineering Research and Applications*, *2*(4), 164–167.

Payne, A., & Frow, P. (2005). A strategic framework for customer relationship management. *Journal of Marketing*, *69*(4), 167–176. doi:10.1509/jmkg.2005.69.4.167

Phan, D. D., & Vogel, D. R. (2010). A model of customer relationship management and business intelligence systems for catalogue and online retailers. *Information & Management*, *47*(2), 69–77. doi:10.1016/j.im.2009.09.001

Pink, D. H. (2011). *Drive: The surprising truth about what motivates us*. Penguin.

Porter, M. E., & Heppelmann, J. E. (2014). How Smart, Connected Products Are Transforming Competition. *Harvard Business Review*, *92*, 64–88.

Position Paper-Hyper-Personalization. (2016). www.nem-initiative.org

Power, J. D. (2017). *Despite Inflammatory Incidents, Airline Customer Satisfaction Keeps Improving, J.D. Power Finds Alaska Airlines, Southwest Airlines Rank Highest in Respective Segments*. https://www.jdpower.com/business/press-releases/jd-power-2017-north-america-airline-satisfaction-study

Priyadarshinee, P. (2020). Examining Critical Success Factors of Cloud Computing Adoption. *International Journal of Decision Support System Technology*, *12*(2), 80–96. doi:10.4018/IJDSST.2020040105

PRNewswire. (2018). *Global $2.2 Bn Artificial Intelligence in Aviation Market 2018-2025: Market to Grow at a CAGR of 46.65%*. https://www.prnewswire.com/news-releases/global-22-bn-artificial-intelligence-in-aviation-market-2018-2025-market-to-grow-at-a-cagr-of-4665-300618741.html

Puccinelli, N., Goodstein, R., Grewal, D., Price, R., Raghubir, P., & Stewart, D. (2019). Customer experience management in retailing: Understanding the buying process. *Journal of Retailing*, *85*(1), 15–30. doi:10.1016/j.jretai.2008.11.003

PWC. (2019). *AI in financial services - Are you meeting the regulators' expectations?* https://www.pwc.co.uk/financial-services/assets/pdf/ai-in-financial-services.pdf

Quan, X. I., & Sanderson, J. (2018). Understanding the Artificial Intelligence Business Ecosystem. *IEEE Engineering Management Review*, *46*(4), 22–25. doi:10.1109/EMR.2018.2882430

Quyen, D. (2020). Efficiency Evaluation of e-CRM System in Banking Sector under Digitalization. *Journal of Advanced Research in Dynamical and Control Systems*, *12*(SP4), 1800–1807. doi:10.5373/JARDCS/V12SP4/20201665

Rababah, K., Mohd, H., & Ibrahim, H. (2011, April). Customer Relationship Management (CRM) Processes from Theory to Practice: The Pre-implementation Plan of CRM System. *International Journal of e-Education, e-Business, e- Management Learning*, *1*(1).

Rai, R., Sahoo, G., & Mehfuz, S. (2015). Exploring the factors influencing the cloud computing adoption: A systematic study on cloud migration. *SpringerPlus*, *4*(1), 197. Advance online publication. doi:10.118640064-015-0962-2 PMID:25977891

Ramzaev, V. M., Khaimovich, I. N., & Chumak, V. G. (2017). *Big Data Analysis for Demand Segmentation of Small Business Services by Activity in Region*. Data Science. doi:10.18287/1613-0073-2017-1903-48-53

Ransbotham, S., Khodabandeh, S., Fehling, R., LaFountain, B., & Kiron, D. (2019). Winning With AI. *Sloan Management Review*, *10*. https://sloanreview.mit.edu/projects/winning-with-ai

RBI. (2017). *Report of the Working Group on FinTech and Digital Banking*. Reserve Bank of India. rbi.org.in

RBI. (2020). *Annual Report 2019-20*. Reserve Bank of India. https://rbi.org.in

Ready, B. (2020). *Navigating your retail business through COVID-19*. https://services.google.com/fh/files/misc/2020_covidretailguide_en-us.pdf

Reinatz, W., Manfred, K., & Wayne, H. D. (2004). The Customer Relationship Management Process: Its Measurements and Impact on Performance. *JMR, Journal of Marketing Research*, *41*(3), 293–305. doi:10.1509/jmkr.41.3.293.35991

REMOTE—A Framework for Teaching Online | Harvard Business Publishing Education. (n.d.). Retrieved January 20, 2021, from https://hbsp.harvard.edu/inspiring-minds/remote-a-framework-for-teaching-online

ReportG. (2019). https://www.gartner.com/smarterwithgartner/3-barriers-to-ai-adoption/#:~:text=More%20organizations%20are%20adopting%20artificial,the%20business%20impact%20and%20benefits

ReportG. (2020). Retrieved from:https://www.gartner.com/smarterwithgartner/2-megatrends-dominate-the-gartner-hype-cycle-for-artificial-intelligence-2020/

Research, I. (2020, July 31). *AI in Fashion market worth $ 2.42 billion in 2026*. https://www.prnewswire.com/news-releases/ai-in-fashion-market-worth--2-42-billion-in-2026--301103837.html

Retail, O., Decision, C., & Science, D. T. (n.d.). Oracle Retail Consumer Decision Tree and Demand Transference Science Cloud Service - Data sheet. Oracle.

Richrelevance, A. W. F. (2019). *Hyper-Personalization: The Pinnacle of Personalization for Marketers*. Academic Press.

Rigby, D. K. (2003). Management tools survey 2003: Usage up as companies strive to make headway in tough times. *Strategy and Leadership*, *31*(5), 4–11. doi:10.1108/10878570310492005

Rigby, D. K., Reichheld, F., & Schefter, P. (2002). Avoid the Four Perils of CRM. *Harvard Business Review*, *80*(2), 101–109. PMID:11894676

Rigby, D. K., & Ledingham, D. (2004). CRM done right. *Harvard Business Review*, *82*(11). PMID:15559450

RIL edtech biz could hit $7-8 bn if it gets 10% market share by CY25: Report. (n.d.). Retrieved July 8, 2021, from https://www.livemint.com/industry/ril-edtech-biz-could-hit-7-8-bn-if-it-gets-10-market-share-by-cy25-report-11624508424422.html

Robertson, T. S., & Gatignon, H. (1991). How innovators thwart new entrants into their market. *Planning Review*, *19*(5), 4–13. doi:10.1108/eb054333

Roggeveen, A. L., & Sethuraman, R. (2020). Customer-Interfacing Retail Technologies in 2020 & Beyond: An Integrative Framework and Research Directions. *Journal of Retailing*, *96*(3), 299–309. doi:10.1016/j.jretai.2020.08.001

Rouhani, S., Ashrafi, A., Zare Ravasan, A., & Afshari, S. (2016). The impact model of business intelligence on decision support and organizational benefits. *Journal of Enterprise Information Management*, *29*(1), 19–50. doi:10.1108/JEIM-12-2014-0126

Routray, Mishra, & Sahoo. (2015). Adaptation of Fast Modified Frequent Pattern Growth approach for frequent item sets mining in Telecommunication Industry. *American Journal of Engineering Research, 4*(12), 126-133.

Rowley, J., & Slack, F. (2003). Kiosks in retailing: The quiet revolution. *International Journal of Retail & Distribution Management*, *31*(6), 329–333. doi:10.1108/09590550310476060

Ruangguru Case Study | Google Cloud. (n.d.). Retrieved June 22, 2021, from https://cloud.google.com/customers/ruangguru

Rust, R. T., & Huang, M. H. (2014). The Service Revolution and the Transformation of Marketing Science. *Marketing Science*, *33*(2), 206–221. doi:10.1287/mksc.2013.0836

Ryan, R. M., & Deci, E. L. (2000). Self-determination theory and the facilitation of intrinsic motivation, social development, and well-being. *The American Psychologist*, *55*(1), 68.

Sakunthala, A. (2020). Role of information technology on CRM implementation in selected industries. *Asian Journal of Management, 11*(4), 413–418. doi:10.5958/2321-5763.2020.00063.3

Saponaro, M., Le Gal, D., Gao, M., Guisiano, M., & Maniere, I. C. (2018). Challenges and Opportunities of Artificial Intelligence in the Fashion World. *International Conference on Intelligent and Innovative Computing Applications (ICONIC)*, 1–5. 10.1109/ICONIC.2018.8601258

Sarea, A., & Taufiq-Hail, G. A.-M. (2021). Evaluation of Compatibility of Cloud-based Applications, Credibility, and Trust Perceptions on the Adoption of Cloud Technology: A Review. *Advanced Machine Learning Technologies and Applications*, 889–907. doi:10.1007/978-3-030-69717-4_83

Saura, J. R., Palos-Sanchez, P. R., & Correia, M. B. (2019). Digital Marketing Strategies Based on the E-Business Model: Literature Review and Future Directions. In A. G. Guerra (Ed.), *Organizational Transformation and Managing Innovation in the Fourth Industrial Revolution* (pp. 86–103). IGI Global. doi:10.4018/978-1-5225-7074-5.ch005

Scherer, M. U. (2015). Regulating Artificial Intelligence Systems: Risks, Challenges, Competencies, and Strategies. SSRN *Electronic Journal*. doi:10.2139/ssrn.2609777

Schwartz, E. M., Bradlow, E. T., & Fader, P. S. (2017). Customer acquisition via display advertising using multi-armed bandit experiments. *Marketing Science, 36*(4), 500–522.

Schwarzmüller, T., Brosi, P., Duman, D., & Welpe, I. M. (2018). How Does the Digital Transformation Affect Organizations? Key Themes of Change in Work Design and Leadership. *Management Review, 29*(2), 114–138. doi:10.5771/0935-9915-2018-2-114

Schweiz, D. (2020). *Pressemappe tonies®. 2016–2017*. Academic Press.

Selden, L., & Macmillan, I. C. (2009). Manage Customer - Centric Innovation Systematically –. *Harvard Business Review*, (May), 108–117. PMID:16579418

Sha Nazim, S., & Rajeswari, M. (2019). Creating a Brand Value and Consumer Satisfaction in E-Commerce Business Using Artificial Intelligence with the Help of Vosag Technology. *International Journal of Innovative Technology and Exploring Engineering, 8*(8), 1510–1515.

Shaw, C., & Hamilton, R. (2016). How to Move to the Next Level of Customer Experience. *The Intuitive Customer*, 161–191. doi:10.1057/978-1-137-53430-9_10

Shopping in 2020: 6 intriguing experiments in digital retail. (n.d.). Retrieved January 3, 2021, from https://www.fastcompany.com/90585138/the-six-wildest-ways-we-shopped-in-2020

Sima, V., Gheorghe, I. G., Subić, J., & Nancu, D. (2020). Influences of the Industry 4.0 Revolution on the Human Capital Development and Consumer Behavior: A Systematic Review. *Sustainability, 12*(10), 4035–4063. doi:10.3390u12104035

Simester, D., Timoshenko, A., & Zoumpoulis, S. I. (2020). Targeting prospective customers: Robustness of machine-learning methods to typical data challenges. *Management Science, 66*(6), 2495–2522. doi:10.1287/mnsc.2019.3308

Singh, H. (2021). Building effective blended learning programs. In *Challenges and Opportunities for the Global Implementation of E-Learning Frameworks* (pp. 15–23). IGI Global.

Singh, R., & Khan, I. (2012). An Approach to Increase Customer Retention and Loyalty in B2C World. *International Journal of Scientific and Research Publications*, *2*(6), 1–5.

Singh, S. (2017a). *Driving traffic and customer activity through affiliate marketing*. IGI Global.

Singh, S. (2017b). Technological Innovations of Marketing in Digital India. *International Journal of Transformation in Operational & Marketing Management*, *1*(1). www.eurekajournals.com

Sobihah, M., Mohamad, M., Ali, N. A. M., & Wan Ismail, W. Z. (2015). E-commerce service quality on customer satisfaction, belief and loyalty: A proposal. *Mediterranean Journal of Social Sciences*, *6*(2), 260–266. doi:10.5901/mjss.2015.v6n2p260

Sodhi, A. (2018). *Hyper-Personalization: A Marketing Primer for Enhanced Customer Experience*. Academic Press.

Soleymanian, M., Weinberg, C. B., & Zhu, T. (2019). Sensor data and behavioral tracking: Does usage-based auto insurance benefit drivers? *Marketing Science*, *38*(1), 21–43. doi:10.1287/mksc.2018.1126

Soni, N., Sharma, E. K., Singh, N., & Kapoor, A. (2020). Artificial Intelligence in Business: From Research and Innovation to Market Deployment. *Procedia Computer Science*, *167*, 2200–2210. doi:10.1016/j.procs.2020.03.272

Sorescu, A., Frambach, R. T., Singh, J., Rangaswamy, A., & Bridges, C. (2011). Innovations in Retail Business Models. *Journal of Retailing*, *87*, 3–16. doi:10.1016/j.jretai.2011.04.005

Spring, M., Hughes, A., Mason, K., & McCaffrey, P. (2017). Creating a competitive edge: A new relationship between operations management and industrial policy. *Journal of Operations Management*, *49*(1), 6–19. doi:10.1016/j.jom.2016.12.003

Srivastava, R. K., Shervani, T. A., & Fahey, L. (1999). Business Processes and Shareholder Value: An Organizationally Embedded View of Marketing Activities and the Discipline of Marketing. *Journal of Marketing*, *63*(4), 168–179. doi:10.1177/00222429990634s116

State, M. (2020). A statistical perspective of ERP and CRM using in EU enterprises. *Journal of Applied Computer Science & Mathematics*, *14*(1), 37–42. doi:10.4316/JACSM.202001006

Statista. (n.d.). *The statistics portal*. https://www.statista.com/

Sterne, J. (2017). *Artificial Intelligence for Marketing*. doi:10.1002/9781119406341

Stieninger, M., Nedbal, D., Wetzlinger, W., Wagner, G., & Erskine, M. A. (2014). Impacts on the Organizational Adoption of Cloud Computing: A Reconceptualization of Influencing Factors. *Procedia Technology*, *16*, 85–93. doi:10.1016/j.protcy.2014.10.071

Sujata, J., Aniket, D., & Mahasingh, M. (2019). Artificial intelligence tools for enhancing customer experience. *International Journal of Recent Technology and Engineering, 8*(2), 700–706. doi:10.35940/ijrte.B1130.0782S319

Swinton, S. M., & Casey, F. (1999). From Adoption to Innovation of Environmental Technologies. *Flexible Incentives for the Adoption of Environmental Technologies in Agriculture,* 351–359. doi:10.1007/978-94-011-4395-0_22

Syam, N., & Sharma, A. (2018). Waiting for a sales renaissance in the fourth industrial revolution: Machine learning and artificial intelligence in sales research and practice. *Industrial Marketing Management, 69*, 135–146. doi:10.1016/j.indmarman.2017.12.019

Talwar, R., & Koury, A. (2017). Artificial intelligence – the next frontier in IT security? *Network Security, 2017*(4), 14–17. doi:10.1016/S1353-4858(17)30039-9

Taylor, M. (2021). *18 CRM statistics you need to know for 2021 (and beyond).* https://www.superoffice.com/blog/crm-software-statistics/#:~:text=The%20CRM%20industry%20has%20seen,with%2010%20employees%20or%20less

Taylor, S. A., & Hunter, G. L. (2002). The impact of loyalty with e-CRM software and e-services. *International Journal of Service Industry Management, 13*(5), 452–474. doi:10.1108/09564230210447931

Taylor, S., & Todd, P. A. (1995). Understanding information technology usage: A test of competing models. *Information Systems Research, 6*(2), 144–177. doi:10.1287/isre.6.2.144

Tech industry leading India's recovery post Covid - The Financial Express. (n.d.). Retrieved February 20, 2021, from https://www.financialexpress.com/industry/technology/tech-industry-leading-indias-recovery-post-covid/2196681/

Tencent-backed online education firm Yuanfudao raises US$1b in new round, Garage - THE BUSINESS TIMES. (n.d.). Retrieved July 1, 2021, from https://www.businesstimes.com.sg/garage/tencent-backed-online-education-firm-yuanfudao-raises-us1b-in-new-round

Teo, T. S. H. (2001). Demographic and motivation variables associated with internet usage activities. *Internet Research, 11*(2), 125–137. doi:10.1108/10662240110695089

The 10 most innovative education companies of 2021. (n.d.). Retrieved June 15, 2021, from https://www.fastcompany.com/90600179/education-most-innovative-companies-2021

The Topic of Discussion. (n.d.). *How specific online discussion methodologies affect outcomes - Packback.* Retrieved July 16, 2021, from https://www.packback.co/pedagogy/the-topic-of-discussion-outcomes-driven-by-online-discussion-depend-on-implementation-method/

Tian, J., & Wang, S. (2016). Signaling Service Quality via Website e-CRM Features. *Journal of Hospitality & Tourism Research (Washington, D.C.), 41*(2), 211–245. doi:10.1177/1096348014525634

Tinabo, R. (2011). Decision tree technique for customer retention in retail sector. *International Conference on Integrated Computing Technology*, 123–131. 10.1007/978-3-642-22247-4_11

Tong, S., Luo, X., & Xu, B. (2020). Personalized mobile marketing strategies. *Journal of the Academy of Marketing Science, 48*(2), 64–78. doi:10.100711747-019-00693-3

Toniebox gives kids hours of screen-free entertainment. (n.d.). Retrieved July 6, 2021, from https://www.fastcompany.com/90556948/european-kids-love-this-screen-free-storytelling-device-now-u-s-kids-can-get-it-too

Tonies – grandcentrix GmbH. (n.d.). Retrieved July 6, 2021, from https://grandcentrix.net/en/references/tonies/

Torrey, L., & Shavlik, J. (2010). Transfer learning. In *Handbook of research on machine learning applications and trends: Algorithms, methods, and techniques* (pp. 242–264). IGI Global. doi:10.4018/978-1-60566-766-9.ch011

Totah, Z. (2020). *9 Critical CRM Trends to Keep an Eye on for 2021*. Retrieved from https://www.selecthub.com/customer-relationship-management/crm-trends/

Training platform Virti raises $10M Series A led by IQ Capital to teach soft skills in VR | TechCrunch. (n.d.). Retrieved July 12, 2021, from https://techcrunch.com/2021/06/29/training-platform-virti-raises-10m-series-a-led-by-iq-capital-to-teach-soft-skills-in-vr/

Travel + Leisure. (2018). *Humanoid Robot, KEMPA, Introduced for Passenger Assistance at Bengaluru Airport*. https://www.travelandleisureindia.in/trending/humanoid-robot/

Turing, A. M. (1950). Computing machinery and intelligence. *MIND - A Quarterly Review of Psychology and Philosophy, 236*, 1–28. doi:10.1093/mind/LIX.236.433

Unleashing the power of AI for education | MIT Technology Review. (n.d.). Retrieved June 17, 2021, from https://www.technologyreview.com/2020/03/04/905535/unleashing-the-power-of-ai-for-education/

us-tmt-fast-, & -winners-list. (2019). *2019 Technology Fast 500 ™ Ranking Recognizing growth.*

Van Doorn, J., Mende, M., Noble, S. M., Hulland, J., Ostrom, A. L., Grewal, D., & Petersen, J. A. (2016). Domo Arigato Mr. Roboto. *Journal of Service Research, 20*(1), 43–58. doi:10.1177/1094670516679272

Van Esch, P., Black, J. S., & Ferolie, J. (2019). Marketing AI recruitment: The next phase in job application and selection. *Computers in Human Behavior, 90*(January), 215–222. doi:10.1016/j.chb.2018.09.009

Vempati, S. S. (2016). *India and the Artificial Intelligence Revolution. Carnegie Endowment for International Peace*. Carnegie India. https://carnegieindia.org/2016/08/11/india-and-artificial-intelligence-revolution-pub-64299

Venkatesh, T., Thong, & Xu. (2012). Consumer Acceptance and Use of Information Technology: Extending the Unified Theory of Acceptance and Use of Technology. *Management Information Systems Quarterly*, *36*(1), 157. doi:10.2307/41410412

Venkatesh, V., Morris, M. G., Davis, G. B., & Davis, F. D. (2003). User acceptance of information technology: Toward a unified view. *Management Information Systems Quarterly*, *27*(3), 425–478. doi:10.2307/30036540

Verhoef, P. C., & Donkers, B. (2005). The effect of acquisition channels on customer loyalty and cross-buying. *Journal of Interactive Marketing*, *19*(2), 31–43.

Verma, S., Sharma, R., Deb, S., & Maitra, D. (2021). Artificial intelligence in marketing: Systematic review and future research direction. *International Journal of Information Management Data Insights, 100002.*

Virti: Home. (n.d.). Retrieved July 12, 2021, from https://virti.com/

Vlačić, B., Corbo, L., Silva, S. C., & Dabić, M. (2021). The evolving role of artificial intelligence in marketing: A review and research agenda. *Journal of Business Research*, *128*, 187–203. doi:10.1016/j.jbusres.2021.01.055

Vladimirovich, K. M. (2020). Future Marketing in B2B Segment: Integrating Artificial Intelligence into Sales Management. *International Journal of Innovative Technologies in Economy*, *4*(31).

Wang, G., Ma, J., & Yang, S. (2014). An improved boosting based on feature selection for corporate bankruptcy prediction. *Expert Systems with Applications*, *41*(5), 2353–2361. doi:10.1016/j.eswa.2013.09.033

Wang, Y., Xiong, M., & Olya, H. G. (2020). Toward an Understanding of Responsible Artificial Intelligence Practices. *Proceedings of the 53rd Hawaii International Conference on System Sciences*. 10.24251/HICSS.2020.610

Wedel, M., & Kannan, P. K. (2016). Marketing analytics for data-rich environments. *JournalofMarketing*, *80*(6), 97–121.

Weijters, B., Rangarajan, D., Falk, T., & Schillewaert, N. (2007). Determinants and outcomes of customers' use of self-service technology in a retail setting. *Journal of Service Research*, *10*(1), 3–21. doi:10.1177/1094670507302990

Weinberg, B. D., Milne, G. R., Andonova, Y. G., & Hajjat, F. M. (2015). Internet of things: Convenience vs. privacy and secrecy. *Business Horizons*, *58*(6), 615–624. doi:10.1016/j.bushor.2015.06.005

Weiss. (2005). Data Mining in Telecommunications. Springer.

Werbach, K., & Hunter, D. (2012). *For the win: How game thinking can revolutionize your business*. Wharton Digital Press.

What Robots Can Do for Retail. (n.d.). Retrieved January 3, 2021, from https://hbr.org/2020/10/what-robots-can-do-for-retail

Why Beautycounter is live-streaming everything inside its new store. (n.d.). Retrieved January 3, 2021, from https://www.fastcompany.com/90580782/why-this-beauty-startup-is-live-streaming-everything-inside-its-new-store

Wilson, H. J., & Daugherty, P. R. (2018). Humans and AI Are Joining Forces. *Harvard Business Review, July-. Augus*, (August), 114–123.

Wilson, H. J., & Daugherty, P. R. (2018, July). Collaborative intelligence: Humans and AI are joining forces. *Harvard Business Review*, 114–123.

Wilson, H. J., Daugherty, P. R., & Morini-Bianzino, N. (2017). The jobs that artificial intelligence will create. *MIT Sloan Management Review*, *58*(4), 14–16. doi:10.7551/mitpress/11645.003.0020

Wirth. (2018). Hello marketing, what can artificial intelligence help you with. *International Journal of Market Research, 60*(5), 435-438.

Wirtz, J., Patterson, P. G., Kunz, W. H., Gruber, T., Lu, V. N., Paluch, S., & Martins, A. (2018). Brave new world: Service robots in the frontline. *Journal of Service Management*, *29*(5), 907–931. doi:10.1108/JOSM-04-2018-0119

Wood, W., & Rünger, D. (2016). Psychology of habit. *Annual Review of Psychology*, *67*(1), 289–314. doi:10.1146/annurev-psych-122414-033417 PMID:26361052

World Economic Forum. (2018). *How to prevent discriminatory outcomes in machine learning*. Working Paper.

World Economic Forum. (2020). *The Future of Jobs Report 2020*. Retrieved from: https://www.weforum.org/reports/the-future-of-jobs-report-2020

Woszczynski, A. B., Roth, P. L., & Segars, A. H. (2002). Exploring the theoretical foundations of playfulness in computerinteractions. *Computers in Human Behavior*, *18*(4), 369–388. doi:10.1016/S0747-5632(01)00058-9

Wu, J., & Wang, S. (2005). What drives mobile commerce? An empirical evaluation of the revised technology acceptance model. *Information & Management*, *42*(5), 719–729. doi:10.1016/j.im.2004.07.001

Wunderlich, N. V., Heinonen, K., Ostrom, A. L., Patricio, L., Sousa, R., Voss, C., & Lemmink, J. (2015). "Futurizing" smart service: Implications for service researchers and managers. *Journal of Services Marketing*, *29*(6/7), 442–447. doi:10.1108/JSM-01-2015-0040

Xie, X., Ding, J., & Hu, G. (2008). Forecasting the retail sales of China's catering industry using support vector machines. *2008 7th World Congress on Intelligent Control and Automation*, 4458–4462.

Yildiz, O. (Ed.). (2021). Advances in Wireless Technologies and Telecommunication *Recent Developments in Individual and Organizational Adoption of ICTs*. doi:10.4018/978-1-7998-3045-0

Yong-Hak, J. (2013). *2013. Web of science*. Thomson Reuters.

Yuanfudao - Global SERS. (n.d.). Retrieved July 1, 2021, from https://globalsers.org/company-profiles/yuanfudao/

Yuanfudao Raises U. S. $2.2 Billion in New Financing, Valuing the Company at US$15.5 Billion, Becoming the Most Valued Ed-Tech Company Worldwide. (n.d.). Retrieved June 19, 2021, from https://www.prnewswire.com/news-releases/yuanfudao-raises-us2-2-billion-in-new-financing-valuing-the-company-at-us15-5-billion-becoming-the-most-valued-ed-tech-company-worldwide-301157837.html

Zaby, C., & Wilde, K. D. (2018). Intelligent business processes in CRM. *Business & Information Systems Engineering*, *60*(4), 289–304. doi:10.100712599-017-0480-6

Zanker, M., Rook, L., & Jannach, D. (2019). Measuring the impact of online personalization: Past, present, and future. *International Journal of Human-Computer Studies*, *131*, 160–168. Advance online publication. doi:10.1016/j.ijhcs.2019.06.006

Zendehboudi, A., Baseer, M. A., & Saidur, R. (2018). Application of support vector machine models for forecasting solar and wind energy resources: A review. *Journal of Cleaner Production*, *199*, 272–285. doi:10.1016/j.jclepro.2018.07.164

Zhang, H., Cao, X., Ho, J. K., & Chow, T. W. (2016). Object-level video advertising: An optimization framework. *IEEE Transactions on Industrial Informatics*, *13*(2), 520–531. doi:10.1109/TII.2016.2605629

Zhang, T., Huang, X., Tang, J., & Luo, X. (2011). *Case Study on Cluster Analysis of The Telecom Customers Based on Consumers' Behavior*. IEEE. doi:10.1109/ICIEEM.2011.6035407

Ziaie, A., Shami Zanjani, M., & Manian, A. (2021). Systematic review of digital value propositions in the retail sector: New approach for digital experience study. *Electronic Commerce Research and Applications*, *47*, 101053. doi:10.1016/j.elerap.2021.101053

Zoltners, A. A., Sinha, P. K., Lorimer, S. E., & Shastri, A. (2019). Article Sales 4 Ways Sales Teams Could Get More Value Out of AI. *Harvard Business Review*, (February), 2–5.

About the Contributors

Surabhi Singh is a Ph.D. from AMU, ADIM, PGDBA-Mktg., MCA and MCOM & International Certifications in Marketing Analytics, Digital Marketing, and Neuromarketing. With an experience of around 19 years in academics, research, teaching, training & consultancy, she is currently associated with IMS Ghaziabad as Associate Professor-Mktg. She is in the Editorial Board of ABDC / Scopus Indexed National and International Journals. With more than 35 FDPs/MDPs/Workshops/Conferences conducted, she has to her credit around 70 papers, Cases, and articles published in International/National Journals/Publications and nine books with National and International Publishing houses. Being an ardent researcher, she has presented research papers/Cases at premier B Schools in the global platforms. She is associated with Global Conferences in their program Review/advisory Committees. She has received around 20 awards and accolades in various national and international forums. She has been guiding doctoral students and examiners for many universities.

* * *

Vikram Bawa has 18+ years of rich experience in leading Transformation programs for Fortune 500 firms across the globe resulting in Revenue Augmentation, better Customer Experience, improved Operational Performance and Brand Recall. He has worked extensively on BPM & Process Automation, CRM & Analytical tools with organizations like Wipro, IBM and HCL in the past. He has worked on (AI/ML) Neural Network based Chatbots, Audio and Voice Emotion Recognition, Cloud (AWS), SAS – Predictive Analytics, Web/ Mobile Analytics, Social Analytics, SAP-ERP and SFDC. Vikram has a bachelor's degree in Computer Science from IIT, Roorkee and an MBA from NTU, Singapore and Kelley School of Business, USA. He spends his free time in the Gym, playing Chess and Table Tennis. He also takes time out to do social service in Mental Health Diagnostics, Prevention and Cure.

Kirandeep Bedi is an Assistant Professor at Amity University, Noida, India. She has done master's from University Business School, Panjab University, Chandigarh,

India and Ph.D. in Commerce. She has over 13 years of teaching and research experience in Finance and Marketing and has published research papers in International & National refereed Journals in the areas of capital structure, profitability, brand equity, supply chain management, emotional intelligence, digital marketing, and many others. She has presented research papers in both national and international conferences and chaired sessions in various conferences. She is associated as an Associate Editor in a number of international, refereed, indexed journals of repute.

Monica Bedi, MBA, Ph.D. is an Associate Professor at University Business School, Panjab University Chandigarh, India. Her area of specialization is Marketing and International Business. She has 18 years of experience in teaching and research. She has published papers in reputed journals in areas such as brand equity, green consumer behaviour, emotional intelligence. She has presented papers in both national and international conferences and chaired sessions in national and international conferences. She has been a member of Graduate and Post-Graduate Board of Studies, Panjab University, Chandigarh, India.

Darshana Desai is an Associate Professor & Head of the MCA Department at Indira College of Engineering & Management, which is an affiliated institute of Savitribai Phule Pune University, India. She received her Ph.D. degree from Gujarat Technological University in August 2017 in the area of IT Management with the subject of Website Personalization. She is having a total of 17+ years of experience in academia and industry. She has published more than 16 research papers and book chapters to her credit with internationally recognized publishers like IGI Global, Taylor & Francis, Springer indexed in Scopus, Pro-Quest, etc., and peer-reviewed Journals. She is interested in interdisciplinary research in the area of Website Personalization, Machine Learning, Artificial Intelligence, Cognitive Science, Data Science, and its application. She has also received a research grant from BCUD, Pune University.

Shailja Dixit has a PhD in Management and is a Gold Medallist in her Management Program. She is working as Associate Professor in the Department of Management at Amity University, Lucknow, India. Her research interests include Social media, Women Entrepreneurship, Consumer Research, Consumer Decision making, Branding, New Product Diffusion. She has more than 15 research papers published in reputed peer reviewed journals. She is currently associated with many reputed Journals.

Mamta Mohan is M.A.(Eco.), MBA (Marketing & HR), and PhD on "FDI in Indian Retail Sector: Policy and Implications." She possesses 26 years of total experience: 6 years of corporate and 20 years of academic teaching & training. Her areas of interest include strategic marketing, consumer behaviour, entrepreneurship, and economic policy. At present she is serving as Professor (Marketing) at Amity University, Noida.

Nidhi S. Natrajan (PhD, MCA, BSc – Maths) is a seasoned faculty, researcher, and trainer in the field of Information Technology and Analytics. She has 15 years of experience and is currently working at Symbiosis International University (SCMS-Noida). She has many research publications to her credit, including Scopus, ABDC and Web of Science. She has conducted training in Analytics including R programming. Served as reviewer for prestigious Journals and also working on project based on MHM. She is a recognized research supervisor to guide PhD students in Dept. of Management at Symbiosis International University, Pune.

M. Prabha completed her PhD in the Department of Management Studies at the National Institute of Technology, Tiruchirappalli, Tamil Nadu, and India. Her research interests include Data Analytics, Machine Learning in human resources management applications.

Rinku Sanjeev (PhD, MBA, MA, EPHRM-IIM Calcutta) is a multi-dimensional personality in the area of academics and behavioral science. She has 19 years of experience and is currently associated with Symbiosis Centre for Management Studies, Noida. She is a recognized research supervisor to guide doctoral students in management stream at Symbiosis International University, Pune. She has published several research papers and book reviews in Scopus, ABDC and Web of Science listed Journals and also been actively involved in research work & projects sponsored by SIU and external bodies. She has authored and edited six books and also serves as a reviewer for reputed journals. Besides this, she has delivered training in organizations like L&T, DMRC, THDCIL, ONGC, and many more in the area of HR, Soft Skill and Life Skill.

José Duarte da Rocha Santos received his PhD in Management from the University of Vigo, Spain. He is also Master of Marketing and has a Bachelor's degree in Business Sciences. Between 1987 and 2002, he has played various roles in sales, marketing, and management of companies in the information technologies sector. From 2003, he has performed functions of management and marketing consultant. Since 1999, he has been a professor in higher education in Portugal in the field of management and marketing. He is currently a professor at the Instituto Superior Politécnico Gaya (ISPGaya) and at the Instituto Superior de Contabilidade e Administração do Porto (ISCAP). He is also a researcher at the Centre for Organisational and Social Studies of Polytechnic of Porto (CEOS.PP). His current research areas include digital transformation, social customer relationship management and social selling.

Sofia Devi Shamurailatpam has a Ph.D. in Economics with specialization in the area of Banking and Financial Economics. Currently she is serving as an Assistant Professor in the Department of Banking and Insurance, Faculty of Commerce, The Maharaja Sayajirao University of Baroda. She has published several research papers in her credit and authored a book entitled "Banking Reforms in India: Consolidation, Restructuring and Performance, published by Palgrave Macmillan, UK (2017). Her major research area of interests includes Economics of Banking, Financial Economics, Economics of Gender, Agricultural Economics and Development Economics particularly Contemporary issues on Sustainability.

Renu Sharma is a research scholar with Amity University. She has 14 years of corporate and 10 years of academic experience. Her research interest lies in retail, consumer emotions and consumer behaviour. Currently, she is working with Footwear Design & Development Institute as Consultant (Retail).

Parag Shukla (M.Com, PGDMM, UGC-NET, and SET) Dr. Parag S. Shukla holds a Ph.D. Degree in the subject of Commerce and Business Management with focus on Strategic Marketing in the area of 'Retailing'. He has been working as an Assistant Professor in the Faculty of Commerce at the Maharaja Sayajirao University of Baroda [MSUB], Gujarat, India since the year 2009. He received his Bachelors and Masters degree and Post Graduate Diploma in Marketing Management with specialization in 'Marketing' from the MSUB, Gujarat, India. His experience includes content analysis with the television and media research industry. He currently teaches courses of management in various Graduate and Post graduate levels in the University. He has presented and published total number of 90 research papers in different areas of Retailing and Marketing in various National and International refereed peer reviewed journals and conference proceedings. He has also authored a book titled as "Retail Shoppers' Behaviour in Brick and Mortar Stores—A Strategic Marketing Approach" which is published by a reputed National Publisher. He is currently working on a research project entitled "An Empirical Investigation of Experiential Value vis-a-vis Usage Attitude of Selected Mobile Shoppers in the State of Gujarat". He has also received accolades for his research papers from various academias. Dr. Shukla is the recipient of the Best Business Academic of the Year Award [BBAY] where he won the Gold Medal for his research paper in the 70th All India Commerce Conference, which is widely recognized in Indian Commerce Education.

Jasmandeep Kaur received her MBA in Finance and Marketing, UGC in NET-Management, and is an Assistant Professor in the Ideal Institute of Management and Technology,Delhi and is a Research Scholar, Amity University, Noida, India. She is having nine years of teaching experience. She has published research papers and authored books with National and International publishers. She is having experience in organizing various Conferences, seminars and is associated with different journals in different capacities.

Ramanjeet Singh Prof. (Dr.) Ramanjeet Singh, Ph.D. (Management), MBA, M.Phil. (Management), M.H.R.M., M. Com (Foreign Trade), M.Sc. (Computer Science), B.Sc., B.Ed., P.G.D.I.B., P.G.D.I.M., P.G.D.I.P.R., P.G.D.C.A., P.G.D.A.P.R., P.G.D.R.M., C.C.P., C.H.R., D.C.U.L. is currently working as Director, ADMAA, Amity University, India. He is having more than 25 years of Corporate, Administrative, Academic & Research Experience in various Institutes, Universities & Organizations around the world. He is the Founding Chief Editor, Editor, Regional Editor, Associate Editor, Guest Editor, Member: International Advisory Board, International Editorial Board, International Editorial Review Board of more than 350 International and National, Refereed, SCOPUS Indexed, Listed Management & Technology Journals across the globe. He has authored more than 150 publications including Books, Research Papers in International & National Refereed, Indexed, Listed Journals, Book Chapters, International and National Conference Proceedings etc.

Sanjeev Singh, with a varied experience of 23 years in corporate, academics and research, is currently associated with Apeejay Institute of Management & Engineering Technical Campus, Jalandhar, as Senior Faculty- Marketing area in MBA Program. He earned PhD, in the area of Retail Service Marketing, and MBA with specialization in Marketing Management. There are several research papers and book reviews publication in his account. He also presented several research papers in different International and National Conferences and Seminars. Having extensive experience of Industry and Academics in the area of Marketing & Sales, he also managed diverse responsibilities in addition to the regular Academic/ Teaching assignments, as Academic Coordinator, Research Project Guide, Project Evaluator and Career Counselor.

Index

A

B

C

D

E

G

H

I

L

M

N

O

P

Q

R

S

T

U

V

X

Y

Z

www.ingramcontent.com/pod-product-compliance
Lightning Source LLC
LaVergne TN
LVHW081327300926
849161LV00008B/1903